NONSENSE AND MEANING
GREEK COMEDY

This book examines the concept of "nonsense" in ancient Greek thought and uses it to explore the comedies of the fifth and fourth centuries BCE. If "nonsense" (*phluaria, lēros*) is a type of language felt to be unworthy of interpretation, it can help to define certain aspects of comedy that have proved difficult to grasp. Not least is the recurrent perception that, although the comic genre can be meaningful (i.e., contain political opinions, moral sentiments, aesthetic tastes), some of it is just "foolery" or "fun." But what exactly is this "foolery," this part of comedy which allegedly lies beyond the scope of serious interpretation? The answer is to be found in the concept of "nonsense": by examining the ways in which comedy does not mean, the genre's relationship to serious meaning (whether it be political, aesthetic, or moral) can be viewed in a clearer light.

STEPHEN E. KIDD is Assistant Professor in Classics at Brown University. He has published articles on Greek comedy as well as other topics like ancient dreams and games. His research interests center broadly around the role of play in ancient life and how such play affects modes of interpretation and evaluation.

NONSENSE AND MEANING
IN ANCIENT GREEK COMEDY

BY

STEPHEN E. KIDD

CAMBRIDGE
UNIVERSITY PRESS

CAMBRIDGE
UNIVERSITY PRESS

University Printing House, Cambridge CB2 8BS, United Kingdom

One Liberty Plaza, 20th Floor, New York, NY 10006, USA

477 Williamstown Road, Port Melbourne, VIC 3207, Australia

4843/24, 2nd Floor, Ansari Road, Daryaganj, Delhi - 110002, India

79 Anson Road, #06-04/06, Singapore 079906

Cambridge University Press is part of the University of Cambridge.

It furthers the University's mission by disseminating knowledge in the pursuit of education, learning and research at the highest international levels of excellence.

www.cambridge.org
Information on this title: www.cambridge.org/9781107674790

First published 2014
First paperback edition 2017

A catalogue record for this publication is available from the British Library

Library of Congress Cataloging in Publication data
Kidd, Stephen E., 1980–
Nonsense and meaning in ancient Greek comedy / by Stephen E. Kidd.
pages   cm
Includes bibliographical references.
ISBN 978-1-107-05015-0
1. Greek drama (Comedy) – History and criticism.   2. Greek language – Semantics.
3. Greek wit and humor – History and criticism.   4. Meaning (Psychology)
5. Wit and humor – Social aspects.   I. Title.
PA3166.K53   2014
882′.0109–dc23
2014003926

ISBN 978-1-107-05015-0 Hardback
ISBN 978-1-107-67479-0 Paperback

Contents

Acknowledgments   *page* vi

   Introduction   1

1 Greek notions of nonsense   16

2 Nonsense as "no-reference": riddles, allegories, metaphors   52

3 Nonsense as "no-serious sense": the case of Cinesias   87

4 Nonsense as "no-sense": jokes, puns, and language play   118

5 Playing it straight: comedy's "nonsense!" accusations   161

   Conclusions   187

References   190
General index   205
Index locorum   207

Acknowledgments

The best parts of this book are from others and I would like to thank all those who have contributed. A deep debt of thanks goes to David Sider, my dissertation advisor at NYU, and the dissertation committee, David Konstan, Markus Asper, Ralph Rosen, and Nancy Worman, for their original ideas and criticisms. Different pieces of the project were later presented at Columbia University, Brown University, and Boston University, and I thank those audiences for their invitations and feedback. Thanks also go to those who read various parts of the book at later stages, including Ralph Rosen, Colin King, Sara Chiarini, and, especially, Ben Sammons who never failed in that true act of friendship: honest (which is to say, negative) criticism. At Cambridge University Press, I would like to thank my editor Michael Sharp, Liz Hanlon, Laura Morris, and the anonymous readers who often were able to articulate the ideas of this book much better than I could. Many thanks also go to Carly Margolis for her invaluable editorial help in the summer of 2013 and my good colleagues at Brown, especially the department chair, Jeri Debrohun, who makes it possible for junior faculty to get work done. To Olya and little Eric too, of course, for the happiness they bring.

Finally, thanks most of all go to Markus Asper, who, in his enthusiasm for the project, provided me first with the confidence to pursue it, and, later in Berlin, the time to bring it to completion. This book probably would not have happened without him and so, if it were possible to dedicate a book on such a trifling subject as nonsense, it would be to him.

Introduction

Like other genres of literature, comedy is full of meaning. Moral imperatives, aesthetic tastes, lofty sentiments, and political opinions can be extracted from the comic text not just by clever interpreters but by ordinary audience members engaged in the communicative act of spectating and listening. Unlike other genres, however, comedy has a long tradition of resistance to such discovered meanings. For every reader who has found in certain comedies a metapoetic discourse regarding the poet's role, or subtle codes of religious initiation, or allegories revealing Aristophanes' politics, or some other system of references or allusions, there is a persistent backlash which insists that not "all" of comedy is meaningful; rather that some of it is just "foolery" or "fun."

Ian Storey, for example, in questioning the alleged political seriousness of Eupolis' *Demoi* articulates comedy's peculiar problem in general terms (2003, 173, my italics):

> Too many critics of *Demoi*, from Körte onwards ("the greatest political comedy of all time"), assume that Eupolis shared this alleged serious approach of Aristophanes and therefore see in *Demoi* comedy's healing response to a time of crisis. *But comedy need not be as serious as that.* Eupolis and Aristophanes were comedians first and foremost. They saw in the Athens of their day, in her people, events, and issues, the material for *brilliant fantasy* and *comic fun*.

Storey's complaint rests on an opposition: there is the "serious" on the one hand, "fantasy/fun" on the other. Something would be lost, such opinion suggests, if all comedy were treated "seriously": indeed, if all comedy contributed to serious meaning, it would not be comedy at all.

The sentiment is widespread and chronic: MacDowell, for example, writes: "[A]s we read the plays, it is reasonable to expect that we shall find, at least occasionally, a scene or passage in which Aristophanes is not just trying to make the Athenians laugh but is making some serious point which is intended to influence them."[1] Here the opposition is similar: there is "some serious point" on the one hand, and "just trying to make Athenians laugh" on the other. The claim is not that there is an opposition between seriousness and laughter, but something more subtle: to unpack MacDowell's "just," when comedy *is* making a serious point it is usually *also* making the Athenians laugh.[2] The perceived non-meaningful part of comedy, however, seems not to be that which is "funny" but rather, that which is *just* funny, *just* fantasy.

Some scholars adopt metaphors of "beneath" or "behind" to describe this relationship between the meaningful and non-meaningful in comedy. Körte, for example, whom Storey cites above for treating Eupolis' *Demoi* too seriously, himself a century earlier censured contemporary scholars for finding too much meaning "behind" the buffoonery of Aristophanes' *Frogs*.[3] Similarly, McGlew describes those who "search behind [comedy's] humor to find its attitudes toward the political questions of the day,"[4] while Malcolm Heath allows that "serious points can be conveyed in comic guise."[5] It is "beneath" not "behind" for Ralph Rosen who writes "the conventional (or read: 'carnivalesque') elements of a comic play compel the audience to find seriousness beneath the surface details of the play,"[6] and De Luca who writes, "By making us laugh at these extremes, Aristophanes also makes us laugh at the arguments which underlie them, and so Aristophanes induces us to question their validity."[7] Whether "behind" or "beneath," it seems that there is some part of comedy that is meaningful, and that somewhere, there is some part where meaning, or at least "serious" meaning, is absent.

---

[1] MacDowell (1995) 5.

[2] Ruffell's (2011) opposition between "funny" and "serious" (e.g., at 55), rather than the more typical "playful" and "serious," may cause him to overlook the nuance of previous scholars who join Ruffell in seeing comedy's meanings (or "interventions" to use Ruffell's more subtle term, e.g., at 26) in, not outside of, its humor.

[3] Körte (1904) 487 (my italics): "Kaibel [*RE* II 981] already made legitimate objections against the view, which has become common since Stallbaum [*De persona Bacchi in Ranis Aristophanis*. Lipsiae 1835], that Dionysus is a personification of the Athenian public: one has here, as often is the case, sought to find too much *behind* the rambunctious exuberance of the buffoonery." "Gegen die seit Stallbaum üblich gewordene Auffassung des Dionysos als Personification des athenischen Publicums hat Kaibel bereits berechtigte Einwendungen gemacht, man hat hier, wie auch sonst oft, zu viel *hinter* dem derben Uebermuth [sic] der Posse gesucht."

[4] McGlew (2002) 12.   [5] Heath (1987) 15.   [6] Rosen (1988) 6 n. 21.

[7] De Luca (2005) xiii. Cf. Wright (2012) 2, my italics: "*Beneath* these features of presentation [i.e., jokes and irony], there is in fact a surprising amount of common ground between comedy and the later critical tradition"; Katz (1976) 353, my italics: "Aristophanes, *amidst much comic foolery*, intended his divine embassy of Poseidon, Heracles and Triballios . . . to remind his audience of the curious troika placed in charge of the Sicilian expedition."

What part of comedy is this? One might immediately turn to "humor" or the "comic," that is, the part of comedy that makes audiences laugh. Perhaps that silly incongruence which seems to trigger jokes will also accommodate this phenomenon which lies outside of serious meaning. However, this overlooks precisely what many of the above scholars are indicating: that the potentially serious parts of comedy are somehow *in* its humor, not separate from it.[8] It is impossible to disentangle a joke about Cleon from a negative judgment about him, since jokes, as has been argued, so often contain judgments.[9] Moreover, the "point" of such jokes seems to be the judgments themselves: Cleon is a cheat, Cleisthenes effeminate, Cratinus a drunk. To consider humor not "serious" or "meaningful" would overlook the fact that humor can be taken seriously and that these serious meanings are in no way separate from the humor itself. This is why it is often comedy's humorous moments (regarding, for example, Cleon's treatment of jurors or Hyperbolus' military policies) that form the core of the "serious" readings of comedy.

Thus, whatever this phenomenon is which is opposed to comedy's "meaning," it cannot be humor.[10] The joke-form slips through the fingers and all that remains is the content of serious judgment. The scholars' sentiments above (or so many other similar views) cannot be alleviated by diagnosing the perceived fun and foolery of comedy as the mere vessel for its ubiquitous significance: for then there would be no part of comedy not prey to interpretation (and thus one has returned to the idea which provokes the Storey (2003)/Körte (1904) backlash in the first place). Nevertheless, there is a reason for this chronic reaction against comedy's seriousness, and, as I will argue, the reason has to do with the nature of comedy itself. Unlike other genres which use language instrumentally to create meaning, comedy often seems to produce a sort of language which escapes meaning – a language which I will be calling nonsense. So too, unlike other genres like lyric or tragedy, where impenetrable statements are received as "obscure" (a token of faith that meaning is "there," but not immediately intelligible), comedy often suggests a different interpretive gesture, which is not to interpret at all. In comedy and perhaps no other genre language can be left as "nonsense," and it is this

---

[8] Silk (2000) 304–12, reviewing Heath's (1987) and Henderson's (1990) senses of "serious," suggests instead that comedy has "serious" artistic goals (see Chapter 3 below for discussion); but this loses sight of the contrast of play vs. seriousness (*OED* s.v. "serious" 3) which is surely at the center of the debate.

[9] See, e.g., Freud (1989[1905]) 5–11 for versions of this view.

[10] For the changing meanings of "humor" through history, see Chapter 4, 119 n. 4. Here I simply mean that the non-serious/non-meaningful part of comedy cannot be humor by virtue of the fact that humor is often taken seriously/found meaningful.

phenomenon, I argue, that is behind the resistance to serious meaning that has
plagued comedy's reception.

What, then, is this "nonsense"? An initial definition might be "meaningless
language," "meaningless communication," or, more broadly, "that which
seems to be interpretable but is not," since not only utterances are called
"nonsense."[11] This "seemingly interpretable" part of the definition is important, since it is clear that "nonsense" is not the same thing as "noise" – that is,
nonsense is not *any* meaningless sound, *any* meaningless phenomenon, but
rather certain phenomena (utterances, gestures, data, etc.) that present themselves as being interpretable, but turn out not to be. So, for example, one
would not call an inarticulate cry "nonsense," but might call an indecipherable
sentence "nonsense." One would not call a bird's chirping "nonsense," but, if
someone continued to chirp in response to an interrogation, one might call
such responses "nonsense." One would never call the stars "nonsense," but
might call the read-outs from machines charting the pulses of these stars
"nonsense." Nonsense must first present itself as being decipherable (e.g., be
written in an alphabet, spoken in recognizable phonemes, occur in a communicative context, etc.) for it to have the possibility of being called "nonsense."

The "meaningless" part of nonsense's "meaningless language" definition
presents more problems. "Meaningless" for whom? By what definition of
"meaning"? When one exerts the slightest pressure on this idea, nonsense
seems to disappear as a useful category altogether. Take, for example, the
case of Noam Chomsky. Chomsky offered the line "colorless green ideas
sleep furiously" as an example of a nonsensical sentence which was still
grammatical.[12] One cannot help but be disappointed: such a sentence might
be "nonsense" according to some standards, but anyone with literary lean-
ings probably finds the sentence rather pleasant and metaphorical. Rather
than lacking meaning, the line is brimming with it, exciting the mind with
imagery and dark, hidden messages. The idealized vacuum that one wishes
for "nonsense" in fact turns out to be semantically rich, and so it is no
surprise that soon after Chomsky declared the sentence nonsensical, others
began to plumb its hermeneutic depths.[13] It seems that meaning is "there"
in such "nonsense," it is just a matter of finding it – and so, problems begin
to arise around this initial definition of "meaningless language."

---

[11] OED s.v. nonsense, A.1.1.b. for "foolish or extravagant conduct"; A.1.3. for "a trivial or worthless
thing." *Ran.* 198–202 for a Greek example. Chapter 1 for discussion.
[12] Chomsky (1957) 15.
[13] Erard (2010). As any Google search of the line will show, it has become a "pop culture artifact" (Erard,
2010, 420).

But perhaps the problem is simply the example itself: Chomsky wanted to create a sentence which was nonsensical but still grammatical, so a safer example might be found in one that is not grammatical at all. Better yet, to be extra cautious, one should find an example of "nonsense" that is not even made up of recognizable words – that is, pure gibberish. This *must* be nonsense, and one can turn to Aristophanes' ingenious character Pseudartabas for an example of this. At the beginning of *Acharnians*, Dicaeopolis is bemoaning the political situation of Athens and watching in disgust as Athenian ambassadors arrive from abroad, clearly tainted by one of Athens' sources of political corruption – Persia and its endless gold. The Persian ambassador Pseudartabas ("False Measure") is about to proclaim his announcement sent from the King of Persia himself. His costume must have been splendid, and the Athenian ambassadors make much ado in presenting the stunning character. But, when the moment arrives for this ambassador to proclaim the royal message to the Athenians, the message is not entirely clear: ἰαρταμαν ἐξαρξαν ἀπισσονα σατρα (100).

The line, scholars generally agree, is nonsense.[14] Although some exceptional linguists have "deciphered" this bit of Persian, most follow the impulse of Martin West that "it is gibberish made from Persian noises" or S. D. Olson that "this is gibberish and intended to be recognized as such."[15] But if Pseudartabas' words are "gibberish" or "nonsense," what does it *mean* that they are "gibberish" or "nonsense"? This is the question that the linguist Jean-Jacques Lecercle poses at the beginning of his book *The Violence of Language* regarding the nonsense-poet Edward Lear's gibberish letter of 1862 ("Thrippsy pillivinx, Inky tinky pobblebockle abblesquabs? – Flosky! . . ."), and at the beginning of his later *Philosophy of Nonsense* regarding Lewis Carroll's *Jabberwocky* ("'Twas brillig, and the slithy toves / Did gyre and gimble in the wabe . . .").[16] If these texts are meaningless nonsense, what does it mean that they are "meaningless nonsense"? Or more precisely: in what sense can they be said to be "meaningless"? Lecercle reminds, for example, that much can be said about such "nonsense" at the level of phonology,

---

[14] E.g., Olson (2002a) ad *Ach.* 100. For discussion of this and other gibberish passages like the ναβαισατρεῦ of *Av.* 1615 and the νοραρεττεβλο on a Greek vase depicting comedy, see Chapter 4. For the language of foreigners in Aristophanes more generally, especially the Scythian in *Thesmophoriazusae*, see Willi (2003) 213–25.

[15] West (1968) 6. Those who have "cracked" the Persian code play an important role in this book, just as do those scholars who have "discovered" pervasive allegorical codes in the works of Aristophanes. Cf. Lecercle's (1994) discussion of Abraham Eddelson who, in 1966, "decoded" Carroll's *Through the Looking Glass* as a cryptogram for the Talmud (5–20). Such interpreters are important because, as readers and interpreters of texts, we are all implicated in their interpretive excess.

[16] Lecercle (1990) 1–6 and (1994) 20–6.

morphology, and syntax. Regarding phonology, Lecercle notices that Lear's gibberish clearly sounds "English," and one could say the same with Pseudartabas' line (e.g., West's "gibberish … from Persian noises"), which, like the Carthaginian's speech at the opening of Plautus' *Poenulus*, seems to reflect the phonemes and sounds of the mimicked foreign language. Even if such phonological cues do not constitute meaning, it still seems that Pseudartabas' utterance is supplying certain information.

So too, morphological cues (e.g., the feeling that -μαν may be a verb-ending of ἰαρταμαν) and syntactic cues (e.g., the feeling that ἀπισσονα may be an adjective modifying the noun σατρα, both accusative) have caused some editors to edit the line with certain word separations.[17] Again, this probably does not constitute "meaning," but nevertheless the Persian gibber-ish offers certain roadmaps of intelligibility rather than communicative silence. However, it is at the level of semantic analysis that Pseudartabas' ἰαρταμαν ἐξαρξαν, Lear's "amsky flamsky," and Carroll's "slithy toves" begin to reveal themselves as "nonsense." The linguist, Lecercle confesses, is impo-tent to analyze these texts at the semantic level, and so, one might say that it is at this level that Pseudartabas' line is meaningless.[18]

But even here, things are not so simple. As Lecercle rightly argues, these "nonsense" words and phrases still activate our minds, they still ignite patterns of associations: Lear's "amsky flamsky" can unleash "am," "flam(e)," "ram," "dam(e)," etc., and in this unleashing, "meaning creeps into the text."[19] One can do the same with Pseudartabas' line: the gibberish does not create an empty blank in the mind, some ideal zen-like calm which one expects from language "signifying nothing," but rather concocts a stormy *excess* of associations (σατρα, σατράπης, ἐτράπην, σὰ τραγήματα, τράμις). This linguistic excess leads Lecercle to conclude that it is not that a line like Pseudartabas' has no meaning, but that it has *too much*. Upon hearing such "gibberish," the mind is alight with associations – even if those associations cannot unify themselves into a single sense. One might argue, then (as Deleuze seems to have argued),[20] that "nonsense" is not really the right word at all for this imagined phenomenon of meaningless language. Utterances which are generally called "nonsense" do not "mean nothing"

[17] The text and word separations are from Wilson (2007). Olson (2002a) chooses not to separate the words, choosing a more absolute form of gibberish; cf. West (1968) 7, who discerns the line's να-series and assimilation of word-endings.
[18] Lecercle (1990) 3: "Here, the linguist's impotence is complete. I am not even sure that the existing English words that I have recognized in the text have their usual meaning."
[19] Lecercle (1990) 4. Cf. Eco (1998) 145–9.
[20] Deleuze (1990) 71 declares that nonsense is not the absence of sense, but *opposed* to "the absence of sense."

but rather mean too much. Furthermore, if this is the case, such "nonsense" ought even to be perceived as a more bountiful language than "sensible" speech itself: there is *more* to analyze, fewer restrictions in the discovery of meaning. In such a scenario, one might follow the various trails blazed by Pseudartabas' vigorous line, and fill articles with its delirious significance, since one is no longer bound by some gravitational, unifying sense which limits all possible associations. In this case, nonsense *qua* "meaningless language," it would seem, does not exist at all. Meaning always prevails.

If this were the whole story of "nonsense" – namely, that nonsense-*qua*-"meaningless language" does not really exist, that everything has meaning, and that the phenomenon formerly known as nonsense ought to bear a different name[21] – there would not be much left to discuss about that old category of "nonsense," except perhaps the wording of its brief, polite eulogy.

But this is not the whole story of nonsense. Whether or not "real" nonsense exists (i.e., truly meaningless language), this uncertainty has not prevented numerous societies from insisting that it does. If one can judge from the large lexicons surrounding this category of "meaningless" or "useless" language, it might even be suggested that many cultures *require* the category. There is the English "nonsense," from the French *nonsens*, which maps nicely to other language equivalents like the German *Unsinn*. But as if "nonsense" were not enough to contain its own pejorative force, English also shares this nonsense terrain among words like "blather," "drivel," "twaddle," and "claptrap." In ancient Greek, a similar proliferation occurs over such "useless" or "meaningless" language: terms like *phluaria*, *lēros*, *phlēnaphia*, and *hythlos*, which I examine in Chapter 1. In Russian, one finds *chepukha*, *chushj*, *yerunda*, etc.,[22] and, in Chinese there is *hu shuo*, *fei hua*, and *xia che*.[23]

This makes the nonsense-problem presented by Lecercle (and Deleuze) somewhat knottier. Whatever one can claim about the "true" state of nonsense language, one cannot overlook that entrenched vocabulary found in a number of societies which declares that certain utterances are without meaning or use. The label of "nonsense," after all, is not applied to utterances which are perceived to have an *excess* of meaning, or even to those utterances which are perceived to lack unity; rather the label "nonsense" claims that the utterance *as a whole* is meaningless, useless, and, so should be

---

[21] E.g., Deleuze's (1990) 71 "absence of sense."   [22] See Pervukhina (1993) 25 for a handy list.
[23] *Hu shuo* means "thoughtless talk" (perhaps originally "barbarian talk"); the others respectively "waste talk" and "blindly pull."

disregarded in its entirety,[24] rather analogous, perhaps, to the category of "waste."[25] On the other hand, once one starts to consider the uses of such "useless" phenomena, they quickly stop being "waste" or "nonsense" – and thus, the fate of Chomsky's colorless green ideas, which turned out to be highly meaningful after all.

Thus, it is necessary to reconsider or refine this initial definition of nonsense as "meaningless language." As the semiotic framework of Lecercle implies above, objective nonsense is out of the question: simply put, words can always mean. Instead, "nonsense" seems to be something more intersubjective: that is, a subjective label that arises between two parties, whether due to communication breakdown or something else. A more appropriate definition of nonsense, then, should be "language perceived as being unworthy of interpretation." After all, the application of the label "nonsense" is hardly confined to perceived gibberish, and this is especially the case when "nonsense" is being applied to comedy.

If nonsense is language perceived as being unworthy of interpretation, one can find an opening for nonsense's related denotation: that is, not the "nonsense" which denotes "no meaning," but the one which denotes "no serious meaning." For surely it is that latter nonsense, not the former, which has a more significant purchase on comedy. Consider, for example, Plato's *Apology*, where Socrates describes *Clouds* in the following terms (19c):

> ταῦτα γὰρ ἑωρᾶτε καὶ αὐτοὶ ἐν τῇ Ἀριστοφάνους κωμῳδίᾳ, Σωκράτη τινὰ ἐκεῖ περιφερόμενον, φάσκοντά τε ἀεροβατεῖν καὶ ἄλλην πολλὴν φλυαρίαν φλυαροῦντα, ὧν ἐγὼ οὐδὲν οὔτε μέγα οὔτε μικρὸν πέρι ἐπαΐω.

> You have seen yourselves in Aristophanes' comedy, a certain Socrates being carried around there, saying that he is walking on air and a great deal of other nonsense, things about which I know nothing, neither a lot nor a little.

The key words of the passage are φλυαρίαν φλυαροῦντα, "speaking empty nonsense." I will have a lot to say about these Greek words in Chapter 1, but for now it is enough to follow LSJ and those translators who turn the phrase as "speaking nonsense." The representative passage that Socrates is referring

---

[24] The relationship between meaning and use is discussed further in Chapter 1. The categories often overlap, e.g., for Wittgenstein (*Phil. Grammar* 1:29: "Is the meaning really only the use of the word? Isn't it the way this use meshes with our lives?"). Cf. Dummett (1976).

[25] I.e., one might rightly claim that there is no such thing as "actual" waste (such objects, after all, *can* be useful: fertilizer for plants, reuseable materials, etc.), but such claims would overlook that vital organizational principle which distinguishes between what is "useful" and what is not; what is worthy of consideration and what is not. For studies on waste, see Laporte (2000); Stockton (2011); Douglas (2002[1966]) 2: "[d]irt is essentially disorder." The nonsense synonym "rubbish" is pertinent here.

to here is the one in which Strepsiades first encounters the great teacher, hanging in a basket (222–4):

Στ. ὦ Σώκρατης.
   ὦΣωκρατίδιον.
Σω. τί με καλεῖς ὦφήμερε;
Στ. πρῶτον μὲν ὅ τι δρᾷς ἀντιβολῶ κάτειπέ μοι.
Σω. ἀεροβατῶ καὶ περιφρονῶ τὸν ἥλιον.

St. So-cra-tes! Socky-pie!
So. What are you calling me for, creature of a day?
St. First off, tell me, please, what you're doing.
So. I'm air-treading and contemplating the sun.

These four lines, including the particular line that Socrates alludes to (ἀεροβατῶ καὶ περιφρονῶ τὸν ἥλιον), are surely not "nonsense" in the same way that Pseudartabas' line (ἰαρταμαν ἐξαρξαν ἀπισσονα σατρα) is nonsense. There is nothing indecipherable about ἀεροβατῶ καὶ περιφρονῶ τὸν ἥλιον, despite the temporary blip from that initial comic coinage. Rather, it seems that Socrates singles out the phrase (and the depiction of him more generally) as one unworthy of interpretation, or, at least, unworthy of serious interpretation. Stephen Halliwell explains the situation in this way: "Plato makes Socrates refer to the 'empty nonsense' (*phluaria*) of his depiction in Aristophanes' *Clouds* not in order to cast comedy as a serious causal factor in the spread of slanders about him, but in order to suggest that those slanders are no more substantial than the distorted fantasies which everyone knows are the stock-in-trade of comic drama."[26] Nonsense, for Halliwell, is something which is not "substantial" and so, through that very insubstantiality, cannot be a "causal factor." One cannot build on nonsense, his words suggest, since such speech disintegrates: it is not of sturdy stuff, like consequential speech.

Yet, although Pseudartabas' "nonsense" and Socrates' "nonsense" are not nonsense in the same way, there are certain similarities the two share, not least the fragile subjectivity inherent in their very status as "nonsense." Like Pseudartabas' gibberish, which has been deciphered by some and so found not to be "nonsense" at all, Aristophanes' ἀεροβατῶ καὶ περιφρονῶ τὸν ἥλιον (and the depiction of which it is part) is far from being "nonsense" in any absolute or objective way. After all, critics have viewed Socrates' portrayal in *Clouds* as playing "the decisive role" in Socrates'

---

[26] Halliwell (2008) 255. Cf. Frese (1926).

condemnation,[27] which is to say that the lines have been found by many
readers to be not "nonsense" at all – as Plato's Socrates would have it – but
quite the contrary, substantial and causal to the highest degree. The
intersubjective aspect of "nonsense," it seems, is central to its discovery
in both instances: whether it is Pseudartabas' gibberish or Socrates'
ἀεροβατῶ καὶ περιφρονῶ τὸν ἥλιον, the discovery of "nonsense" is that
which separates certain utterances from potential chains of meaning.

Thus, as I have been arguing, there is some part of comedy which is perceived to
lie outside of its meaning and this part is its "nonsense." This "part," however,
does not seem to be *in* the comic text at all. That is, there is no passage which
one can point to in comedy and objectively label "nonsense" since nonsense to
one person may be highly meaningful to another. Whether it be Pseudartabas'
gibberish or the foolery of *Clouds*, the question of nonsense instead seems to be
a question of interpretation. Detecting certain formal features like repetition or
grammatical oddities is ultimately of little help: nonsense can only be found by
analyzing certain comic passages and asking what is lost when they are
interpreted. This lost "part" is what I am calling nonsense.
     Nonsense is *of* not *in* comedy and, as I will argue, its discovery is a central
pleasure of the genre. What is lost when comedy is interpreted is precisely
this discovery of nonsense. If interpretation is the discernment of consequence in an utterance or action, that mode which deprives utterances and
action of their consequence – namely, the mode in which nonsense is
found – is its opposite. The choice of interpretation excludes that option,
and in that exclusion, comedy experiences its central loss.
     This argument begins in Chapter 1 "Greek Notions of Nonsense" where I
define a concept of nonsense via ancient Greek usage of "nonsense" terms.
Exploring the semantic territory of words like *phluarein* and *lērein* in prose
writers like Isocrates, Xenophon, and the Hippocratic corpus, I notice that
although the term "nonsense" is most frequently used as a pejorative in
rhetorical contexts (e.g., "my opponent is speaking nonsense"), the two
contexts in which it is not pejorative – and so shed the most light on what
the pejorative aspect is trying to convey – are the contexts of mental illness
and play. In the Hippocratic corpus, when patients are suffering from some
sort of fever or mental impairment, they are said to "speak nonsense." On
the other hand, in contexts of sympotic play, when one is fooling around,
joking, or making small talk, one might also be said to be "speaking

---

[27] Henderson (1998)b 5; Halliwell (2008) 255 n. 94 for similar views; cf. Ruffell (2011) 6–8; Wright (2012)
    112–13.

nonsense." Somehow, for the same reason that such "nonsense" is viewed negatively in medical contexts, it is viewed positively in the contexts of play: namely, because it is "useless" speech.

This tension between play and mental illness which Chapter 1 demonstrates to be in the semantic domain of "nonsense" becomes the foundation for the book's overarching argument about comedy's special relationship to meaning. What follows may be seen as being divided between these two aspects of nonsense: while Chapters 2 and 3 consider the pleasures of nonsense (i.e., its relationship to play), Chapters 4 and 5 consider the discomforts of nonsense (i.e., its relationship to mental illness). So, if Chapters 2 and 3 ask what is lost when the comic text is found meaningful (a certain experience of play), Chapters 4 and 5 suggest a certain gain in the discovery of comic meaning, a gain not generally noticed: namely, an assurance against mental illness.

In Chapter 2, I consider comedy's metaphors, allegories, and riddles, and argue that often the discovery of these tropes' references seems to miss the purpose of the tropes themselves. If the "reference" of a riddle is its answer (i.e., the reference of "a creature with one, two, and three legs" is a "man"), and the "reference" of an allegory is what it is allegorizing (i.e., the reference of Alcaeus' "ship" is the "state"), and the "reference" of a metaphor is its tenor (i.e., the reference of Pindar's "dream of a shadow," is "man"), then it can be argued that comedy indulges in "reference-free" language: riddles without answers, allegories without allegorized, and metaphors without tenors. Examples range from the dog trial of *Wasps*, the allegorical chorus of Eupolis' *Cities*, the personified Harvest of Aristophanes' *Peace*, and riddles from the comic fragments of Antiphanes. I argue that in these examples it can be seen not only that nonsense arises when tropes are deprived of their references, but that it is precisely when language is most reference-free that comedy attains some of its most climactic points.

Chapter 3 pursues this idea in broader terms. When scholars or audiences claim that there is "nonsense" in comedy it is usually in regard not to specific "reference-free" tropes but to something much broader and vaguer, often in terms of whole parts of plays or even whole plays. This is not the "nonsense" which denotes "no sense" but, like Socrates' usage of the term earlier, the "nonsense" which denotes "no serious sense." The relationship between terms like "sense" and "serious sense" – or for that matter "reference" in Chapter 2 – is less important for the project than delineating that central act of interpretation which they all share. Whether the term be "reference," "meaning," or "serious content," the discovery of nonsense consists in rejecting that part of the utterance beyond the utterance itself.

Chapter 3 tackles that larger question of nonsense – namely what happens when comedy is deprived of its "serious meaning" or "serious content" – and does this by considering the example of a *komoidoumenos*[28] being mocked. How would it have been possible for a *komoidoumenos* like the dithyrambic poet Cinesias, who was mocked year after year for his lousy music and loose bowels, not to take such mockery "seriously"? I consider passages from Pherecrates' *Mousikē*, Aristophanes' *Birds* and *Gerytades*, as well as a number of comic fragments where the hypothetical audience member Cinesias was faced with this interpretive choice: is it "serious" or "just" nonsense? I then extrapolate from this particular case study to more general questions of comic interpretation.

The chapter ends with a useful theoretical model offered long ago by Gregory Bateson, and since that time, increasingly recognized in the field of ethology: the concept of a "play signal." As something not *in* but *of* certain utterances and actions, this play signal offers a nice theoretical distillation of what comedy may lose when it is interpreted. I argue that the recognition of the play signal can be understood as the realization of nonsense. Interpretation, on the other hand – whether it be Cinesias' interpretation in the face of a potential insult or the interpretation of a scholar analyzing one of these Cinesian passages – overwrites that realization. Here the answer to the question of what is lost when a comic text is interpreted finds its most direct answer.

This might have been a natural place to end the investigation, but the question of nonsense in comedy is not so simple and the complication has to do with nonsense's other connotation from Chapter 1: not play but mental illness. If the realization "this is nonsense" or "this is play" were all comedy needed to achieve, why is it that comedy is not entirely Pseudartaban gibberish or Socrates on stage playing with words like *aerobateo*? The reason, I argue, is that play with language carries with it certain problems that play with aggression (like that against Cinesias in Chapter 3) does not. While a danger of aggressive play is that it will become "real," a danger of language play is that the "real" is nowhere to be found: that is, one has entered a state of delirium.

In Chapter 4, "Nonsense as No-Sense," I consider such language play in comedy and make the simple observation that the same verbal phenomena which are usually marshaled as "comic techniques" by those studying humor (e.g., repetition, rambling speech, wordplay), often produce very

---

[28] I.e., a person lampooned in comedy.

negative reactions as well (irritation, anger, disgust).[29] The richness of "sense" found in aggressive play ("let's kill Socrates," "don't vote for Cleon") is often absent in language play and this may help to explain the negative reactions that arise against it. However, this should not cause one to overestimate the role of sense or meaning in comedy's enjoyment: the perception of nonsense, despite its potentially negative effects, is still a comic goal. Examples include repetition from *Thesmophoriazusae*, word-coinage from *Ecclesiazusae*, rambling speech from Antiphanes' *Cleophanes*, and puns from *Birds*. I will also add to the relationship between play and nonsense some more theoretical substance from Freud who is also interested in the difference between language play and aggressive play, often formulating jokes as "concealing" nonsense in sense.

In Chapter 5, I examine the relationship between nonsense and comedy from a different perspective, via the actual accusations of "nonsense" that occur on the comic stage. Why is it that characters scold each other for cracking jokes, and why do these scoldings often take the particular form of "stop speaking nonsense!"? This leads to a more general problem: why, if comic spectators desire comic buffoonery, is there a need at all for a "straight" or serious character who balances and offsets that comic buffoonery? Usually described as providing "set-ups" or "feeds" for the clown's joke, the straight character's role is far broader: as I argue, such characters prevent the comedy from devolving into senselessness, and the accusation of "nonsense!" is precisely to identify that danger.

The rejection of interpretation, or, as I am calling it, the discovery of nonsense, is a central pleasure of comedy. But as with the earlier distinction between "nonsense" and "noise," by "rejecting interpretation" I do not mean rejecting all interpretive effort, since this would make it impossible, for example, to "get" a "joke." Instead, by "rejecting interpretation" I mean rejecting what might be interpreted (which surely must require some sort of hermeneutic activity). It may be that to register a sense like "Cleon is a scoundrel" or "Socrates is a quack" is at times a requirement of comedy, preventing the encroachment of that other, less pleasurable form of nonsense found in Chapter 1. On the other hand, to privilege such "sense" as the whole of comedy, a source of pleasure rather than a safety net for it, is to fall into that repeated trap, the very

---

[29] Consider the recent event (February 13, 2011) when the CBS TV-reporter Serene Branson suffered a brain malfunction on air (originally thought to be a stroke, later diagnosed as a rare form of migraine) and began to speak gibberish. The responses to the videos posted online ranged from being deeply disturbed by the event to outright mockery. For a similar range of responses, see Freud (1989 [1905]) 257; Lucian *Lit. Prom.* 4 for an ancient example.

privileging of meaning which produces the now familiar reaction: namely, that not all of comedy is meaningful and some of it is "just" fun.

As I emphasized earlier, in exploring this "nonsense" part of comedy, I will not be identifying certain passages of comedy and calling them, objectively, nonsense. At no point will I be demarcating certain swaths of comic text with red flags and demanding that they no longer be interpreted. Such is not the nature of this project, nor does it congrue with my understanding of nonsense which, as I see it, is irreducibily subjective.[30] Instead, I will be looking at passages that raise this question of interpretation (is it meaningful or is it nonsense?) in an interesting way. For that reason, if the question arises "but for *whom* are these passages nonsense?" the answer is quite simply: for whomever they are nonsense. The objective basis for this invitation to the subjective is that century of scholarship I listed at the beginning of this introduction. Rather than considering such scholars simply wrong or misguided, I find their repeated articulations of comedy's non-meaningful part acute, sympathetic, and theoretically interesting.[31] The goal of this book is simply to pursue systematically something which has been observed about comedy for a long time by such scholars.

When considered in this way, one of the most productive aspects of this study of the "non-meaningful" part of comedy may be that it cuts across party lines in the usual debate of comic scholarship. While the debate over comedy's meaning is usually construed as the opposition between the Gomme camp on the one side (comedy is just entertainment)[32] and the de Ste. Croix camp on the other (comedy contains serious political messages), certain members from both sides seem to agree that "some" part of comedy is "just" funny, "just" fun.[33] De Ste. Croix himself articulates this non-meaningful part of comedy most beautifully of all, associating it with the genre itself. He writes: "Scattered through the play are passages which demand to be taken seriously, even if they are mixed in with pure comedy."[34] Pure comedy? One must assume that this perceived "pure comedy" is that which is opposed to those "passages which demand to be

---

[30] Although at times through the course of this book, I will refer to "nonsense" in a more shorthand way, one can always prefix "perceived" to it.

[31] Cf. Ruffell (2011) 20 who argues that past scholars' separation of "serious meaning" is due to a lack of "solid theoretical grounding." If I understand his position, it seems that there is no "just silly" or "meaningless" part since *all* of comedy is an ideological intervention. This remarkably efficient view only puts into a starker light the fact that comedy, unlike other genres, does create this persistent impression of not being serious or meaningful.

[32] The debate, of course, is much older: Gomme's (1996[1938]) review provides history into the late nineteenth century.

[33] For the most recent discussion of the debate, see Olson (2010 a).   [34] De Ste. Croix (1996 [1972]) 62.

taken seriously." The term even suggests that this age-old battle over comedy's meanings has little to do with the "comedy" part of comedy at all: "pure" comedy, according to de Ste. Croix, lies elsewhere.[35] Thus, the stakes are high, I would argue, in the pursuit of the non-meaningful part of comedy: nonsense or non-meaning is associated with the very essence of the genre.

[35] See Lowe (2008) 10 for the perception of a paradox in the genre: "This is not to say that comedy is primarily interesting for its serious content; there would be at least something of a paradox in claiming that comedy is significant precisely when it is not being funny." Cf. Silk's (2000) 159 observation of "comedy at its most comic," discussed below in Chapter 4.

CHAPTER I

Greek notions of nonsense

Is the meaning really only the use of the word?
Isn't it the way this use meshes with our lives?

Wittgenstein *Philosophical Grammar* I: 29

The Greeks had a number of ways of describing "nonsense," that is, language perceived as having no use. One might be said to φλυαρεῖν, from the earlier verb φλύω meaning to "babble":[1] like some bubbling brook, or boiling pot, one's words (or phonemes) flow disorderly out of the mouth as useless *phluaria*.[2] Similarly spluttering (albeit less common), are words like φληναφάω, φλεδονέω, and παφλάζω, the last describing the speech of Aristophanes' bombastic Paphlagon at *Knights* 919.[3] One might also be said to ληρεῖν (like φλυαρεῖν, probably onomatopoeic),[4] to ὑθλεῖν,[5] or to στωμύλλεσθαι,[6] all covering English words like "to blather,"

---

[1] Beekes (2010) s.v. φλυαρέω calls the verb an "enlargement of φλύω" and Chantraine (1968–80) s.v. φλύαρος: "La parenté avec φλύω 'dire des niaiseries' . . . et τὸ φλύος 'bavardage' est évidente; mais la formation est obscure . . ." Archilochus, according to Herodian, wrote φλύος ἐπὶ φλυαρίας "*phluos* for *phluaria*" (Arch. fr. 284 West). So too, one finds in Aeschylus and the *Prometheus* author instances of the related *phlusai*, being used similarly to *phluarein*. Aesch. *Sept.* 661: ἐπ' ἀσπίδος φλύοντα σὺν φοίτωι φρενῶν; *PV* 504: οὐδείς, σάφ'οἶδα, μὴ μάτην φλῦσαι θέλων. Hutchinson (1985) ad *Sept.* 661: "The stem is connected with *fluo*, and is used of liquids bubbling up, bursting forth." The schol. glosses ad loc. φλύοντα] φλυαροῦντα "σὺν φοίτωι φρενῶν] σὺν μανίᾳ."

[2] Timocreon of Rhodes, in perhaps the earliest surviving usage, writes Κηΐα με προσῆλθε φλυαρία οὐκ ἐθέλοντα "Nonsense from Ceos came upon me unwillingly" (10 West), ridiculing Simonides.

[3] Beekes (2010) s.v. φλέδων and φληναφάω connects φλεδ-/φλην- as a case of pre-Greek nasalization. Chantraine (1968–80) s.v. φλεδονεία: "En réalité, on a affaire à un thème φλεδ- (φληδ- avec allongement) reposant sur II *bhl-ed-*, cf. III *bhl-d-* dans φλαδεῖν et παφλάζω . . . Au départ, la racine est *bhel-* '(se) gonfler, couler en bouillonnant' qui peut être suffixée en *d (φλεδ-) ou en *u (φλύω)."

[4] Beekes (2010) s.v. λῆρος. Chantraine (1968–80) s.v. λῆρος: "Et.: Obscure. En coupant λῆρος, on tente de faire entrer ces mots dans une série plus ou moins vague de termes se rapportant à la voix, à des cris bâtis sur *lā-*, . . . lat. lamentum."

[5] Beekes (2010) s.v. ὕθλος says there is no convincing etymolology. Chantraine (1968) s.v. ὕθλος suggests the possibility of rain (rather like the fluid sources of *phluaria*): "Persson, *Studien* 8, évoque ὕει 'il pleut', ce qui peut passer pour un simple jeu de mots."

[6] Beekes (2010) s.v. στωμύλος: "Traditionally compared with στόμα . . ."

"to drivel," "to talk nonsense." More abstractly, one might be said literally to "say nothing [of sense]" (οὐδὲν λέγειν),[7] to speak in vain (λέγειν μάταια or μάτην) or speak empty things (λέγειν κενά); to indulge in certain forms of μωρολογία or κενολογία, or, more colorfully, to "fall from an ass" (ἀπ᾽ ὄνου πίπτειν).[8] In a related category, there is speech which somehow loses its qualitative force through its being quantitatively too much – I mean "garrulity" like ἀδολεσχία, and λαλιά. Due to its sheer volume, such speech becomes mere twitters (τερετίσματα), their speakers compared to birds.[9]

In this chapter, I will not analyze all of these terms, but instead will focus on the two most common ones, those most often translated as "to speak nonsense" – φλυαρεῖν and ληρεῖν – in order to depict the broad range of denotations and connotations that "nonsense" has for the Greek mind, and, in that process, define nonsense more clearly.[10] There are two things which I would like to show in this chapter (i.e., the chapter's "use"): first, that to call something "nonsense" is a pragmatic act which deprives an utterance of force and meaning, and second, that certain formal features can contribute to the impression of nonsense more readily than others. These seem to be two separate ideas, even exclusive of one another, but they are interrelated as well, and one cannot provide an adequate picture of nonsense without telling both stories simultaneously. That is, when one sees "nonsense" as a pragmatic act – i.e., the choice not to interpret something that could be interpreted – it follows that *anything* can be called "nonsense" (so long as it complies with the speaker's agenda in calling it "nonsense"). But this very inclusivity of "nonsense" demands some type of nonsense to be perceived as "actual" nonsense (e.g., language with specific formal features), which provides the metaphorical material for the pejorative's broader use. If one approaches nonsense from the opposite angle, however, and isolates linguistic features whereby a statement might be registered as nonsense (e.g., repetition, rambling speech), the question of interpretation is immediately present since one person often discovers meaning or use for an utterance which is identified as nonsense by another. This is, of course, a central problem for any discussion of meaning, as I argued in the introduction.

---

[7] This important idiom is mirrored by the corresponding τι λέγειν "to say 'something,'" i.e., "to speak sensibly," "to say something worthwhile," etc. In form, this is probably the closest Greek comes to the English "nonsense," inasmuch as the οὐδέν of οὐδὲν λέγειν (just as the τι of τι λέγειν) refers to that extra-linguistic speech-element which English often calls "sense."

[8] For "fall from an ass," see, e.g., Plato *Laws* 701c, discussed below.

[9] Chantraine (1968–80) s.v. τερετίζω: "Et. Repose sur une onomatopée. Frisk se demande si c'est un arrangement pour τιριτίζω et évoque τιτίζω à côté de τέττιξ." For a list of birds as metaphorical labels for chatterers, see Alexis 96 KA.

[10] LSJ s.v φλυαρέω "talk nonsense"; φλυαρία "nonsense, foolery"; λῆρος "nonsense! humbug!"

The development of these two aspects of nonsense in this chapter will be set in counterpoint: one story is followed until the other becomes necessary. So, in the first section, I explore the use of the accusation "nonsense" in classical rhetoric, especially in the writings of Isocrates, where it becomes clear that "nonsense" implies a certain type of falsehood. I distinguish this falsehood from other forms of falsehood like lying or mistakes, and argue that the unique pejorative force of "nonsense" is that it suggests some sort of mental incompetence. While the accusation "lies" alerts the listener to the dangers of the speaker, the accusation "nonsense" renders that speaker danger-free, indeed without any potency at all, as though the speaker were abnormal and socially impotent.[11]

This leads into the following section where it is shown that when *phluarein* and *lērein* are used in a non-pejorative way, it is precisely to describe the speech/behavior of those who are mentally impaired – either those who are drunk (which still bears an element of the pejorative), or those who are delirious with fevers (which bears no pejorative trace). When combining the rhetorical/pejorative uses with the medical/non-pejorative uses, an abstract definition of nonsense may be reached: "a useless type of language/behavior, similar to the language/behavior of those who are mentally impaired." But up to this point, the argument is purely in the abstract, so now the reactive story must begin, since, as helpful as the definition is, it is still merely linking one abstract idea ("nonsense") to another abstract idea ("the speech/behavior of the mentally abnormal"). One desires concrete examples: e.g., what does such "nonsense" speech sound like, and what formal features might suggest the "nonsense" of delirious speech? Here I begin with some ancient descriptions of mental illness – especially *mania* – in order to flesh out the abstract definition, and then turn to Plato and Isocrates to elicit some possible features of nonsense, such as rambling speech and repetition. The social aspect of the "nonsense" definition ("to speak/behave like one mentally ill") is never abandoned but continually developed, since the perceived linguistic features of nonsense (repetition, rambling speech) still operate within the social continuum whereby certain people may be labeled as aberrant, or falling below the mental norm.[12]

One extra step is required before concluding the chapter, which is simply to show that φλυαρεῖν and ληρεῖν were not *only* pejorative or non-pejorative

---

[11] For the *phluaria* of Pl. *Ap.* 19c, see the discussion in Introduction.

[12] Those who treat nonsense as a formal category still enumerate linguistic features like repetition, rhyming, etc. see Stewart (1979). Cf. discussion of such linguistic features (e.g. repetition, homophony) in Chapter 4.

descriptions of delirious speech. Nonsense as language or activity cut off from and bearing no relationship to reality – when viewed in a positive light – is very similar to the category of "play" (*paidia*), and thus one finds these words appearing in social or festive contexts without any negative valence. One might, of course, think of many "uses" for play (as do Plato and Aristotle),[13] which might undermine any claim regarding nonsense's status as "useless." But play's perceived uselessness (especially from the player's point of view) is its foundational myth: that is, if one felt one's play were useful, it would stop feeling like "play" (and this perceived uselessness is what imbricates play with nonsense). By the end of this chapter, there should be a clear definition of Greek nonsense, a few examples of what might readily have been termed "nonsense" in ancient Greece, and an idea that words like φλυαρεῖν and ληρεῖν, on occasion, obtain a positive sense for precisely the same reasons as their negative sense – namely, that they denote a useless language/behavior similar to that of the mentally ill which bears no relationship to reality. With this in hand, it will be possible to relate "nonsense" to Greek comedy in the following chapters.

One last note before beginning: despite my interest in exploring a "category" of "nonsense," I hope not to seem complacent or blind to the differences between terms like the English "nonsense" and the Greek *phluaria* (or, for that matter, the Greek *phluaria* and the Greek *hythlos*, etc.). "Nonsense" is admittedly an imperfect term which cannot directly map on to Greek concepts, since English "nonsense" is probably less pejorative than the above Greek terms. So too, the English "nonsense" carries some baggage from twentieth-century analytic philosophy[14] and quite a bit of baggage from Victorian "nonsense literature" (which, in turn, evokes a growing eighteenth/nineteenth-century idealization of children in Europe).[15] The Greek can bear no such connotation with a literary genre (although relating the Italian *phluax* play to *phluaria* has experienced a recent revival)[16] nor did the Greeks ever idealize children

---

[13] For the educational uses of play see Pl. *Resp.* 4.424e; 7.536d–537a; *Leg.* 643b–c; Arist. *Pol.* 7.17, 1336a33–4; cf. Halliwell (2008) 20.

[14] E.g., Wittgenstein's 1921 *Tractatus* which defines as nonsense many seemingly meaningful propositions like "one is a number." See Hochberg (2003).

[15] For studies on English "nonsense" as informed by "nonsense literature" (e.g., Lewis Carroll, Edward Lear), see Sewell (1952); Stewart (1979); the thorough bibliography and discussion of various senses of "literary nonsense" in Tigges (1988) 6–46; more recently, cf. Lecercle (1990); Menninghaus (1995); Malcolm (1997); Trahair (2007); Antonelli and Chiummo (2009); Tarantino and Caruso (2009).

[16] Although Pollux (9.149) had connected *phluax* to *phluaria*, for most of the twentieth century the root was considered to be *phleō* (to teem) as most considered the genre to be connected to ancient south Italian rites of Dionysiac fertility (cf. *RE* s.v. "phluax"). After Taplin (1993) showed that a number of

and childish "nonsense" in the way the Victorians did (e.g., Lewis Carroll, Edward Lear). Yet, "nonsense" is still a useful translation for these Greek words, since (unlike, e.g., "blather" or "babble") it is broad enough to capture the range of applications of words like *phluaria* and *lēros* – which not only refer to useless speech, but (just as with English "nonsense")[17] also expand metaphorically to include useless actions and even useless objects.[18]

If one turns to the differences between Greek words for "nonsense," it can be seen, for example, that, while a doctor might report that a fevered patient began to *phluarein* or *lērein* ("to talk nonsense"), he would not say that the patient began to *hythlein* or *phlēnaphan* – a clear distinction between these words.[19] From a diachronic perspective, words like *lalia* and (possibly) *phluaria* are adopted to bear specific rhetorical meanings in the second sophistic, which never gained such specificity before that period. As much as possible, I will provide references in the footnotes to sentences where one word for "nonsense" is elsewhere substituted for another, where one word is distinguished from another, or where one is used in a certain sense only at a late date, in order to give a sense of diachrony for what is largely a synchronic study of classical Greek word usage.

"Nonsense!" as rhetorical accusation

Greek words for nonsense, like English words for nonsense ("rubbish," "blather," "twaddle," etc.), are generally pejorative. They tend to arise in accusations – for example, "my opponent's argument was complete

---

south Italian vases were not "*phluax* vases" after all, and that the genre was indeed Hellenistic (followed, e.g., by Gutzwiller (2007) 123–4), the ancient "nonsense play" etymology regained its status. Cf. Olson's (2007) introduction and Halliwell (2008) 116 n. 41 implying the connection.

[17] OED *s.v.* nonsense, A.1.1.b. for "foolish or extravagant conduct"; A.1.3. for "a trivial or worthless thing."

[18] E.g., food that provides delightful scent but no sustenance is called λῆρος (Alexis fr. 263 KA), wind-eggs (eggs without chicks) as φλυαρία (*CGFPR* fr. 62), medicine which has no effect as φλυαρία in Galen (*De Comp. Med.* 13.391), and dildos (which provide pleasure but not procreation) as φλυαρία, λῆρος, and ὕθλος (Austin *CGFPR* fr. 62, *Lys.* 159); cf. Pherecrates' Λῆροι. So when one wishes to apply *phluaria* or *lēros* more metaphorically/pejoratively to an object, it is precisely this aspect of uselessness which is being implied. As such it often sums up a list of objects, e.g., "ports, dockyards, and walls, and such nonsense": Pl. *Grg.* 519a3, *Phd.* 66c3, *Symp.* 211e3, *Ap.* 19c4. See also Epictetus 3.3.19, Lucian *Alex.* 47.17, Philo *De Spec. Legibus* 1.176.4.

[19] See section on "Nonsense and mental impairment" below for medical citations. Cf. Worman's (2008) section on "Socrates' crude blather" (186–212) where she connects words like *phluaria* and *lērēmata* to "lowbrow" talk (190, 227). For discussion of such words for "nonsense" in comedy, see Chapter 5; cf. Beta (2004) 148–74.

nonsense"[20] – accusations which depict stated facts or opinions as being so incorrect that they bear no discernible relationship to reality. Although these pejorative terms are particularly familiar from comedy, I will refrain from that discussion until a later chapter, in order to obtain a clear picture of nonsense outside the comic genre. In this section, I would like to examine how these nonsense-words are used in Greek oratory and compare the accusation of "nonsense" with other accusations. Since an orator generally wishes to persuade an audience that his own depiction of reality is true, while his opponent's depiction of reality is false, he will discover different ways to describe the falsehood of his opponent's speech.[21] Thus one finds under this broad category of "false speech" accusations such as "lies," "mistakes" "deceptions," "trickery," but also "nonsense."[22] Although all of these accusations might be categorized under the "not true" rubric, the force of each of them is quite different. To call someone's speech "nonsense" is to deprive that speech of all potency; to call someone's speech, for example, a "lie," is to grant that speech the ability to injure, break the law, commit outrage. While the latter has the important rhetorical effect of alerting the listener to the dangers of the speaker, the former has the opposite effect: rendering the speech not dangerous or potent at all, but utterly sterile. To call an utterance "nonsense" even hints that the speaker is somehow mentally weak – which, as will be seen, is a suggestion that is often collocated with the "nonsense" label. As such, the nonsense-speaker is not worthy of being taken seriously, is somehow extra-social and thus extra-legal – an implied status which provides "nonsense" with a pejorative force altogether different from that of other accusations of falsehood.

Since words like *phluarein* and *lērein* are frequent in classical prose, I will not examine every instance. Instead I will choose two instances that construct neat oppositions for defining these words (since usually nonsense-words can be difficult to isolate). Both examples are from an orator who has

---

[20] See, e.g., Isoc. *C. soph.* 11.5: βουλοίμην ἂν παύσασθαι τοὺς φλυαροῦντας; Dem. *De Pace* 10.10: νομίζω δὲ τὸν λέγοντα ληρεῖν; Dem. *Exordia* 48.3.1–2: εἰ . . . προσθήσειν αὐτοῖς οἴονταί με, ληροῦσιν. Just as often, it appears as an anticipated accusation from a rival speaker: Aeschin. *In Ctes.* 252.1: ὅτι δ᾽ οὐ ληρῶ, ἐκεῖθεν τὸν λόγον θεωρήσατε; Dem. *Ad Lept.* 20.2: ἀλλ᾽ ἐὰν δείξῃ πέντε, ἐγὼ ληρεῖν ὁμολογῶ.

[21] This is not the same as saying that an orator always wants to depict his opponent as "lying": see Brock (2004) 145 on Hesk (2000).

[22] For lies and deception ψεύδω, ἀπάτη, διαβάλλω (for the last see Chadwick, (1996) 87–94). For representations of deception and lying in classical Greek oratory, see Hesk (2000); at 10 n. 33 "Whilst *apatē* denotes an intentional lie or trick, *pseudos* can denote either an intentional or an unintentional falsehood." Somewhere between the danger of lies/deception and the impotence of nonsense one might locate words like φενακισμός and ἀλαζονεία which recall Black's (1983) "humbug" definition "deceptive misrepresentation" but "short of lying" or Frankfurt's (2005) definition of "bullshit" – see below at 31.

a particular knack for antitheses and thus is particularly useful for lexicography – Isocrates. Examples from other orators will be found in the footnotes, and it should be noted that the substitution of *lērein* for *phluarein* (and vice versa) is common. The first instance is from the end of Isocrates' *Panathenaicus*. Isocrates, in praising the history of Athens and criticizing Sparta's ancestors, addresses the opinion of a former student which depicts a reality opposed to that of Isocrates' speech.[23] The student's opinion is that "the Spartans discovered the best way of life" (205: τούτους φάσκων εὑρετὰς γεγενῆσθαι τῶν καλλίστων ἐπιτηδευμάτων). Since this is the opposite of what Isocrates has been claiming in the speech, it is clear that he must call this proposition false, but the antithesis he constructs in doing so is telling: "if, on the one hand, you happen to be speaking true things, . . . if, on the other hand, you happen to be speaking nonsense" (205–6: εἰ μὲν τυγχάνεις ἀληθῆ λέγων... εἰ δὲ σὺ μὲν φλυαρῶν τυγχάνεις ...). Why does not Isocrates simply employ the more obvious opposite of ἀληθῆ λέγων, namely ψευδῆ λέγων, "speaking things *not* true," or, perhaps, even further, "lying"? Obviously, there must be an aspect of φλυαρῶν here which denotes the falsity of the statement "the Spartans discovered the best way of life." But to call the statement "nonsense" is to say something more than that simply it is false, or that it is an incorrect depiction of reality. Although this opposition will be returned to, Isocrates' antithesis can be a starting point for defining the accusation of "speaking nonsense" (φλυαρῶν): that it is something opposed to "speaking true things" (ἀληθῆ λέγων). While a true statement accurately reflects reality, *phluaria* does not. In a reality where Spartans did not discover the best life, the statement "the Spartans discovered the best life" is *phluaria*.[24]

The second opposition that Isocrates constructs with *phluaria* – from the speech *Philip* – is different from that of the *Panathenaicus* but nonetheless pertinent. This antithesis regards not the truth-status of speech, but speech's ability to *do* things: either oratory can *do* something – e.g., rally the Greeks against Persia – or it can *do* nothing – e.g., be a rhetorical set-piece. This is most clearly and briefly articulated in *Philip* 13: τοὺς βουλομένους μὴ μάτην φλυαρεῖν, ἀλλὰ προὔργου τι ποιεῖν ("those who

---

[23] A simple reading of what becomes later a complicated interchange between teacher and student regarding interpretation. For the hermeneutic issues of the later interchange, see Eden (1987), von Reden and Goldhill (1999) 277–84, Roth (2003) – but these do not affect my simple lexicographical argument.

[24] For a similar pairing of a "nonsense" word with a "false/lying" word, see [Dem.] *In Aristog.* 1.70.5: ἡμεῖς ληροῦμεν, μᾶλλον δὲ ψευδόμεθα "we are speaking nonsense, rather we are lying." Note also that later in the passage Isocrates substitutes *phluarein* with *lērein*: ἔπειτ᾽ εἰ μὲν εὐλόγεις αὐτοὺς μηδὲν ἀκηκοὼς τῶν ἐμῶν, ἐλήρεις μὲν ἂν ... (*Panath.* 206.6–7).

desire, not to talk vain nonsense, but to do something useful").²⁵ Just as "speaking nonsense" (φλυαρεῖν) was opposed to "speaking true things" (ἀληθῆ λέγων) above, here it is opposed to "doing something useful" (προὔργου τι ποιεῖν). Proper speech must do something of use (προὔργου: literally, "for a work, deed" πρὸ ἔργου), Isocrates is claiming. There is an expectation that there must be something beyond the speech itself, some deed or action in real life that speech helps to effect. While proper speech provokes an action and participates in the chain of causes and effects, nonsense eschews such participation by "doing" nothing beyond itself.²⁶ This "useful/useless speech" opposition appears similarly in the *Panegyricus*, where Isocrates urges orators not to continue speaking on minor forensic issues or oratorical set-pieces, but to use their powers to rally the Greeks against Persia.²⁷ He writes (188):

> τοὺς δὲ τῶν λόγων ἀμφισβητοῦντας πρὸς μὲν τὴν παρακαταθήκην καὶ περὶ τῶν ἄλλων ὧν νῦν φλυαροῦσιν παύεσθαι γράφοντας πρὸς δὲ τοῦτον τὸν λόγον ποιεῖσθαι τὴν ἅμιλλαν...
>
> those of you competing in speeches [must] stop composing orations on "deposits"²⁸ or on the other themes which people now *phluarousin*, and center your rivalry on this subject ... [i.e., Panhellenic unification against the East]

There is the right kind of speech – that which has use – and the wrong kind of speech, that which has no further use beyond itself. He emphasizes this in the following lines: οὐ πρέπει περὶ μικρὰ διατρίβειν, οὐδὲ τοιαῦτα λέγειν ἐξ ὧν ὁ βίος μηδὲν ἐπιδώσει τῶν πεισθέντων "It is not proper to waste time on little things, nor to speak the sorts of things from which the life of the

---

²⁵ The context of these excerpts is here less important than their lexicographical value. Nevertheless, the opposition that Isocrates is drawing is the difference between addressing a crowd in a democracy and addressing a monarch. It is the latter he has come to realize that is προὔργον τι ποιεῖν. For notes on the passage, see Laistner (1927) 128–9, although his interests lie elsewhere than the meaning of φλυαρεῖν.

²⁶ See also Isoc. *Antid.* 3.1–2 ἡγούμενος τὰς μὲν ἐκείνων φλυαρίας οὐδεμίαν δύναμιν ἔχειν.

²⁷ Cf. Isoc. *Helen* 12 for the περὶ τῶν ἄλλων ὧν νῦν φλυαροῦσιν: namely encomia of bees and salt. Norlin (1928) 240 n.b.: "In general, he seems here to be thinking of such rhetorical *tours de force* as Lucian caricatures in his *Encomium on the House Fly*"; also Bonner (1920) 386. Note also the interchangeability of *phluarousi* and *lerousi* which Bonner notes, citing Isoc. *Panath.* 11: "He is advising aspirants for oratorical distinction to do exactly what he himself did throughout his own professional career, viz., to avoid forensic oratory (οὐδὲ περὶ τῶν ἰδίων συμβολαίων οὐδὲ περὶ ὧν ἄλλοι τινὲς ληροῦσι = πρὸς μὲν τὴν παρακαταθήκην καὶ περὶ τῶν ἄλλων ὧν νῦν φλυαροῦσι) and deal with topics of national importance."

²⁸ Bonner (1920) ad loc. says that the article in τὴν παρακαταθήκην is generic and not specific, referring to "a general topic for rhetorical exercises," not a specific speech. Although Norlin follows this reading, Mathieu and Brémond (1987[1938]) 187 overlook this in their note. Buchner (1958) 26–7 does not comment.

persuaded will derive no benefit." It is a strong opposition: speech which confers benefit on its listeners, and speech which does not – i.e., the sort which people "nowadays" blather (φλυαροῦσιν), according to Isocrates. Like the example from *Philip*, nonsense here is that which does not "do something useful" (προὔργου τι ποιεῖν).

Thus, the first opposition claims that nonsense is speech which is not "true." The second claims that nonsense is speech which does nothing "useful" and confers no benefit (τοιαῦτα λέγειν ἐξ ὧν ὁ βίος μηδὲν ἐπιδώσει τῶν πεισθέντων). If one briefly considers these usages, it is not difficult to see the relationship between them. In the first example, where the statement "the Spartans discovered the best life" is called *phluaria* – for the very reason that the statement is untrue, it cannot "do something useful" (προὔργου τι ποιεῖν). If the statement were shown to be true, one might presumably then engage in some activity affected by this statement, e.g., mimic the Spartan way of life, study Spartan customs, or reconsider one's politics. The truth-value of the statement is directly related to its applicability: if a statement is true, it can be used to confer something further beyond itself. Because the statement "the Spartans discovered the best life" is not true – is "nonsense" – it cannot confer any such further effect (something which clearly distinguishes *phluaria* from other falsehoods like lying – but this will be discussed below). So too, in the second opposition, although one would not readily oppose oratorical displays to truth-values, there is still a reasonable connection. For Isocrates' purposes, these oratorical displays for issues of lesser importance are not adequately responding to the circumstances of real life (e.g., a fragmented Greece, a powerful Persia). By engaging in less important issues (like the "deposit" speeches) or in oratory which does not participate in political realities, these speeches are engaging in certain acts of falsehood or quasi-fictions.[29] Such speeches do not directly deal with real-life situations; they do not provide a true depiction of reality; and for that reason (to come full circle) they can confer no further use. As useless language, they are *phluaria*.

One might roughly define *phluaria* from the two oppositions that Isocrates constructs as "a type of false and useless speech." To zero in a little further on this idea, it will help to consider its relationship to other false speech – for example, "lying." Staying with the example "the Spartans discovered the best way of life" as "nonsense," one might ask: if nonsense is

---

[29] Not that Isocrates is calling his own past set-pieces *phluaria* – it is simply the substance of the present opposition of *others'* rhetoric. For the relationship between falsehood and fiction in Greek thought, see Gill (1993); Bowie (1993). For more bibliography with discussion, see Hesk (2000) 176–88.

simply language which incorrectly depicts reality and is therefore of no use, cannot one say that the same "useless" effect is produced by lies? That is, presumably if one knows that the student's statement is a lie – just as if the statement were nonsense – one will not then proceed to "use" the statement. But something else would be suggested by the accusation "lies." If Isocrates had said that his former student was "lying" when he claimed "the Spartans were the discoverers of the best way of life," he would be suggesting that the student knew the correct version of reality (i.e., that the Spartans were not the discoverers) but told an incorrect version on purpose. Further, that the purpose of lying was likely to effect something beyond itself (προὔργου τι ποιεῖν), some hidden agenda – e.g., so that the persuaded listeners admire the Spartans or the pro-Spartan speaker, or (eventually, through a series of such false persuasions) perhaps even vote for a pro-Spartan politician. The pejorative force of "lying" is entangled with the personal affront involved in lying – that personal affront which makes lying and deception punishable by law in certain contexts.[30] One who is per-suaded by a lie is presumably acting no longer to his own advantage but to that of the liar. The pejorative force of *diabolē*, *apatē*, etc. lies precisely in that extra-linguistic danger.

But what is the pejorative force of calling the statement "the Spartans discovered the best life" nonsense? A clue may be found in how Isocrates continues: εἰ δὲ σὺ μὲν φλυαρῶν τυγχάνεις . . . οὐκ ἔστιν ὅπως οὐ μαίνεσθαι δόξεις ἅπασι τοῖς ἀκούσασιν, οὕτως εἰκῇ καὶ παρανόμως οὓς ἂν τύχῃς ἐπαινῶν. "But if you happen to be speaking nonsense . . . it is not possible that you will not seem to be *raving* to everyone listening, so randomly and lawlessly praising whomever you chance upon" (*Panath.* 206). This is certainly something different from lying, and even extends beyond an unintentional falsehood. If the one who is "talking nonsense" (φλυαρῶν) is similar to someone who is "raving" (and this is a relationship that will be explored in the following section), the suggestion is that not just the speech but the speaker has an impaired sense of reality. One does not need to look far to discover a parallel for this. In Xenophon's *Anabasis* one finds that a speech which is described as "foolish, naïve" in *oratio obliqua* is called "nonsense" in direct speech (1.3.16): μετὰ τοῦτον ἄλλος ἀνέστη, ἐπιδεικνὺς μὲν τὴν εὐήθειαν τοῦ τὰ πλοῖα αἰτεῖν κελεύοντος . . . ἐπιδεικνὺς δὲ ὡς εὔηθες εἴη ἡγεμόνα αἰτεῖν "after him another arose, showing the foolishness of the speaker who had bid them ask for ships . . . and showing

---

30 For ἀπάτη, see Lipsius (1984[1905–15]) 381; ψευδογραφῆς and other ψευδ-offenses Lipsius (1984 [1905–15]) 443–6; ψευδομαρτυρίων 778. For discussion of laws against deceit, see Hesk (2000) 51–64.

how foolish it would be to ask for a guide." When this speaker breaks into direct speech, he summarizes these "foolish" plans as nonsense (1.3.18): ἀλλ᾽ ἐγώ φημι ταῦτα μὲν φλυαρίας εἶναι. The pejorative force of "nonsense" here is not just that the speaker is incorrectly depicting reality – for a liar also can do so, as well as someone who is simply mistaken – but that the speaker is misrepresenting reality in the way that a foolish or naive person would. So too, with the statement "Spartans have discovered the best life": when Isocrates calls this nonsense, he is saying that it is such a radically misconstrued statement of reality that only someone with an impaired sense of reality could say it (e.g., one raving, or "foolish").[31]

Thus, it appears that someone who is accused of nonsense is participating in some sort of false and useless language. On the one hand, this "nonsense" is opposed to "speaking true things" (ἀληθῆ λέγων), on the other hand, it is opposed to speech which "does something useful" (προὔργου τι ποιεῖν), and, further, such "nonsense" seems to connote the speech of the mentally abnormal. It is here that one can begin to distinguish "nonsense," not only from ψευδῆ in the sense of "lies," but from ψευδῆ in its more general sense of "incorrect things, things which are not true." A key passage for this will be Xenophon's description of mental illness where he defines mental illness in terms of social majorities: the mentally ill make the sort of mistakes that most people do *not* make (and so, similarly, nonsense might be said to consist of such higher-order mistakes). But before turning to that passage of Xenophon, it is necessary to examine nonsense briefly in less pejorative and more descriptive contexts – that is, among medical writers. When *phluaria* or *lēros* is being used in a non-pejorative sense, it is precisely to describe the mental impairment of medical patients.

Nonsense and mental impairment

Phluarein and *lērein*[32] appear frequently in the Hippocratic corpus (fifth/ fourth century BCE)[33] and their use is always as symptoms for mental abnormalities, especially fevers. To take a typical example, this one considering the symptoms of the disease *lēthargos*: "The disease called *lēthargos*: he

---

[31] See also Dem. *Phil.* 3.20.8: ἂν δὲ ληρεῖν καὶ τετυφῶσθαι δοκῶ, Isoc. *Antid.* 90.4: ληρεῖν ἂν φαίη καὶ μαίνεσθαι.

[32] The corpus does not use other nonsense terms like *hythlos* or *ouden legein*, which suggests a less colloquial register for *phluarein* and *lērein*.

[33] Phillips (1973) 35, regarding the Hippocratic corpus as contained in Littre: "To attempt to date them closely is for the most part a foolish enterprise; all that can be said is that they appear to belong to the second half of the fifth century, with some continuation into the early fourth."

is taken with a cough, and he spits up a lot of wet saliva, and he φλυηρέει, and whenever he stops φλυηρέων, he sleeps, and he passes a bad-smelling stool."[34] It is clear that *phluaria* here is a symptom just as objective as excessive saliva or coughing, and this points to the conception that *phluaria* has certain formal features whereby it can be identified. *Phluarein* (just as *lērein*)[35] must be indicating a sort of delirium,[36] and, as such, the word often arises alongside weakness of the body (καὶ δυσθενεῖ καὶ φλυηρέει, *Morb.* 2.67.5; καὶ φλυηρέει ἐνίοτε, καὶ οὐ δύναται ἑωυτὸν κατέχειν, *Morb.* 3.13.6) as though weakness of the body (δυσθενεῖ) and weakness of the mind or tongue (φλυηρέει) went hand-in-hand (a paired *akrasia* which also arises with *methē* – drunkenness: see below).

For that reason, the (medical) meaning of *phluarein/lērein* is very close to verbs of madness like *mainesthai* or *paraphronein*.[37] For example, the following prognosis:

> If, looking up and speaking he is in his senses and does not speak/behave nonsensically (φθεγξάμενος παρ' ἑωυτῷ γένηται καὶ μὴ φλυηρῇ), he will lie down drowsy this day, but on the next will become healthy. But if, standing up he vomits bile, he will rave (μαίνεται) and in five days die indeed, if he does not sleep.[38]

It is clear that "speaking or behaving nonsensically" (φλυηρῇ) comes very close to "raving" (μαίνεται) here: that is, μὴ φλυηρῇ seems to be the opposite of μαίνεται. Both verbs point to mental impairment and, for that reason, *mainesthai* or other verbs of madness often appear together with *phluarein*

---

[34] *Morb.* 2.65.1–3: νοῦσος ἡ καλουμένη λήθαργος· βὴξ ἴσχει, καὶ τὸ σίαλον πτύει πουλὺ καὶ ὑγρόν, καὶ φλυηρέει, καὶ ὅταν παύσηται φλυηρέων, εὕδει, καὶ ἀποπατέει κάκοδμον.

[35] LSJ s.v. ληρέω 2: "of a sick person, *to be delirious*." Cf. Hippoc. *Epid.* 1.3.13(3).6–7 alongside Herophon's fever (πυρετὸς ὀξύς) and temporary insanity (παρεφρόνησεν), "'Έκτῃ, ἐλήρει· ἐς νύκτα ἱδρώς· ψύξις· λῆρος παρέμενεν." See also *Epid.* 7.1.56, 1.3.13(1).15, 3.1.1.3, 3.2.5.8, 7.1.25.8, 7.1.25.13, 7.1.25.20–3, 7.1.26.16, 7.1.109.5, 5.1.80.1. But more often used is the compound *paralērein*.

[36] "Deadly fever" πυρετὸς ὁ φονώδης, at *Morb.* 2.67.1. Linked with non-deadly, minor fevers in *De Diaeta* 84: πυρετοὶ ἐπιγίγνονται φαῦλοι, καὶ φλυαρεῖ and *De Iudicationibus* 11.13–14: ἀλλ' ἀχθῆ καὶ ὀδύνη ἔχῃ τὴν κεφαλήν, καὶ φλυηρέῃ, ἐπικάθηρον αὐτόν where fever is ἡ λιπυρίη (11.12). Also connected to fever at *Epid.* 4.1.20.

[37] For all practical purposes, I am treating different madness words as equivalent since I am only interested in the symptom "talking nonsense" and not other aspects of disease (e.g., whether it is caused by black bile, how long it lasts, etc.). As Padel (1995) 21 notes, in tragedy at least, these "madness" words are roughly interchangeable: "*Paranoia, anoia*, above all *oistros, lussa*, and *mania*, are tragedy's main madness nouns . . . In tragedy, they seem roughly interchangeable with each other. They are not different sorts of madness, but different words for the same thing. Someone who has *paranoia* has *mania*."

[38] *Morb.* 2.22.6–10: Οὗτος ἦν μὲν ἀνατείνας τοὺς ὀφθαλμοὺς καὶ φθεγξάμενος παρ' ἑωυτῷ γένηται καὶ μὴ φλυηρῇ, τὴν μὲν ἡμέρην ταύτην κεῖται κωμαίνων, τῇ δ' ὑστεραίῃ ὑγιὴς γίνεται· ἢν δ' ἀνιστάμενος χολὴν ἐμέῃ, μαίνεται, καὶ ἀποθνήσκει μάλιστα ἐν πέντε ἡμέρῃσιν, ἢν μὴ κατακοιμηθῇ.

or other verbs of nonsense.[39] Although it will be discussed later how nonsense differs from madness, for now it is simply the similarity that needs to be noticed.

Along the same descriptive/medical lines, these nonsense-verbs are also used to describe the effect of excessive alcoholic intoxication. Although one of truth's greatest friends, many Greeks would claim, is wine – "wine and truth,"[40] goes the dictum; "wine is the window to the soul,"[41] "wine shows the mind,"[42] to say nothing of the later *in vino veritas*[43] – there is also the notion that wine, excessive wine, causes one to *lērein*, to *phluarein*, to *mōrologein*. When someone reaches a certain point of inebriation, he or she is not revealing "truth," but simply "talking nonsense," "blathering," "saying stupid things." For that reason, when Peter, in *Acts*, is asked why his fellow disciples are speaking a strange gibberish (i.e., speaking in tongues), he must give assurance that the disciples are not drunk, "for it is only 9:00 a.m." (Acts 2.14–16; cf. Romans 8.23). It is in this sense that words like *phluarein*, *lērein*, and *mōrologein* seem to be used, and not in the sense of drunkenness causing one imprudently to reveal secrets. The fragments (from a passage of Plutarch) which have been ascribed variously to Aristotle or Chrysippus are as follows:

οἰνώσεως μὲν ἄνεσιν μέθης δὲ φλυαρίαν[44]
Drinking gives rise to relaxation, inebriation to *phluaria*.

τὴν μέθην λέγουσιν εἶναι λήρησιν πάροινον[45]
They define inebriation as drunken *lērēsis*.

---

[39] See Herodotus 3.35: Cambyses interchanges madness and nonsense to describe the Persians' opinion: Πέρσαι ... λέγοντες ταῦτα παραφρονέουσι and Πέρσαι φανέονται λέγοντες οὐδέν. Cf. Galen *De Diff. Puls.* 4.8.611.13–14: ἀρά γε παίζων ἢ μαινόμενος τὰ τοιαῦτα ληρεῖ and ps.-Callisthenes *Hist. Alex. Mag.* 2.10.9 τὰς κενὰς φλυαρίας σου ... τε μανίας. Diog Laert. 7.118.8 διὰ μελαγχολίαν ἢ λήρησιν. See also the oratorical examples cited above.

[40] See Gow (1950) 504 ad Theoc. 29.1 for list of ancient citations.

[41] Alc. fr. 333 Lobel/Page: οἶνος γὰρ ἀνθρώπω δίοπτρον. Cf. also Aesch. fr. 393 Radt: κάτοπτρον εἴδους χαλκός ἐστ', οἶνος δὲ νοῦ.

[42] Thgn. 500: ἀνδρὸς δ' οἶνος ἔδειξε νόον; cf. Pl. *Symp.* 217e with Dover's note: "[the line] obviously means that drunken men, through carelessness, and children, through natural candour, tell the truth."

[43] See Rösler (1995) who argues that Theocritus' χρὴ μεθύοντας ἀλάθεας ἔμμεναι (Id. 29) ought to be translated as a sympotic obligation not a necessity of alcohol's effects – turning to an example of a present-day group psychotherapy session (108). The other (and opposite) function of wine – to cause some to ληρεῖν – is not discussed.

[44] From Plut. *De Garr.* 503f1–2. Rose has claimed this passage for Aristotle (fr. 102). Aristotle avoids the term *phluaria* in extant writing, except in the early Platonic *Protrepticus*.

[45] From Plut. *De Garr.* 504B1–4 (οἱ δὲ φιλόσοφοι καὶ ὁριζόμενοι τὴν μέθην λέγουσιν εἶναι λήρησιν πάροινον· οὕτως οὐ ψέγεται τὸ πίνειν, εἰ προσείη τῷ πίνειν τὸ σιωπᾶν· ἀλλ' ἡ μωρολογία μέθην ποιεῖ τὴν οἴνωσιν) and *Quaest. conv.* 716f1–2 (τὴν γοῦν μέθην οἱ λοιδοροῦντες φιλόσοφοι λήρησιν πάροινον ἀποκαλοῦσιν). Helmbold and O'Neil (1959) 17 claim it for Chrysippus.

ἀλλ' ἡ μωρολογία μέθην ποιεῖ τὴν οἴνωσιν.[46]
It is *morologia* which makes drinking inebriation.

All three of these statements – and it does not matter much to my argument whether these fragments originated with Aristotle or Chrysippus or some other philosopher – point to an important phenomenon. In each case "speaking nonsense" (or possibly nonsensical behavior) is the touchstone for inebriation, as if "nonsense" were some objective feature, a symptom by which one might diagnose drunkenness (just as nonsense is a symptom for mental disorders caused by fevers). And so these lines have been translated as "silly talk in one's cups," "foolish talk," "vinous babbling," "foolish twaddling," and so forth.[47] So too, Plutarch glosses the second quotation with τὸ δὲ ληρεῖν οὐδέν ἐστιν ἀλλ' ἢ λόγῳ κενῷ χρῆσθαι καὶ φλυαρώδει (*Quaest. Conv.* 716f2–3) "and *lērein* is nothing other than using empty nonsense (*phluarōdei*) speech." Although this merely defines abstractions with more abstractions, it is clear that what is being defined here is not the confessional speech of *oinos dioptron*, but rather a type of "empty speech," speech devoid of truth-claims, truth content, or use.[48]

To sum up, when used in contexts of both fevers and drunkenness, the words *phluarein* and *lērein* become purely descriptive, lacking their rhetorical, pejorative senses. They are used as hard data – symptoms – whereby one might tell the difference between a healthy person and a sick person, a sober person and a drunk person. This suggests that there is a perception in ancient Greece of "actual" nonsense and, further, that this idea of "actual" nonsense (e.g., the language of delirium) is what is informing the pejorative accusation "nonsense." If this is so, it can be seen that the mental illness often simultaneously suggested by orators when accusing an opponent of nonsense, is precisely what is being hinted at by the accusation of "nonsense" itself.

Definition of nonsense

When one considers the usage of *phluarein* or *lērein* as non-pejorative (e.g., in the Hippocratic corpus regarding fevers but also in descriptions

---

[46] Although Rose cites the whole passage under Aristotle fr. 102, Helmbold and O'Neil (1959) 8 rightly, in my view, attribute only this last sentence to Aristotle (504b4); Aristotle prefers the term *morologia* rather than, e.g., *phluaria*.

[47] Plut. *Mor.* 504b1–2 "foolish talk," 716f2–3 "vinous babbling," 503f "foolish twaddling" (Babbitt, trans.). For ancient citations relating drunkenness and madness, see Olson ad *Ach.* 1166–8.

[48] For more on Stoics and drunken nonsense, see Philo's discussion in *De Plant.* and Schofield (1983) 41–2. For the possibility that Plutarch is referring to sympotic *willed* nonsense (which is considered both positive and pleasurable), see the section "Nonsense and play" below.

of drunkenness), it clarifies how the terms are being used metaphorically in rhetorical contexts. It is along these medical lines that the pejorative force of the accusation "nonsense" can be understood. To return to the argument: the accusation "nonsense" cannot convey the personal affront that "lying" or "deception" does, since, whereas the liar knowingly passes a false statement as true in order to serve a hidden agenda, the nonsense-speaker, *qua* mentally incompetent, has no hidden agenda – he or she is simply too "simple" *euēthēs* (as the character from Xenophon's *Anabasis* suggests above), his or her speech too random to be calculated. While the accusation "lies" identifies the hidden dangers and potencies of the liar, the pejorative force of "nonsense" is to deprive the speaker of any such potency at all.

Although the two categories are in stark contrast to one another, the complications involved must be noted. To return to Isocrates' "the Spartans discovered the best way of life" – just as any proposition can be called a "lie," any proposition can also be called "nonsense." For that reason, it is not difficult to find examples of someone calling a propositional statement a "lie" but later "nonsense," or toggling back and forth between the two terms. But this should not cause one to conflate nonsense with other forms of falsity. Rather, when a speaker toggles between terms one should be aware of the sensitive calibrations that are occurring within the speech. For example, when Isocrates writes to Philip how Philip is being slandered (73) αἰσθάνομαι γάρ σε διαβαλλόμενον ὑπὸ τῶν σοὶ μὲν φθονούντων "For I perceive that you are being slandered by those who are envious of you," and then lists the number of slanders against him, only to sum up these very slanders as "nonsense" (ταῦτα φλυαροῦντες "the ones blathering these things," 75), one need not think that φλυαροῦντες and διαβάλλοντες are somehow synonymous. Rather, by calling these slanders "nonsense," Isocrates is playing a careful game of calibration. He can distance himself from the statements in a way that he could not with the word διαβάλλοντες. While all slanders have the potential to be believed – which, of course, is their primary danger – nonsense has no such potential. By calling the slanders "nonsense," Isocrates is saying that he (along with Philip) knows the accusations to be not simply false, but completely unrelatable to reality: the sort of language that fools or madmen speak. It is a moment of careful, calculated deflation while enumerating the threats against Philip: if he were simply to enumerate all the slanders that the Greeks were spreading, he would be constructing a hostile worldview for Philip. By slipping in the idea that it is all just *phluaria* Isocrates can defuse this threatening picture as mere foolishness. It is my view that all occurrences of *phluaria/lēros* should be treated this way, and that the aspects it shares with other forms of falsehood does not extend beyond its status as an incorrect depiction of reality. The citations that conflict with this view are quite late and rather anomalous.[49]

Thus, "nonsense" as an accusation suggests useless language, language which bears no relationship to reality and, as an accusation, one which renders the speaker impotent (unlike "lies" which alerts one to the dangers of the liar) *as if* the speaker were a fool (εὐήθης) or insane (μαινόμενος). There is a rather vague middle ground of falsehood which should be noted – not outright lies but not exactly nonsense either. Here one can locate *alazoneia, phenakismos*, and recall Max Black's "a deceptive misrepresentation, short of lying" ("humbug")[50] or Harry Frankfurt's distinction of a falsehood which misrepresents neither the "state of affairs . . . nor the beliefs of the speaker" but the "speaker's enterprise" ("bullshit").[51] But even here, that element of deception, however slight, is what distinguishes words like *alazoneia* and *phenakismos* from "nonsense." Nonsense, on the other hand, should be defined as follows: a certain type of false and useless speech/behavior, similar to the speech/behavior of the mentally impaired.

"Nonsense": some concrete examples

In achieving an abstract definition of nonsense not much has been achieved since one abstract idea has simply been substituted for another: "nonsense" is like the kind of speech/behavior produced by the "mentally abnormal." But then, one might ask, who are the "mentally abnormal"? The answer, presumably, in the circularity of abstractions would be: "the type of people who speak nonsense." Some concrete examples of what might have been

---

[49] The only passage where *phluarein* seems to mean "denigrate" is 3 Ep. John 10 λόγοις πονηροῖς φλυαρῶν ἡμᾶς, which is the only instance I have found of *phluarein* + acc. (recipient of *phluaria*) + dat. (the *phluaria* itself) and is thus quite anomalous. The passages that Halliwell (2008) 116 cites ("[*phluarein*] is sometimes associated with denigration") – Xen. *Hell.* 6.3.12 and Isoc. 5.79 – both use *phluarein* rhetorically to deprive a perceived denigration of its force (as has been discussed in this section on the rhetoric of nonsense). For the "passive" forms (see Philo *Leg.* 363.2, Diog. Laert. 7.173.7) which are best translated into English as "being made a fool of" or "having been made a fool of," I would argue that this points not to an active sense of *phluarein* "to mock" but rather to an extension of "talking like a fool" to "being made to seem like a fool": for the lack of a real passive voice in Greek, see Conrad (2002).

[50] Black (1983) 143 defines "humbug" as a "deceptive misrepresentation, short of lying, especially by pretentious word or deed, of somebody's own thoughts, feelings or attitudes." He suggests possible synonyms for such falsehood as "hokum," "drivel," "buncombe," "imposture," "quackery," "balderdash," and "claptrap."

[51] Frankfurt (2005) 53–4: "What bullshit essentially misrepresents is neither the state of affairs to which it refers nor the beliefs of the speaker concerning that state of affairs. Those are what lies represent, by virtue of being false . . . What [the bullshitter] does necessarily attempt to deceive us about is his enterprise. His only indispensably distinctive characteristic is that in a certain way he misrepresents what he is up to."

termed "nonsense" in ancient Greece would help to escape this circle of abstractions. While it is possible to see the accusation "nonsense" as a pragmatic act in rhetorical contexts (i.e., not to interpret an interpretable statement in order to deprive that statement of force), in medical contexts it became clear that doctors appeared to be registering "actual" nonsense, as if there existed formal features or concrete examples of such nonsense speech/behavior. So it is worthwhile to examine some descriptions of mental impairment, since, in the Hippocratic corpus, "speaking nonsense" was presumed to be so objective and recognizable that no further description was deemed necessary (just as with other symptoms like "excessive saliva" or a "cough"). Although I argued in the introduction that I wish to abandon any idea of objective nonsense, the existence of perceptions of "actual" nonsense (e.g., in the medical writers) is central to this study of interpretation.

In Xenophon's *Memorabilia* (3.9.6–7), Socrates provides some examples of mental illness, explaining that such impairment consists of not the sorts of mistakes everyone makes, but those that only a few make.[52] His examples are of someone thinking that he is so large that he stoops to pass through city-gates (ἐάν τε γάρ τις μέγας οὕτως οἴηται εἶναι ὥστε κύπτειν τὰς πύλας τοῦ τείχους διεξιών), or someone who thinks that he is so strong as to try to lift a house (ἐάν τε οὕτως ἰσχυρὸς ὥστ' ἐπιχειρεῖν οἰκίας αἴρεσθαι). Either language or behavior can be imagined here: e.g., someone expressing concern about hitting the huge city gates, or literally crouching so as to pass through them. What the language and behavior have in common is the impossible (ἀδύνατα) – i.e., what is considered impossible by most people is considered possible by the mentally impaired, what is not actual is considered actual. Their language and behavior reflect a reality which is not there. Another example: the third-century BCE historian Hegesander reports a certain Menecrates who dressed as Zeus, called himself Zeus, and had a cult following of those he had "healed" – a following who, in turn, adopted the names of other gods. In writing a letter to Philip II, Menecrates explained that he is Zeus, the healer of the world, and therefore greater than Philip, to which Philip supposedly responded Φίλιππος Μενεκράτει ὑγιαίνειν "Dear Menecrates, be sane!"[53] – pointing to the fact that Menecrates was speaking *ouden hygies*, a term which is often translated as "nonsense," but obviously

---

[52] Xen. *Mem.* 3.9.6–7: ἃ μὲν οἱ πλεῖστοι ἀγνοοῦσι, τοὺς διημαρτηκότας τούτων οὐ φάσκειν μαίνεσθαι, τοὺς δὲ διημαρτηκότας ὧν οἱ πολλοὶ γιγνώσκουσι μαινομένους καλεῖν.

[53] Hegesander fr. 5, *FHG* iv.414, from Ath. 7.289c–e. For Menecrates, who was apparently also ridiculed in Alexis' *Minos* (156 KA) and Ephippus' *Peltasts* (17 KA) – which is also from the same passage of Athenaeus – see Weinreich (1933); Rosen (1968) 104–7.

carries the connotation of poor mental health.[54] It should be noted that the syntax of Menecrates' letter is perfectly fine, but that it is the abnormal content that causes the response ὑγιαίνειν. One last example to add some more concrete substance to the abstraction of "mental impairment": the fourth-century philosopher Heraclides Ponticus tells of a certain Thrasyllus, who in his delirium (διετέθη ποτὲ ὑπὸ μανίας) would venture every day to the Piraeus since he believed that all the ships there were his. He took so much joy in tracking his ships, logging their comings and goings, that when he was treated, and his mania abated, real life was a comparative disappointment.[55] Like the hypothetical man who says he is too large to pass through the city-gates, or Menecrates who claims that he is Zeus giving life to all, Thrasyllus' behavior (and presumably his language) is comprehensible, but expresses *adynata*, things that are impossible. For that reason the language/behavior is dismissed as aberrant. It does not seem implausible that these examples are equally applicable to the delirious mistakes of the fevered Hippocratic patients who are said to "speak nonsense." A delirious patient, one might imagine, also could say things like "I am Zeus" or "I am too large for this room," since such "nonsense" expresses a reality that is not actual, not there. If this is the case, Xenophon's initial definition can help to differentiate "nonsense" from "mistakes" more generally: one who is "speaking nonsense" is making not the mistakes that "most people" make, but those that very few make.

Many more examples of potential nonsense could be elicited: one could turn to the possible "nonsense speech" of demented characters in tragedy – for example, Pentheus' καὶ μὴν ὁρᾶν μοι δύο μὲν ἡλίους δοκῶ, / δισσὰς δὲ Θήβας καὶ πόλισμ' ἑπτάστομον[56] – but in tragedy, the gravitational pull of the interpretive response is at its strongest, so the examples are best resisted.[57] "Much madness is divinest sense," after all, and this is one of the major differences between *mania*/madness and *phluaria*/nonsense.

---

[54] Also note Philip's wordplay on ὑγιαίνειν for the usual *khairein* or *eu prattein*; noted by Gulick ad loc. with parallel cited Plut. *Ages.* 21. For *ouden hygies* translated as "nonsense," see, e.g., Sommerstein (2001) ad. *Plut.* 274.

[55] Heraclides Ponticus fr. 56 Wehrli from Ath. 12.554e. Thrasyllus' behavior is also reported in Ael. *VH* 4.25. For the trope of never being happier than when deluded, see also Hor. *Epist.* 2.2, 128–40, who reports someone who was happiest when he was deluded, thinking he was hearing performances in an empty theater. For discussion, see Rosen (1968) 95–6.

[56] Eur. *Bacch.* 918–9, although some consider this drunkenness rather than delirium (it matters little for my argument). Cf., e.g., Clem. Al. *Paed.* 2.2.24 (although he may be mistaken in line attribution since he calls the speaker μεθύων ὁ Θηβαῖος ἔλεγεν γέρων) and *Prot.* 12.118.5 where the line is attributed to a certain παροινοῦντα καὶ . . . παρανοοῦντα. For discussion, see O'Brien-Moore (1924) 140–2; Dodds (1960) 182; Seaford 1987.

[57] For madness in Greek tragedy, see O'Brien-Moore (1924) 74–149; Padel (1995). Mad or possessed characters: Aeschylus' Orestes (*Cho.*) and Cassandra (*Ag.*); Io in *PV*; Sophocles' Ajax; Euripides' Orestes (*Or.* and *IT*), Heracles. For epic, see Hershkowitz (1998) 16, who well conveys this

Although the above examples of mental illness may help to flesh out part of the "nonsense" definition in the previous section, it should be noted that none of these examples is actually referred to as *phluaria* or *lēros*. Moreover, I do not want to suggest that "madness" and "nonsense" are the same concepts: although the delirium described in medical writers (*phluarein*, *lērein*) often draws very close in meaning to verbs like *mainesthai*, *paraphronein*, they cannot be equivalent since there are certain contexts where one verb of delirium cannot be substituted for another. "Madness" is different from "nonsense" in two respects. First, madness is often interpreted as "meaningful" (i.e., "divine" madness, the divine truth of madness): the possessed oracles, the words of Cassandra, no matter how abstruse, are considered interpretable language, language that is referring to actual events, language that if adopted can lead to right action – in a word, "useful" language.[58] This does not fit Isocrates' definition of nonsense, since such madness does what *phluaria* cannot: it can "do something useful" (προὔργου τι ποιεῖν).

The second way in which "nonsense" is different from "madness" is that there is a real sense of madness being dangerous – *mainomenoi* have a tendency to throw rocks, attack people without reason, and cause pollution to those who come in contact with them (to say nothing of Hercules).[59] So too there are the harmful economic consequences of insanity/senility (*paranoia*) which Athenian law tries to prevent regarding inheritance.[60] *Phluarein/lērein*, on the other hand, although expressing a delirium similar to madness, suggests a more sterile form of madness – that is, it neither can be useful, nor can it be violent (the rhetorical force of the words showing precisely this, as has been shown: to render the speaker *not* dangerous or potent). The Hippocratic patients that "babble" or "talk nonsense" neither reveal eternal, divine truths, nor behave violently. Medically speaking, "nonsense" is used to describe the kind of mental aberration which cannot threaten, either with violence or with meaning.

Thus, although nonsense is not equivalent to madness, it is still worth keeping the above examples in mind as possible instances of what a Greek

---

hermeneutic response of the meaning of madness in serious literature, e.g., "poetics of madness, or the meaning created *by* madness in the texts under investigation" including the "meta-madness" of the poet's being mad, 61–7.

[58] See Dodds (1973[1951]) 64–101, "The blessings of madness." Pl. *Phdr.* 244a, *Timaeus* 71d–e; cf. Hershkowitz (1998) 16 on epic.

[59] See Ar. *Ran.* 555–67, *Vesp.* 1482–91; Ps.-Pl. *Alc. II* 139d; Arist. *EN* 7.5, 1148b25–27 for a man who killed and ate his mother διὰ μανίαν; cf. Rosen (1968) 100–1; Diggle (2004) 374–5.

[60] Dover ad *Nub.* 845 on *paranoia*: "It seems that if a man was incapacitated by insanity or senility his son could obtain through a law court the right to administer the family's property." Cf. Aeschin. 3.251, Xen. *Mem.* 1.2.49, Pl. *Leg.* 929d–e, Arist. *Ath. Pol.* 56.6, Isaeus 1. For the law, see Lipsius (1984 [1905–15]) 355; also Glotz (1929) 232–262; Hershkowitz (1998) 12; Harrison (1968) 80–1.

doctor might have called "nonsense" (*phluaria, lēros*) – Xenophon's hypothetical man crouching through the gates, trying to lift a house, Menecrates
proclaiming that he is Zeus, Thrasyllus that he is the owner of all the ships
in the Piraeus – since all of these examples correspond with the "nonsense"
definition: that of speech/behavior which is useless, reflecting a reality that is
highly discrepant from reality. These examples provide some flesh to the
abstractions of nonsense's definition: if nonsense is a type of false or useless
speech/behavior similar to that of the mentally abnormal, it can now be said
that nonsense is a type of false or useless behavior similar to the speech/
behavior of Xenophon's man, Menecrates, and Thrasyllus. All participate in
a type of exertion (whether in speech or action) which is to no effect, for no
real purpose. It should be noticed, however, that "nonsense" as a subjective
result of interpretation is still very much present – Xenophon speaks of
nonsense/sense in terms of intersubjective minorities and majorities (ἃ μὲν
οἱ πλεῖστοι ἀγνοοῦσι … ὧν οἱ πολλοὶ γιγνώσκουσι μαινομένους καλεῖν,
Mem. 3.9.6), and the cult following of Menecrates (a minority) clearly
interprets his language/behavior differently than do Philip and the Greek
majority. Nevertheless, it is helpful to observe the various perceptions of
nonsense in society, and in the next section, it will be seen that such
observations often tie nonsense to certain linguistic features.

Nonsense and linguistic features

Looking at "nonsense" as a rhetorical accusation reminds that *anything* can
be nonsense. Any speaker can accuse another (or herself/himself) of "nonsense," whether the accused's utterance be a declarative statement with
truth-values (e.g., "the Spartans discovered the best way of life") or types
of utterances outside truth-commitments, like commands or questions. But
"nonsense" is often tied to certain formal features as well and it seems that
certain sorts of language increase the chances of receiving the label "nonsense" more than others. So one might categorize the above examples as
"speaking in opposites," the type of opposites which everyone "knows to
be false" as Xenophon says – e.g., "I am Zeus" when I clearly am not Zeus,
"I am larger than the city gate" when clearly I am of more modest stature.
But "speaking in opposites" is not exactly a formal linguistic feature since it
requires an extra-linguistic reality to oppose. In what follows I will elicit two
perceived features of nonsense from classical texts: one from a passage in
Isocrates which suggests nonsense as excessive repetition, the other from a
passage of Plato which suggests nonsense as excessively rambling speech. To
consider nonsense in this way is not to leave behind the idea of mental

impairment since the kind of language the delirious Hippocratic patients "babble" or "blather" should be the ever-present litmus test. But it is not hard to imagine a fevered, delirious person rambling with very little chain of thought or such a person constantly repeating a phrase or idea in his delirium, and such speech warranting the symptomatic label of "speaking nonsense."

In the *Antidosis*, Isocrates detects something which might be taken as a linguistic feature of nonsense. He is considering the idea of repetition – that it is difficult to say anything new since everything has already been said before. He muses on how life is easier for law-makers who merely need to collect laws that have succeeded elsewhere, while the orator, if he were to do the same (namely, repeat what had already succeeded elsewhere), would be accused of "shameless nonsense" (83.7–8: λέγοντες μὲν γὰρ ταὐτὰ τοῖς πρότερον εἰρημένοις ἀναισχυντεῖν καὶ ληρεῖν δόξουσι "for those saying the same things as were said before will seem to speak shameless nonsense"). Obviously, Isocrates is referring to something like repeated arguments or "cliché," but what exactly does "cliché" or a repeated argument have to do with "speaking nonsense"?[61] To say something which has already been said is presumably "useless" language since nothing new is being created, but Isocrates' label of "nonsense" (ληρεῖν) seems to be suggesting something more. Why does something become "nonsense" if it has already been said? It does not matter whether one translates this phenomenon as a cliché, or some other form of repetition: in either case, the idea being articulated is that a statement loses its force through its being repeated.

Something similar to this idea is articulated in Plutarch's *De Garrulitate*. He relates an anecdote about Lysias (504C), wherein one of Lysias' clients reports that when he read Lysias' speech once it seemed to be outstanding, but when he read it through multiple times it seemed dull and ineffective (ἀμβλὺν καὶ ἄπρακτον). Lysias supposedly responded with a laugh and said, "are you planning to recite it more than once to the jurors?" (οὐχ ἅπαξ μέλλεις λέγειν αὐτὸν ἐπὶ τῶν δικαστῶν;). While this anecdote about Lysias is different from Isocrates' anxiety (Isocrates' fear of repetition may be more along the lines of cliché; Lysias' client's concern is that a speech loses its effectiveness through repetition), the two are related. What makes Isocrates' cliché ineffective is that it has been said/heard before; what makes Lysias' speech ineffective for the client is that it too has been said/heard before. Such repetitive excess is not along the lines of the positive use of repetition

---

[61] Regarding repeated arguments, one might envision, e.g., a debate or even a trial with multiple *sunēgoroi* sharing the work on one side of the case: merely repeating what a previous speaker said in that debate/trial would be useless and make no new contribution to the enterprise.

for rhetorical force (anaphora, anadiplosis, etc.), or the positive use of repetition for magic and religious incantations. Rather what is being suggested is the negative effect of excessive repetition – that when a speech or utterance is repeated enough times and, through that repetition, no new extra-lingual idea is being produced, it cannot *do* anything (ἄπρακτον), it becomes blunt (ἀμβλὺν), and, in Isocrates' term (as language which *does* nothing), it becomes nonsense (ληρεῖν).

Related is repetition not of the same words, but of the same idea. In a rhetorical treatise of the late second century CE, one finds that a speaker who gives too many examples (*peritta*, sometimes translated as "redundancy")[62] for one idea is guilty of *phluaria*.[63] The grammarian's example of this mistake, oddly enough, is Thersites (Ps.-Dion. Hal., *Ars Rhet.* 11.8):

> Ὅμηρος ταῦτα ἐπεσημήνατο· "Θερσίτης δ' ἔτι μοῦνος ἀμετροεπὴς ἐκολῴα"· τίς τῆς ἀκαίρου περιττότητος ἡ αἰτία; ἐὰν γοῦν τοῦ Θερσίτου παρέλῃς δύο ἔπη, Νέστορος γίνεται δημηγορία.

> Homer showed this: "Thersites alone jabbered immoderately." What is the reason for this untimely excess? If you take away two sentences of Thersites, you'll get a speech of Nestor.

According to this grammarian, what is ἀμετροεπής about Thersites is not the abusive quality of his speech, but the *quantity*. If Thersites – according to this rhetorician – had given two fewer examples for his thought (γνώμη), he would have been as fine a speaker as Nestor. Instead, by repeating this thought over and over again, through a multitude of examples, he creates nonsense (φλυαρία), which is precisely what makes him laughable (for more examples of *phluaria* producing laughter, see below). He sums up the moral of the Thersites story as "we learn a great and illustrious lesson, not to think that the excellence of rhetoric be in the volume of what is spoken" (ὥστε ἤδη μάθημα μανθάνομεν μέγα καὶ λαμπρόν, μὴ ἐν τῷ πλήθει τῶν λεγομένων ἡγεῖσθαι τὴν ἀρετὴν τῆς ῥητορικῆς, 11.8.34–7). Although this is different from the repetition that Isocrates or Plutarch mentions

---

[62] For that reason also translated by LSJ as "redundancy," although the quotation from [Pl.] *Axiochus* (LSJ *s.v.* περισσός ΙΙ.3) does not require this translation.

[63] Ps.-Dion. Hal. discussing mistakes in expressing a thought (γνώμη). A speech giving too many examples becomes "nonsense," too few becomes "inadequate," and self-contradicting examples "dangerous": ἡ γνώμη τριπλῆν ἐξέτασιν ἔχει· μὴ περιττά, μὴ ἐλλείποντα, μὴ ἐναντία. τὰ περιττὰ φλυαρία, τὰ ἐλλείποντα ἀσθενῆ, τὰ ἐναντία κίνδυνος (11.8). The meaning is clearer when read with the author's other discussion on gnomic excess in 10.4 (as suggested by Russell (1978), 126: οἱ δὲ ὅπως πλεῖστα εἰς ἕκαστον τῶν ὑποκειμένων ζητημάτων ἐροῦσι, σκοποῦνται οὐκ εἰδότες, ὅτι τὰ μὲν φύσει ὁμολογούμενα καὶ τὰ τοῖς ἤθεσι διεγνωσμένα καὶ τὰ ἔθεσι κεκριμένα βραχείᾳ ἀποφάσει τὴν ἰσχὺν ἔχει, ἐὰν δέ τις μηκύνῃ, ψυχρότερα καὶ ἀσθενέστερα αὐτὰ ἐξεργάζεται). For the relationship between these two treatises and their date and authorship, see Russell (1978); Heath (2003).

(the excessive repetition of an idea vs. the excessive repetition of words), these different types of repetition are perceived to be features of nonsense.

If one returns to the classical period, it can be seen that while Isocrates suggests that one way of producing nonsense is through repetition, Plato suggests that another way is through a sort of rambling speech. In *Laws*, Plato explores a proverbial expression for "speak nonsense" which is to "fall from an ass"[64] (701c5–d2):

> δεῖν φαίνεται ἔμοιγε οἱόνπερ ἵππον τὸν λόγον ἑκάστοτε, ἀναλαμβάνειν, καὶ μὴ καθάπερ ἀχάλινον κεκτημένον τὸ στόμα, βίᾳ ὑπὸ τοῦ λόγου φερόμενον, κατὰ τὴν παροιμίαν ἀπό τινος ὄνου πεσεῖν, ἀλλ᾽ ἐπανερωτᾶν τὸ νυνδὴ λεχθέν, τὸ τίνος δὴ χάριν [ἕνεκα] ταῦτα ἐλέχθη).[65]

> It seems to me necessary to constantly pull up on the argument point-by-point like a horse, and not, like one with an unbridled mouth, borne forcefully along by the argument, "to fall from some ass" (= "speak nonsense") as the proverb goes, but to ask about what was just spoken, indeed, why these things were spoken.

The Athenian's injunction is that each point in an argument be checked to see what is being added logically to the overall argument. If one does not do this, one risks allowing the argument to act like "an unbridled horse" – that is, to run off in unintended directions, adding nothing to the overarching argument. Such an argument, then, without the signposts of an overarching, logical structure, risks "nonsense" (ἀπό τινος ὄνου πεσεῖν). As with Isocrates, one can find more expressions of this idea in later writers, but it is along the lines of the Athenian's notion that the ideas of "nonsense" (*phluarein*, *lērein*) and "garrulity" (*lalein*, *adoleskhein*) converge: when one speaks too much and loses track of the central thread, garrulity becomes nonsense.[66] Along these lines, when Aelius Aristides defines "garrulity," he says (*Pros Plat.* 53):

---

[64] For the proverbial expression, cf. *Nub.* 1273, τί δῆτα ληρεῖς ὥσπερ ἀπ᾽ ὄνου καταπεσών "why do you talk nonsense like one who fell from an ass?" The origin of the proverb is obscure: that it is a pun from ἀπὸ νοῦ πεσεῖν originates in the Suda and is proposed by LSJ (*s.v.* ὄνος 4). This possibility is rejected by Dover (1989[1968]) ad loc.

[65] England (1921) ad loc. notes that mss. A, L and O have νοῦ, while O² has ὄνου: "The mistake was probably not accidental, but due to a misunderstanding of some grammarian's note to the effect that often – e.g., the passage from the *Clouds* – ἀπ᾽ ὄνου was meant to be heard as ἀπὸ νοῦ." Cf. MacDowell ad. *Vesp.* 1370.

[66] For the pairing of "garrulity" words with nonsense words, see Alexis 9.10 KA λαλεῖν τι καὶ ληρεῖν (the meaning of this passage is discussed below). Plut. *De Garr.* 504b5: unlike the drunk who only speaks nonsense when drunk the garrulous man (ὁ δ᾽ ἀδόλεσχος) πανταχοῦ ληρεῖ; Plut. *De Garr.* 510c χαίρεις λαλῶν καὶ φλυαρῶν, *Quaest. Conv.* 716f4 λαλιᾶς δ᾽ ἀτάκτου καὶ φλυαρίας; Aristid. *Pros Plat.* 130.9 φλυαρίαν τινὰ καὶ λαλιὰν ἐπεδείκνυτο; Plut. *Quomodo adul.* 22a9 φλυαρεῖς τοσαῦτα καὶ

λαλιᾶς μὲν οἶμαι διὰ κενῆς ληρεῖν καὶ εἰς μηδὲν δέον καὶ διατρίβειν τηνάλλως, λόγων δὲ ἀληθινῶν τῶν καιρῶν καὶ τῶν πραγμάτων στοχάζεσθαι καὶ τὸ πρέπον σῴζειν πανταχοῦ.

I think it is the mark of garrulity to babble in vain and pointlessly, and fruitlessly to waste time, but it is the part of true speeches to aim at opportunity and action, and everywhere preserve propriety.

Just as the Athenian suggests that one might produce nonsense by not asking what each sub-argument is for, so Aristides says that speech which does not everywhere maintain what is appropriate but instead speaks about nothing necessary risks nonsense (διὰ κενῆς ληρεῖν). Because such speech seems to be random (60: φλυαρεῖν εἰκῇ) rather than rational (53: λόγων τῶν ἐμφρόνων), not aiming at anything (53: στοχάζεσθαι), it risks becoming qualitative nonsense through garrulous quantity. Only in this sense can verbal quality and quantity be in inverse proportion (as Plutarch writes in *De Garrulitate*).[67] When a long speech becomes excessively rambling, and one loses the central thread, the center of the widening gyre cannot hold and the utterance becomes nonsense (ἀπό τινος ὄνου πεσεῖν). One can find a fine example of Plato's excessive rambling in the *Lalos* ("chatterbox") of Theophrastus' *Characters*. It is not the quantity alone that ruins the nature of the speech but its rambling nature (and this aspect of *lalia* provides its later usage as a rhetorical term).[68] Here is Theophrastus' rambling *lalos* (7.7):

> If one inquires what happened at the assembly, he relates in addition (προσδιηγήσασθαι) also the battle which occurred in the time of the orator Aristophon and the one among the Spartans in the time of Lysander, and those public speeches which he himself delivered which were well received, and at the same time throwing in (παρεμβαλεῖν) an accusation against the masses, so that those listening either interrupt, nod off, or depart leaving him behind.

The *lalos* does not "check in" (as Plato's Athenian suggests) to see how each instance is helping to add to the main theme of "what happened at the

---

καταδολεσχεῖς ἡμῶν, Dion. Hal. *Comp.* 26.44 τὸν ἀδολέσχην τοῦτον λέγω καὶ φλύαρον, 26.46 ὅμοιον εὑρίσκω τῷ φλυάρῳ καὶ ἀδολέσχῃ and many more. The rather late date of these suggests that ληρεῖν and φλυαρεῖν may be converging with words for garrulity *after* the classical period.

[67] See 503b–c: "for just as they say that those who have lots of sex have sterile sperm, so the speech of chatterers (ἀδολέσχων) is ineffectual and fruitless (ἀτελὴς καὶ ἄκαρπός)."

[68] See Menander Rhetor's discussion (late second/early third CE) of *lalia* as a charming type of speech (Russell and Wilson (1981) 388–94), especially 391: "It is also to be noted, as a general principle, that a 'talk' (*lalia*) does not aim to preserve a regular order as other speeches do, but allow the treatment of the subject to be disorderly. You can put anything you please in first or second place. The best arrangement in a 'talk' (*lalia*) is to avoid proceeding always on the same track, but to display a continuous disorder." Translation is Russell and Wilson's.

assembly."[69] It is not simply the quantity of words which makes the *lalos* "fall from an ass" and "speak nonsense," but the excessively rambling nature of his lengthy speech.

Thus, while Isocrates suggests that nonsense can be produced through pointless repetition, Plato suggests that nonsense can be produced through pointless rambling. If one continually says the same things as before one risks nonsense; if one rambles without any central theme, one also risks nonsense. Both of these formal features congrue with the abstract definition of nonsense (a certain type of false or useless speech like that of the mentally impaired) as well as the Hippocratic, medical sense of "delirious babble." It is possible that the linguistic features which render the utterances of the fevered or drunk symptomatic are precisely features like repetitiveness or rambling speech.

Nonsense, illness, laughter

Looking at the medical aspects of "nonsense" has introduced the concept of nonsense as a symptom. Like a cough or excessive saliva, "delirious babble" or "talking nonsense" is treated as though it were so recognizable that no further description or definition is deemed necessary in the Hippocratic texts. In reconstructing that missing Hippocratic description, I have suggested two possible linguistic features of such "delirious" language – excessive repetition and rambling – teasing these features out of Isocrates' and Plato's usage of nonsense-terms. Alongside such excessive linguistic aberrations, I also suggested possible examples of delirious nonsense from descriptions of mental illness: e.g., Thrasyllus in the Piraeus or Menecrates' "I am Zeus." These examples exhibited a language or behavior reflecting an environment which was not real or actual (in fact, highly discrepant from the actual environment), and exertions which were to no purpose or effect. These concrete examples and formal features of nonsense can further develop the abstract definition: while disorganized ramblings, repetitive speech, and, more generally, speech/action regarding a non-existent reality trigger the medical diagnosis "nonsense," that medical diagnosis provides the metaphorical material for nonsense's extension as a pejorative term.

Before leaving behind this section, it is worthwhile to note one more shared feature between mental abnormality and nonsense: in antiquity, both were often found laughable. Regarding "nonsense," Diodorus Siculus, for

---

[69] Diggle (2004) 266: "if [others] want the latest news from the Assembly, he will give it, then add what they do not want . . ."

example, tells of someone convulsing with laughter (διαχυθεὶς ἐπὶ τῷ ῥηθέντι) after hearing what he considered to be nonsense (λῆρος) from a general.⁷⁰ Josephus wonders whether to laugh at an indiscreet etymology which he considers to be nonsense (καταγελάσειε τῆς φλυαρίας) or to despise its shamelessness;⁷¹ Plutarch tells of a teacher who was clearly laughing (δῆλος ἦν καταγελῶν) while listening to a theoretical speech and, finally, could not contain himself, calling the speech complete nonsense (φλυαρίαν ... πολλὴν).⁷² Dionysius of Halicarnassus thinks that poetry that resembles the garrulous nonsense (τῷ φλυάρῳ καὶ ἀδολέσχηι) of some prose is worthy of laughter (γέλωτος ἄξιον).⁷³ There are many similar examples of this reaction of laughter in the face of perceived nonsense,⁷⁴ and what these examples share is laughter arising not from intentionally funny statements (e.g., jokes or anecdotes) but rather from statements which are perceived to be so distant from reality that they are found laughable (a laughable effect, of course, unintended by the earnest "nonsense"-speaker). Although I will map out this relationship between perceived nonsense and the laughable in Chapter 4, for now it can be seen that these citations are, again, examples of interpretation: the alleged "nonsense" statements are neither repetitive nor rambling, nor do they, in the words of Xenophon, make the sorts of mistakes that only a few make. But in that pragmatic act of calling a statement "nonsense" and depriving that statement thereby of all force and meaning, it is as if something else needs to replace what would have been the exertion of interpretation – which, in this case, is laughter.

Similarly, just as nonsense was often considered laughable, it should also be recalled that certain forms of mental impairment *itself* provided a source of laughter. In the *Bacchae*, Dionysus induces Pentheus' madness, so he says, to make him a laughing-stock before the Thebans (854: χρηίζω δέ νιν γέλωτα Θηβαίοις ὀφλεῖν), and although it is not stated explicitly in the above examples – e.g., Xenophon's man crouching through the city gates,

---

⁷⁰ Diod. Sic. 37.18.1: "Convulsed with laughter at this remark (διαχυθεὶς ἐπὶ τῷ ῥηθέντι), the Cretan said: 'In the eyes of the Cretans citizenship is just high-sounding claptrap (εὐφημούμενός ἐστι λῆρος)'" (trans. Walton and Geer).

⁷¹ *Contra Apionem* 2.22 regarding Apion's etymology of "sabbath" as an Egyptian word for groin disease.

⁷² Plut. *Quaest. Conv.* 738f13–15.   ⁷³ *De Comp. Verb.* 26.46–7.

⁷⁴ Cf. Plut. *Arist.* 10.8 where the Spartans laugh at Aristides for his mistaken accusations (οἱ δὲ σὺν γέλωτι ληρεῖν αὐτὸν ἔφασκον), *Mor.* 472a5 where young pigment-grinders mock someone for babbling ignorantly about art (παιδάρια καταγελᾷ σου φλυαροῦντος). See also Dio Chrysostom 66 who says not to pay attention to the nonsense of the crowd (τῆς τῶν πολλῶν φλυαρίας) but laugh at their garrulity (ἀλλὰ τῆς μὲν ἐκείνων ἀδολεσχίας καταγελᾷ). See also Philo *Quod omnis probus liber sit* 104.4, and Thersites in Dionysius of Halicarnassus, discussed above. The doubling of γέλωτα καὶ φλήναφον seems only to occur in late antiquity.

or Thrasyllus' bustling about the Piraeus – it seems unlikely in light of other ancient evidence that the response to these mentally deranged characters was one of sympathy. Not simply Philip's playful response to Menecrates' letter (or the further treatment reported by Athenaeus), but a range of evidence notes that the deranged were often social butts for their nonsense speech and nonsense behavior (again, as if in the act of *not* interpreting, something else needs to take interpretation's place). Euthyphro, for example, claims that when he gives his prophecies in court, he is ridiculed as a madman (*Euthphr.* 3c καταγελῶσιν ὡς μαινομένου) and later Aesop playing with nuts is laughed at as if he were crazy (Phaedrus 3.14.1–3 "quasi delirum risit"). Less metaphorically, Philo tells of a certain Carabas (*In Flaccum* 36–7) who would spend day and night naked in the streets, and was a "plaything" for boys and teenagers (ἄθυρμα νηπίων καὶ μειρακίων σχολαζόντων):[75] they would dress him up as a king with a play costume and pretend to be his bodyguards. In Plutarch, the citizens laugh at Mithridates who seemed like a madman riding around on a horse exclaiming "all this is mine!" ἐμὰ ταῦτα πάντα ἐστί.[76] It is doubtful that Thrasyllus, for example, bustling about the Piraeus (before his family returned from Sicily to give him proper medical treatment), was treated any differently than Euthyphro's being ridiculed "as a madman," or the children playing with Carabas. Sympathy's ambit was more limited in the ancient world.

In fact, laughing at the mentally ill was something of an institution in much of the ancient world. I mean the ancient habit of keeping "fools" – a practice of maintaining the mentally (and/or physically) handicapped for the purposes of entertainment, which is in fact at the root of the English "fool" as well.[77] Seneca writes (*Ep.* 50) of his wife's fool (*fatua*) Harpaste who was entrusted to him after her death. Although he cannot understand why people generally delight in such "freaks" (*prodigiis*), he can at least indulge himself in reporting her latest nonsense: she has gone blind but does not realize it, and, for that reason, keeps asking to change her living quarters which are "too dark." Clearly, this anecdote – which might strike modern readers as somewhat offensive – is meant to entertain and raise a laugh. Harpaste's nonsense-language (i.e., language reflecting a

---

[75] For children following the mentally deranged, see also Artemidorus 3.42: ἐπειδὴ καὶ παῖδες τοῖς μαινομένοις ἀκολουθοῦσι. For a modern example of making fun of mental defects, see the character Denny Dimwit in 1950s US cartoons.

[76] *Pomp.* 36.5–6.

[77] As the OED reminds, "fool" points to an important, albeit obscured moment of English comic entertainment: definition 2a is "a jester, clown" while definition 4 is "a weak-minded or idiotic person." But in 2a it is admitted "The 'fool' in great households was often actually a harmless lunatic or a person of weak intellect, so that this sense [2a] and sense 4 are often hard to distinguish."

non-existent reality) is indicative of her mental deficiency, and her mental deficiency to a typical Roman was inherently funny.[78] Although it must be admitted that this practice of keeping "fools" for entertainment may have passed by archaic and classical Greece (the institution may have developed in Pharaonic Egypt, was adopted by the Ptolemaic court, and then passed on to Rome),[79] laughing at the mentally abnormal was surely as much a Greek pastime as it was for the rest of the ancient world.[80] For this reason, it is protecting Greece too much to interpret deformed dancers on archaic vases as merely "pretending to be deformed" for comic effect.[81] So, it was not just "nonsense" which was found funny in the ancient world, but mental illness itself, and it is worthwhile here simply to note the relationship: the two categories, nonsense and mental illness, inform each other.

Nonsense and play

There is still one aspect to the picture of ancient "nonsense" which is missing. So far, it seems that nonsense is something that is only engaged in *unwillingly*: either one is inebriated, one is delirious with fever, or one is perfectly rational and earnest but being accused of speaking "nonsense" by an opponent. No Greek would actually *want* to produce nonsense, let alone be accused of it, the picture seems to say. Although this is largely correct, there is a context in which classical Greeks claim to engage willingly in "nonsense," and that is the context of play (*paidia*). In fact, nonsense and play share a good amount of lexical territory, and it is not difficult to see why: like nonsense, play is an activity that, by definition, lies outside

---

[78] See Garland (1995) 46–8 for more discussion of Roman examples; Martial 12.93 for a "diminutive cretin," 8.13 for complaining that the idiot entertainer is a "fake," i.e., not a real "fool," 14.210, *moriones* in 3.82. For Tiberius' fool, see Suet. *Tib.* 61.

[79] See Garland (1995) 49 for the evidence.

[80] For various societies in which mentally retarded people are stoned, beaten, and jeered at for public amusement, see Dettwyler (1991) 382.

[81] See Stark (1995) 104: "it is possible that they twist their feet on purpose to imitate a limp, assuming they are not actually physically disabled." For plates, see Garland (1995) pl. 20., who notes that the practice of exposure can only affect the population so much (13). "Though natural attrition and the practice of exposure accounted for the deaths of many congenitally disabled infants, however, some parents must have found themselves with problem cases on their hands, either because symptoms of abnormality did not manifest themselves at birth or because they were only acquired postnatally. Likewise mental deficiency and growth disturbance are not evident at birth." Note also deformed Thersites, and the gods laughing at Hephaestus' ποιπνύειν which Halliwell (2008) 61–4 treats far too genteelly as "play-acting," 63; but as Halliwell (2008) 63 n. 30 notes *contra* Garland (1995) 86, Plut. *Mor.* 35a–c rejects the idea that Homer thought deformity laughable.

"seriousness" – it has no intended use or consequence beyond itself.[82]
So too, like nonsense, play can acquire a pejorative sense for precisely that
reason: namely, that it is not serious, not useful, not of the real world.[83] The
purpose of this section is to show that speaking nonsense was considered a
source of pleasure (and laughter) for many of the same reasons that *play*
was considered a source of pleasure (and laughter). I will begin this argument by focusing on a classical sympotic epigram which depicts a group of
symposiasts who "talk nonsense" (φλυαρεῖν) as a source of enjoyment, play,
and laughter. I will then turn to some other passages where nonsense-words
either combine with or replace *paidia* and argue strongly for their relationship: the same reason that play is pleasurable is why nonsense is pleasurable;
both are forms of exertion (either in behavior or language) without any
real-life purpose, necessity, or effect.[84]

In a sympotic epigram which has been assigned dates from the fifth
century to the end of the fourth,[85] there is a collocation of words which
suggest a certain pleasure in nonsense: φλυαρεῖν, γελώς, and παίζειν. The
epigram constructs a neat opposition between not-serious (3–6) and serious
(7–10) and argues that the proper symposium ought to devote a balanced
amount of time to each type of behavior. Here is the epigram:

> Χαίρετε συμπόται ἄνδρες ὁμ[. . . ˙ἐ]ξ ἀγαθοῦ γὰρ
>   ἀρξάμενος τελέω τὸν λόγον [ε]ἰς ἀγα[θό]ν.
> Χρὴ δ᾽, ὅταν εἰς τοιοῦτο συνέλθωμεν φίλοι ἄνδρες
>   Πρᾶγμα, γελᾶν παίζειν χρησαμένους ἀρετῆι,
> ἥδεσθαί τε συνόντας, ἐς ἀλλήλους τε φ[λ]υαρεῖν
>   καὶ σκώπτειν τοιαῦθ᾽ οἷα γέλωτα φέρει.
> ἡ δὲ σπουδὴ ἐπέσθω, ἀκούωμεν [τε λ]εγόντων
>   ἐν μέρει˙ ἥδ᾽ ἀρετὴ συμποσίου πέλεται.

---

[82] Huizinga (1949) 7–13 for play as an activity separated from "seriousness," but 5–6 for how even "non-
serious" play can be taken seriously, e.g., professional sports (so too one can think of all the athletes
who die in ancient Olympic bouts as serious consequence, but unintended). Cf. Halliwell's discussion (2008) 19–38, at 24: "To be playful is, by definition, to step outside (or, at least, to suspend)
'seriousness.'"

[83] See, e.g., Pl. *Cri.* 46d4, discussed below.

[84] Necessity (*anankē*) being especially important for Aristotle: for the idea that all things necessary
are unpleasant, and things not necessary pleasurable (e.g., *paidiai* and *hypnos* and *anapauseis*), see
Rh. 1370a.

[85] The epigram, one of other sympotic poems of a papyrus found in the tomb of a Greek soldier at
Elephantine, has a hand that has been "dated to 300/280 BC." See Cameron (1995) 74, who thinks the
poem not "much older than the date of the writing" and Nisbet (2003) 26 n. 16. For a fourth-century
date, see Page (1941) 445, (1981) 443; West (1974) 15; Ford (2002) 33. For a fifth-century date, see
Gentili and Prato (1985) 2.130; Halliwell (2008) 114: "probably of late classical date, just possibly
earlier." Ed. Pr. is Schubart/Wilamowitz–Moellendorff (1907) 2.62, Pl. VIII for image. See Ferrari
(1988) 219–25 for commentary.

Τοῦ δὲ ποταρχοῦντος πειθώμεθα· ταῦτα γάρ ἐστιν
ἔργ᾽ ἀνδρῶν ἀγαθῶν, εὐλογίαν τε φέρει.

Hello, symposiasts . . .! From a good beginning I'll begin and finish with a
good ending. Whenever we come together as friends for such an occasion, we
should laugh and play in a good way, and take pleasure in each other's
company, and talk nonsense to one another, and mock the sorts of thing that
bring laughter. But let seriousness follow, and let us listen to each other
speaking in turn: that's what makes a symposium good. And let's obey our
drinking-master, for this is the pastime of good men, and confers a good
reputation.

At issue here are the four lines of "play," especially the "to talk nonsense"
(φλυαρεῖν) of line five. Clearly this "nonsense" cannot be denoting the
negative mental impairment of drunkenness discussed above, since what
is being depicted is a willed form of behavior enjoyed within the bounds of
social norms. Although most translate *phluarein* along the lines of "speaking
nonsense," a few suggest it means something more like mockery.[86] As I have
argued above, the latter cannot be the case – at least, not exactly[87] – since
although the accusation "nonsense" can arise alongside other accusations
(like "slanders" or "denigration"), this only suggests the careful calibrations
of the speaker (recall Isocrates referring to Philip's slanders as "nonsense").
Similarly, although mockery and *phluarein* might arise together in the
context of play, their meanings are distinct: while mockery often veils an
underlying criticism or a hidden agenda, "speaking nonsense" (φλυαρεῖν), as
has been shown, never has such a meaning. The person who "talks nonsense" is too simple (εὐήθης) to veil anything (indeed if there were some
hidden, underlying meaning his statement would no longer be *phluaria*).
But what then does "talk nonsense" (φλυαρεῖν) mean in this context,
whether it be translated as "ineptias dicere" or "engage in foolish talk"? It
may be that such talk indeed resembles the nonsense which has already been
discussed: what makes it "foolish" is precisely that it is rambling, repetitive,
and bearing no relationship to the real world. Unlike Plato's earlier injunction, one is not constantly "checking in" to see how statements add to
the overarching theme or argument, and may even be indulging in the

---

[86] For those who translate φλυαρεῖν along the lines of "nonsense," see Gentili and Prato (1985) 130:
"ineptias dicere;" Gerber (1999) 489: "engage in foolish talk with one another;" Nisbet (2003) 26
n. 16: "engage in horseplay (*phluarein*, 'messing about')"; Collins (2004) 66: "jest at one another." For
mockery, Rosen (2007) 112–13 translates it as "insult": "and insult and jeer in such a way as to bring
laughter"; Halliwell (2008) 114, reading a hendiadys with σκώπτειν translates "send up each other
with mockery"; Page (1941): 445 "make sport of each other."
[87] As I will argue in Chapter 3 mockery might be subsumed under "speaking nonsense," but this does
not mean that *phluarein* denotes "to mock."

disorderly logic of "falling from an ass." One may even be making statements that purposefully bear no relationship to reality ("I am Zeus," "I am
larger than this room"), and deriving pleasure from such "foolishness."

A parallel for the "nonsense" of this anonymous sympotic epigram can be
found in a fragment of Alexis, where the verb used is not *phluarein* but its
close synonym, *lērein*. In the Alexis fragment, Aesop has just praised Solon
for instituting the mixing of wine in symposia, and Solon explains what the
right form of (Greek) drinking entails (fr. 9 KA): μετρίοισι χρωμένους
ποτηρίοις / λαλεῖν τι καὶ ληρεῖν πρὸς αὑτοὺς ἡδέως "with a moderate
amount of drink to chat a bit and talk nonsense with one another pleasantly." Olson comments on the passage: "The use of ληρέω indicates that
the talk is inconsequential even if enjoyable" while Arnott explains *lērein* as
"joking and frivolous nonsense."[88] The talk need not be completely "foolish" (e.g., "I am Zeus") in order to be "inconsequential": one might think,
for example, of the category of "small talk" (e.g., speaking about the weather
without any hoped-for results of meteorological conclusions) or Frankfurt's
description of a "bull-session" where "usual assumptions about the connection between what people say and what they believe is suspended."[89] But
Plato's earlier description of "nonsense" talk (which does not constantly
observe what is being added to the overarching argument) is of great value
here: sometimes discussions are engaged in to take away something useful
(e.g., a philosophical conclusion, a new political opinion); but in certain
contexts (like sympotic play) there is a resistance to such a form of talk, and
rather one indulges in a type of language which does not "do anything
useful" (προὔργου τι ποιεῖν, in Isocrates' words). Of course, it may be
argued that this type of "inconsequent speech" bears little relationship to the
sorts of "delirious nonsense" that have been discussed up to this point. But,
if one considers *how* one might produce "inconsequent speech," that is,
what methods one might employ to create a speech in hopes that it *not* be
taken seriously, many of the features that have been discussed (e.g., speaking in opposites, repetition, rambling) seem like ready possibilities. More
parallels for this sympotic appreciation of *phluarein* and *lērein* can be found
in later writers.[90]

From this perspective, "nonsense" draws very close to the register of
"play," and so it is not surprising that in the sympotic epigram that began

---

[88] Olson (2007) 308; Arnott (1996) 79. Lucian must have had such usage in mind when Lexiphanes
attempts the sympotic συνυθλήσομεν (14).

[89] Frankfurt (2005) 35–7; the reason for this suspension is so that speakers "enjoy a certain irresponsi-
bility" and can "convey what is on their minds without too much anxiety that they will be held to it."

[90] See Plut. *Mor.* 54f4, 73b12, 787b10.

this section *paizein* is listed alongside *phluarein*. But not only does "nonsense" resemble "play" when "nonsense" is being used in this (rare) positive sense; "play" often resembles "nonsense" when "play" is being used in a pejorative sense. This is an interesting relationship because the positive and negative aspects of the words can be seen as two sides of the same coin: for the very reason these activities are denigrated, they are considered pleasurable. Both "play" and "nonsense" are useless and without any real-world effect.

In the *Protagoras* (347c–d), Socrates offers a parallel to the sympotic epigram and the passage of Alexis discussed above, but casts the "play" half of the symposium in a more negative light. Here it is the serious discussion of symposia that must be emphasized, and the "play" and "nonsense" that must be jettisoned. He discusses the drinking parties of the common-fold (τῶν φαύλων καὶ ἀγοραίων) who need flute-girls and sympotic music to help them carry on their conversations. But gentlemen, *kaloi kagathoi*, have no need of "this nonsense and play" (ἄνευ τῶν λήρων τε καὶ παιδιῶν τούτων), but content themselves with orderly conversation, each in turn, no matter how much they have had to drink. The underlying assumption of the serious symposium is that good conversation ought to *get somewhere* (e.g., philosophical conclusions), and that good conversation ought to *do* something (e.g., persuade listeners to action). *Lēros*, like *paidia*, by its nature does nothing, gets nowhere (it does not "do anything useful"). For that reason, just as the second half of the sympotic epigram suggests, such nonsense/play must be avoided by serious symposiasts.[91]

In the *Crito* (46d4), Socrates provides an example of *phluaria* and *paidia* that is more poignant: condemned to die, Socrates discusses with Crito whether the new circumstances ought to change their views. It is a touching moment: it is as if death, that most serious subject, creates a new frame for arguments – all was fun and games until (Socrates') death came into the picture, at which point ideas must be reconsidered more seriously.[92] He asks Crito whether now, in the face of death, they ought to maintain their former opinions: "were we right before I was condemned to death, whereas now it has become clear that we were speaking in vain for the sake of argument (νῦν δὲ κατάδηλος ἄρα ἐγένετο ὅτι ἄλλως ἕνεκα λόγου ἐλέγετο), but really it was just games and nonsense (ἦν δὲ παιδιὰ καὶ φλυαρία ὡς ἀληθῶς;)?"[93]

---

[91] Cf. Xenophanes B1 West.

[92] As Aristotle writes in *Rh.* 2.5, one fears what is close at hand: in this scene, death is no longer an abstract, distant topic for the students, but an impending reality.

[93] Halliwell (2008) 116 n. 41 translates this pairing as a hendiadys (as he does with the sympotic epigram): "playful bluster."

This is a fine articulation of what nonsense (*phluaria*), and for that matter play (*paidia*), is: it is not for the sake of anything other than itself. Play is for its own fun, and nonsense here is simply for the sake of language itself (ἄλλως ἕνεκα λόγου ἐλέγετο). It is as if Socrates is suggesting the idea that people can speak and play, but when actual, impending death comes into the picture – when reality and real loss become evident – it is time to use language to more serious ends.[94]

What separates these passages of Plato from the more positive view of nonsense is their vantage point: the anonymous epigram and passage of Alexis which stress the need for non-serious behavior in sympotic conversation offer nonsense in a positive light, but the Socratic dialogues which (at least seem to) desire serious progress, serious concentration on a philosophical problem, reject that very nonsense, simply because it is not a serious use of language. What is important to note is that both Plato and the sympotic epigram are still referring to the same phenomenon: for Socrates at these moments nonsense is *not* desired because it gets nowhere, says nothing, will bear no philosophical import; but for the symposiast of the same period, nonsense is desired for precisely the same reasons – because the language gets nowhere, says nothing, and bears no philosophical import. There is an underlying notion that language ought to have a use, bring some sort of advantage (i.e., better understanding of death, more appropriate action). Proper language will lead towards that advantage or use, while nonsense is that language which does not bring the advantage that language-*qua*-tool brings. This opposition is often expressed explicitly, not just in Plato and Isocrates, but in later writers as well (e.g., "not nonsense, but for the sake of use," οὐ γὰρ φλυαρίας, ἀλλ' ὠφελείας χάριν).[95]

There are other examples of this relationship between play and non-sense,[96] but let one more suffice. Here, rather than the conjunction of the two words, it seems that *phluaria* is replacing the very concept of play, e.g., a cordoned-off activity often done by children that has no serious effect or consequence in real, adult, life.[97] A young Cyrus in Xenophon's *Cyropaedia*, having just gone off on a hunt in the wilderness – putting his life in danger (i.e., a "serious" risk) and bagging real prizes (i.e., a perceived "serious"

---

[94] Cf. *Phdr.* 276d where Socrates discusses writing philosophy as play or a pastime (*paidia*). For the role of play in Plato's philosophy more generally, see Gundert (1965); Plass (1967); Ardley (1967); Jouet-Pastre (2006); for Socrates' depicted relationship with play/irony/laughter, see Halliwell (2008) 276–302.

[95] Strabo 1.2.19.8–9.

[96] Philo *Legatio ad Gaium* 168.6, Achilles Tatius 7.11.8.4–5, Lucian *Anach.* 32.11, Plut. *Mor.* 54f4, 73b12, 787b, Philostr. *VA* 5.14.13. For "childish nonsense" Plut. *Mor.* 701a2–3. Aesop 93.2 as reconstructed by Hausrath (1970).

[97] For the notion that play exists inside a "magic circle," the central text is Huizinga (1949).

consequence) – declares: "How we were merely playing (ὡς ἄρα ἐφλυαροῦμεν), boys, when we used to hunt animals in the park (ἐν τῷ παραδείσωι). To me anyway it seems like hunting animals that are tied up. For, in the first place, they were in a small space (ἐν μικρῷ χωρίωι) . . ." (1.4.11). With his emphasis on real vs. pretend danger, on the real world vs. an enclosed space, the young Cyrus – already destined and eager for great and serious things – could have easily replaced ἐφλυαροῦμεν with ἐπαίζομεν. Although he is disparaging his former activity as trifles (or games), it is only from the vantage point of a serious person eager to enter into serious life. Later, once that life has been entered into, he will occasionally return to that space of trifles and play, where that very inconsequence is a source of enjoyment (and laughter) rather than an object of denigration.[98]

Thus, as Plutarch reminds, there is something pleasurable, something to be desired, in having time for games and nonsense (σχολὴν ἄφθονον ἐν παιδιαῖς καὶ φλυαρίαις),[99] and I need not argue here why games and play were considered pleasurable by most Greeks. Their very existence is testimony to their being enjoyed and valued. I would simply like to remind how the pejorative aspect of play (like nonsense) informs its enjoyment. When one thinks of Greek games (and many of our games) it is noticeable how "useless" and "foolish" they are – not only are they without use or value in the real world, but they are often extraordinarily repetitive and in many cases can be played under considerable mental impairment (e.g., drunkenness). *Kottabos* can be played and probably was played after a good deal of inebriation, a time when the brain is so impaired that one cannot engage in dialectic or geometry or more complicated pastimes, but certainly can fling the dregs of wine at a target over and over again.[100] The repetitiveness and simplicity of games is remarkable: *ostrakinda* (the modern "tag"), *ephetinda* (the modern ball-game "catch"), *posinda* (~morra), *khalkinda* (spinning a coin), and so forth require no complicated thought and thus can be played by children or the inebriated.[101] They all consist of extremely simple,

---

[98] See, e.g., the pretend battle at 2.3.17–19 of clods and cudgels, παίοντες σὺν πολλῷ γέλωτι καὶ παιδιᾷ discussed in Chapter 3.

[99] Plut. *Mor.* 787b7–12, in arguing that public life is not all sweat and toil, but also filled with enjoyable processions, theatrical events, etc., turns to the comparison of war: οὐδὲ γὰρ αἱ στρατεῖαι παρατάξεις ἀεὶ καὶ μάχας καὶ πολιορκίας ἔχουσιν, ἀλλὰ καὶ θυσίας ἔστιν ὅτε καὶ συνουσίας διὰ μέσου καὶ σχολὴν ἄφθονον ἐν παιδιαῖς καὶ φλυαρίαις δέχονται.

[100] For discussion of *kottabos*, see Rosen (1989) 355–9.

[101] See *RE* s.v. "Spiele" and Van Leeuwen's (1968[1900]) note ad. *Eq.* 855. For *ostrakinda*, Plato Com. fr. 168 KA which describes the game; also Ar. *Eq.* 855, Pl. *Phdr.* 241b, *Rep.* 521c; also called *nux/hemera* the game was a tag-game played by two sides. For *ephetinda* Cratin. fr. 456 KA; for *posinda* Xen. *Eq. Mag.* 5.10, Ar. *Plut.* 816.

goal-oriented activities that are repeated over and over again. Although the simplicity, "foolishness," and pointlessness of games cannot fully explain their pleasure, it certainly explains part of it: for the very reason games are denigrated, they are enjoyed.[102] It is in this context that the pleasurable nonsense of Alexis and the anonymous symposiast should be understood.

Conclusions

In defining these Greek terms for nonsense, a considerable amount of ground has been covered since nonsense shares lexical territory with a number of concepts, including lies, mistakes, madness, and play. To conclude, I will briefly summarize how nonsense is, and is not, like the concepts with which it has come into contact. In the section on nonsense as rhetorical accusation it was shown that Isocrates considers "nonsense" to be a certain form of falsehood, but that nonsense differs from other falsehoods (like lies) in that it cannot "do anything useful." While lies serve the liar's hidden agenda (and this is the potential danger of the liar), nonsense can have no hidden agenda. The unique pejorative force of "nonsense" is that the nonsense-speaker is similar to one who is mentally impaired, an extra-legal, extra-social character with no potential effect on the outside world.

This led into the following section in which some medical texts were examined (as well as texts discussing alcoholic intoxication) to observe how these "nonsense" words were being used in non-pejorative contexts. It became clear that, in such contexts, words for "nonsense" often drew very close to words for "madness" – since both were suggesting actions and speech detached from reality. However, the difference between nonsense and madness was that while madness can often express divine truths and threaten danger, nonsense can neither threaten danger nor express truth. "Nonsense" can only suggest mental incompetence or impairment (through fever or drunkenness), but never the divine inspiration (or the violence) that both madness and alcohol create in other contexts.

The final category with which "nonsense" shared lexical range is that of "play." What the two concepts share is a sort of activity or speech that is inconsequential, separated from reality, and, even more, often "silly," "foolish," "useless." The categories are different because "nonsense" is much

---

[102] I discuss "play" more in Chapter 3. See Arist. *Rh.* 1370a18–1371a explaining that games are pleasurable because winning is pleasurable; that even when one does not win, there is still the *phantasia* of winning which is pleasurable. This is part of an overarching connection between desire and pleasure (e.g., 1370a17–18).

more pejorative than play is – in fact, it is when "play" is being used pejoratively that it most resembles "nonsense." On the one hand, this is because *paidia* at its root evokes not the mental impairment of illness or drunkenness (although, as I argued, this aspect is not completely absent), but another group of (perceived) mentally inferior people – children, as the *paizein* root suggests.[103] On the other hand, "nonsense" seems to be more pejorative than "play" simply because nonsense is play observed from a technological vantage point (i.e., questioning what the "use" of the activity or utterance is). This technological perspective, then, is also why "nonsense" is more interwoven with questions of communication and meaning than "play" is: if the underlying demand behind language, actions, and objects is that they be useful, nonsense *qua* meaningless language is negative because a meaningless utterance is a useless utterance.

Although sharing lexical range with falsehood, mistakes, mental impairment, and play, nonsense has been shown to be its own particular category: a sort of false and useless speech/behavior (or even object) which is disconnected from reality. With this definition of nonsense in hand, as well as some examples and formal features of nonsense, it is now time to consider nonsense's relationship to comedy.

---

[103] See Halliwell (2008) 19–20.

CHAPTER 2

Nonsense as "no-reference": riddles, allegories, metaphors

οὐκ ἂν οὖν, ὦ φίλε, πάνυ γέ τι σπουδαῖον εἴη ἡ δικαιοσύνη, εἰ πρὸς
τὰ ἄχρηστα χρήσιμον ὂν τυγχάνει.　　　　　　　Plato, *Republic* 1.333e1[1]

In the introduction to this book, I argued that there is a persistent voice
in comic scholarship which insists that *some* part of comedy is beyond
the scope of serious meaning, that *some* part is just "silliness" or "fun."
The problem is that this "silliness" is not particularly easy to locate once one
starts looking for it: the very jokes or humorous scenes which strike
audiences as funny are also the central sources for comic scholarship's
serious readings. Jokes about Cleon, Hyperbolus, and Euripides provide
more than enough evidence for historical theories regarding Aristophanes'
politics, his aesthetic values, or the morals of his milieu. It seems that once a
silly joke explodes into laughter, all that remains is a judgment or serious
opinion. But what happened, then, to the supposed silliness? As I argued in
the introduction, that non-meaningful part of comedy is not some phan-
tom, but a central feature of the comic genre, what I have been calling
"nonsense." Like the *phluaria* and *lēros* discussed in the last chapter, this
"nonsense" is a sort of false speech or action which is perceived not to reflect
reality and so, considered to be useless and to be discarded in its entirety.
It is very much the opposite of meaningful speech.

The nonsense that I will be examining in this chapter is specifically
language without reference. My notion of "reference" is influenced by
Gottlob Frege's (1980[1892]) distinction between "sense" (*Sinn*) and "reference" (*Bedeutung*) in logic, and Paul Ricœur's (1977) application of this
distinction to literature. For Frege, the reference (*Bedeutung*) is the object in
nature that the word/sentence names, while the sense (*Sinn*) is the inexistent
thought that the word/sentence expresses. For example, "north of the
north pole" (or to use one of Frege's examples, the phrase "the celestial

---

[1] "Justice, my friend, wouldn't be a serious thing at all, if it is useful only with respect to useless things."

body most distant from the Earth") has a sense, but no reference: one can grasp the thought, even if the thought designates no existent object. Although for Frege, the great majority of fiction and poetry also lacks a *Bedeutung* – e.g., since Odysseus does not really exist, neither his name nor the sentences he is in have a *Bedeutung* (62) – Ricœur expands the sense/ reference distinction for the purposes of literature and metaphor (216–56).[2] My application of these terms "sense" and "reference" is purely for reasons of organization: in this chapter, I examine nonsense as no-reference, e.g., "north of the north pole"; in a later chapter, I will turn to nonsense as no-sense, e.g., "north of the north of the."[3]

"Language-without-reference" is a rather broad category, and one might pursue the topic in a number of directions. In order to be as clear as possible, I will limit my discussion here to three familiar tropes: riddles, allegories, and metaphors. By "reference," I mean that which a statement refers to: so, for example, a riddle's reference is its solution; an allegory's reference is what it allegorizes; a metaphor's reference is its tenor. What I will be arguing in this chapter is that, in comedy, one often finds these tropes deprived of their references, that is, riddles without solutions, allegories without allegorized, metaphors without tenors. To give some examples: in that famous riddle of the Sphinx "a creature which walks on four legs in the morning, two legs at noon, and three in the evening," its equally famous solution, "man," is what I will be calling the riddle's reference. In that allegory of Alcaeus about the ship tossing on stormy seas, what is allegorized by the ship – "the state" – is what I will be calling the allegory's reference. In Pindar's metaphor of man as "a dream of a shadow" the tenor of the metaphor – "man" – is what I will be calling the metaphor's reference. What I will be arguing, effectively, is that comedy initiates these tropes only to declare that the references have disappeared: the Sphinx's riddle proceeds without solution, Alcaeus' ship remains an image without meaning, and "shadow of a dream" is rendered empty sound. In locating such reference-free language in comedy, I argue, one discovers a certain form of nonsense.

---

[2] The *Bedeutung* in Ricœur's (initial) terms can reference the world *of the text*, i.e., a sentence from the Odyssey has a *Bedeutung* since Odysseus exists within the world of the poem. But Ricœur's initial expansion becomes obscured by his ultimate interests, when he requires the *Bedeutung* again to apply to the real world.

[3] Cf. Frege 1980[1892] 58, that sense can be produced by any "grammatically well-formed expression." For anyone well versed in the tormented twentieth-century applications of sense/reference (especially, e.g., their relation to connotation and denotation), my organizational principle will only add further torment: my use of the terms are (unapologetically) loose. For discussion of the *Nachleben* of the Fregean distinction, see Baker and Hacker (1984).

Objections may arise here regarding the subjective nature of this word "nonsense." As I emphasized in Chapter 1, nonsense, like meaning, can be treated as an objective category only up to a point, since what is nonsense to one person is highly meaningful to another. The examples of references I provided above, it may be claimed, are too straightforward: there may be many (often unsatisfactory) solutions to an "unsolved" riddle, just as there may be multiple interpretations of obscure metaphors; regarding allegories, some feverish readers discover them everywhere. The authority is not mine to entitle certain metaphors or allegorical figures as "reference-free": more ingenious interpreters will (and have) "solved" such riddles.

This objection, however, is not the obstacle to my argument but its substance, since these two mutually exclusive reactions – interpretation (where one actively seeks meaning) and nonsense-realization (where one decides that no meaning exists) – provide the dialectic that delineates nonsense's contours in this chapter. If an obscure phrase is taken as nonsense, the opportunity for possible meanings, perhaps even profound ones, will be lost. But if that same phrase is interpreted and quarried for its hidden depths and references, a different sort of opportunity, I argue, is lost. Meaningless language has a particular effect that meaningful language does not: it causes more irrational reactions in lieu of the cerebral interpretive response – discomfort, frustration, rage, laughter, and others.[4] Like some blunt object, nonsense falls upon the ears as something impenetrable, insoluble; a quandary arises of how to react to language that is devolving into mere sound. What I argue is that the very act of surrendering interpretation is what is achieved in discovering nonsense, and it is precisely that effect that comedy often attempts to produce.

Since the type of nonsense studied in this chapter is specifically language without reference, the question of interpretation will be foremost, as the existence or non-existence of a reference is ultimately subjective. The chapter begins with a section on riddles, particularly those in two plays by the fourth-century BCE comedian Antiphanes. A close contemporary of Aristotle, Antiphanes is able to imagine a possibility of language that the philosopher, in the *Poetics*, does not: that is, meaningless language, language without reference. The particular form under dispute is the riddle: for Aristotle the most "riddled" riddles have the potential to be obscure; for Antiphanes such riddles have the potential to be nonsense. The difference

---

[4] All such reactions can be elicited by meaningful statements as well, but the difference lies in tying such reactions to the meanings of the statements themselves rather than some perceived absence of meaning.

between these two outcomes is critical: "obscurity" suggests that the riddle still has a solution (a reference) although the language is difficult to discern; "nonsense" suggests that the riddle has no solution at all, but is rather a form of reference-free language. I argue that this semantic option (nonsense) is the particular domain of comedy rather than other genres. While riddling language (for example, the phrasing of oracles and dithyrambs) has the potential effect of obscurity in Aristotle's world, in comedy that obscurity is realized as nonsense. The penetrating interpretations that obscurity demands are precisely what comedy rejects.

That rejection is thematized in the opening of Aristophanes' *Peace* which is briefly considered at the end of the "riddles" discussion. There Aristophanes acknowledges the opening obscurity of his play, and ventriloquizes the interpretive response to the play's opening via a pair of imagined spectators. The opening is described as a riddle demanding solution and the two spectators offer conjectures. Their speculations, however, are derided, and interpretation itself is rendered an object of laughter and contempt. The effect of this, I argue, is suggestive: it offers the audience a laughable image of the interpretation of on-stage obscurities. Serious hermeneutics, it seems, ought to be surrendered.

Thus, resistance to interpretation is not merely a phenomenon of comic scholarship but a recurring program in comedy itself. This argument is developed further in the following section which considers comic allegory. Not concealment of the reference (which is the domain of the riddle), but transparency to the reference is allegory's aspiration. For example, it is quickly obvious in *Knights* that the master "Demos" represents the Athenian "people" and the Paphlagonian slave represents Cleon (and other comic allegories operate in the same vein). But once that transparent meaning-structure is created, the dismantling immediately begins. Certain elements are injected without any obvious references, and remain as blemishes on the allegorical clarity. But these destabilizations of the meaning-structure are not formal mistakes of an otherwise functional allegory, but rather often seem to be the allegory's *raison d'être*, as if the allegory were simply the opportunity for reference-free language. The examples are drawn from the dog trial of *Wasps* (where the prosecuting dog represents Cleon, the defendant dog the general Laches), and the female chorus of Athenian allied-states in Eupolis' *Cities*.

In the final section, I consider an extended metaphor from *Peace*. As with the comic allegories where the reference is initially transparent but soon dismantled, the *Peace* metaphor slowly decays until the reference is obscured altogether. It is here that the conclusions of the chapter's arguments can finally be drawn. One cannot refer to this reference-free metaphor (or the other phenomena discussed in this chapter) as an obscurity, a formal mistake, or an authorial failure. Rather such reference-free language appears to be a positive, productive element in the comedian's palette: it occurs often at climaxes of language as if the perception of nonsense had been the goal all along. The effect is not necessarily laughter (for this is the desideratum of humor), but rather a form of submission where the audience is momentarily compelled to abandon the habitual interpretive act. If one returns to the questions that began this book, it will become clearer why such resistance to serious meaning has been a recurrent feature of comic scholarship: the resistance to meaning is an essential feature of comedy itself.

Finally, a brief note about treating these three meaning-structures (riddle, allegory, and metaphor) as a group. I am not the first to do so: Newiger in his study of Aristophanic metaphor and allegory heavily relies upon Hegel who also handles these three under a single category, namely, "comparisons which start from the meaning (*Bedeutung*)"[5] – that is, what is *meant* produces the image in riddle, allegory, metaphor and not vice versa (which, for Hegel, would require fables and parables). Nor is the fluidity between these terms a modern phenomenon: Aristotle describes the relationship thus in the *Rhetoric* (1405b4): "From good riddles (ἐκ τῶν εὖ ᾐνιγμένων) one can take good metaphors (μεταφορὰς ... ἐπιεικεῖς): for metaphors pose riddles (αἰνίττονται), and therefore a good riddle can furnish a good metaphor,"[6] while in the *Poetics* he describes a riddle (αἴνιγμα) as language consisting entirely of metaphors (1458a25).[7] So too regarding allegory: although the word did not exist in Aristotle's day,[8] Cicero later describes allegory in this way (*Orator*, 94): "When there have been more metaphors in a continuous stream, another kind of speech clearly

---

[5] The translation is by Knox (Kegel (1975) 395–421). The original classification is "Vergleichungen, welche in der Verbildlichung mit der Bedeutung den Anfang machen" (1966[1835]) 383–407; also grouped here are similes and an intermediary *Bild* (Knox: "Image") which is, roughly, an extended metaphor. Fables, proverbs, parables, etc. are categorized under "comparisons originating from the external object," but I would contest this distinction applies more to "fable" than to ancient *ainos* which often comes quite close to allegory. Newiger's introduction (1957, 1–9) is in large part quotations of and agreement with Hegel.

[6] Cope (1973[1877]) ad loc. contrasts Cicero who thought of the relationship between metaphors and riddles more destructive than productive: *De or.* 3.42.167 "est hoc (translatio) magnum ornamentum orationis, in quo obscuritas fugienda est: etenim hoc genere fiunt ea quae dicuntur aenigmata."

[7] Or, technically, he describes language consisting entirely of metaphors as a riddle.

[8] The word is not attested before the first century BCE. See Innes (2003) 20: "Though [Aristotle] does not know the term allegory, proverb and enigma come under 'saying what is not said' (ἐκ τοῦ μὴ ὃ φησι λέγειν: *Rh.* 1412a22ff.) and are linked to metaphor." Cf. the Derveni commentator's use of *ainigma* (Struck, (2004) 25–39), and Plato's use of *hyponoia* (*Resp.* 2.378d6–7).

arises: and the Greeks call this kind 'allegory' (ἀλληγορία)."[9] Metaphors from riddles, then, and allegories from metaphors, according to some ancient thinkers. This is not to merge these terms together here behind some obfuscating fog, but simply to recognize the fluidity between their boundaries, and explain the rationale behind treating them as a group: namely, their artificial (and thus visible) relationships to their references. For one interested in the possibility of reference-free language, the artificial structures of riddles, allegories, and metaphors make for good hunting grounds: if one can locate riddles without answers, allegories without allegorized, metaphors without tenors, one has found reference-free language, which is one species of nonsense.

Riddles without solutions

The possibility of linguistic obscurity is not foreign to Greek theories of language. Philosophers like Heraclitus, for example, receive the charge of obscure language from a number of ancient critics, and Aristotle, in the *Poetics*, suggests obscurity as an outcome of language that is overly metaphorical.[10] But obscurity is not the same thing as nonsense, since the charge of "obscurity" still contains an expectation of "pre-existent . . . meaning" behind a "dark filter," while a charge of nonsense suggests that, "behind" the language, there is nothing at all.[11] Still, the two concepts are related, and one might expect that where there is obscurity, nonsense too may be close at hand. Take Aristotle's discussion of lexis in the *Poetics* (1458a26, my italics):

> The style that makes use of uncommon words is a lofty one, avoiding the commonplace. By "uncommon" I mean an unusual word, a metaphor, a word-extension and everything not ordinary. *But if one writes entirely in this way, there will be either a riddle* (αἴνιγμα) *or a solecism* (βαρβαρισμός); if made up of metaphors, it is a riddle, if unusual words, a solecism. For this is the idea of a riddle: describing something by an impossible combination of words (τὸ λέγοντα ὑπάρχοντα ἀδύνατα συνάψαι).[12]

---

[9] For discussions and parallels, see Boys-Stones (2003) 2 (whose translation this is) and Innes (2003) 19–20.

[10] Arist. *Rh.* 3.5, 1407b11 and Demetr. *Eloc.* 192 regarding Heraclitus. The *Poetics* passage on overly metaphorical language is discussed below.

[11] For this view of obscurity, see Hamilton (2003) 2 quoting White (1981) 18. Both reject this view in favor of an actual, positive darkness which has its own existence beyond being "merely as a *moment* toward some elucidation or ultimate clarification," Hamilton at 7.

[12] Fyfe (1927) translates *barbarismos* as "jargon" presumably in the sense of *OED* 5: "A barbarous, rude, or debased language or variety of speech." Lucas (1968) 209 explains the word as "Greek as it might be

These two options – the riddle or the solecism – cover a broad range of language deviance, but fall short of anything like meaningless language. Just like the foreigner who has simply chosen inept terms to express his ideas, the riddler merely conceals his underlying thought, or fails to make that thought clear. What is *not* expressed here is that language might have the potential to mean nothing at all.[13] Yet here, with riddles, one approaches the Aristotelian limit, since the only thing that separates an obscure riddle from nonsense is the expectation of that riddle's underlying meaning. The question one would like to pose to Aristotle is whether there is such a thing as a riddle without a solution, for surely this, then, would make a good candidate for nonsense.

Although Aristotle does not answer this question in the *Poetics*, it is handled by his close contemporary, the comic playwright Antiphanes. In two separate plays an obscure riddle is posed, but the mode of viewing riddles is altogether different from Aristotle's. For Antiphanes, riddles can indeed exist without answers, and the term he uses to describe this phenomenon is, indeed, "nonsense." This nonsense (*qua* riddle-without-answer) creates two different responses – in one listener it produces laughter, in another rage – as if by rejecting the act of interpretation some more basic form of reaction must occupy its place.

In Antiphanes' play called *Gut* (or possibly *Man from Cnoithideus*),[14] a speaker describes his experience with the sympotic pastime of riddles (122 KA = Ath. 448f–449b):

> ἐγὼ πρότερον μὲν τοὺς κελεύοντας λέγειν
> γρίφους παρὰ πότον ᾠόμην ληρεῖν σαφῶς
> λέγοντας οὐδέν, ὁπότε προστάξαι τέ τις
> εἰπεῖν ἐφεξῆς ὅ τι φέρων τις μὴ φέρει,

---

used by a foreigner not brought up to speak it." Regarding *ainigma* he writes "'a puzzle,' because it is in the nature of metaphors that their meaning is not always obvious at first sight, and this enigmatic quality is one of the causes of the effectiveness of metaphors, only it must not be overdone."

[13] This could be because of Aristotle's instrumental view of language, for which see Cope ad *Rh.* 3.13, 1404b1, or because Aristotle is interested in studying only healthy specimens (*Politics* 1.20 1254a36) not the fevered or insane who, as Chapter 1 has demonstrated, are the ones likely to produce Greek "nonsense." In *De Interpretatione*, as well, only syllables can be meaningless (οὐδὲ . . . σημαντικόν), not whole sentences (16b30). The central text for "fallacies" (i.e., language not mapping on to reality) is *Sophistici Elenchi* which will be discussed in Chapter 4. As with the abacus, Aristotle writes, mistakes are made because there are a limited number of words but an unlimited number of things. Following this metaphor, one wonders what effect the absence of the concept of the number "zero" might have had on Greek conceptions of "nonsense"; cf. Rotman (1987) and Kaplan (2000) for the history of "zero" in Western thought; West (1982) 85 regarding the pronunciation of οὐδείς ("no-thing" rather than the hypostatized "nothing").

[14] The transmitted Greek titles are *Gastrōn* and *Knoithideus*. There are recent discussions of sympotic riddles in Kostantakos (2000a) 146–56, Pütz (2007) 192–210, Hunter (1983) 200–7. Cf. Schultz, *RE* 1A.99–101 "Rätsel." For Antiphanes, see especially Kostantakos (2000a), (2000b).

ἐγέλων νομίζων λῆρον, οὐκ ἂν γενόμενον
οὐδέποτέ γ᾽, οἶμαι, πρᾶγμα παντελῶς λέγειν,
ἐνέδρας δ᾽ ἕνεκα. νυνὶ δὲ τοῦτ᾽ ἔγνωχ᾽ ὅτι
ἀληθὲς ἦν· φέρομεν γὰρ ἄνθρωποι δέκα
ἔρανόν τιν᾽, οὐ φέρει δὲ τούτων τὴν φορὰν
οὐδείς. σαφῶς οὖν ὅ τι φέρων τις μὴ φέρει,
τοῦτ᾽ ἔστιν, ἥν θ᾽ ὁ γρῖφος ἐνταῦθα ῥέπων.
καὶ τοῦτο μὲν δὴ κἄστι συγγνώμην ἔχον·
ἀλλ᾽ οἷα λογοποιοῦσιν ἐν τῷ πράγματι
οἱ τἀργύριον μὴ κατατιθέντες. ὡς σφόδρα
ὁ Φίλιππος ἄρ᾽ ἦν εὐτυχής τις, νὴ Δία . . .

Earlier, I used to think that people who bid one to tell [or "explain"[15]] riddles over drinks were clearly raving and talking nonsense; when someone asked us to guess one after the other "what someone brings but does not bring" was, I used to laugh, thinking it drivel – that he was meaning something, I suppose, which could never happen at all, just to catch us. But now I've recognized that it was true: for we ten people bring a certain contribution, but no one brings the payment of these things [i.e., carries them]. Clearly then "what someone brings but does not bring" is this, and the riddle was hinting towards these things right here. And one can indeed excuse this: but the sorts of speeches that are made in fact by those not paying the money! How truly lucky Philip was, by Zeus!

Antiphanes' speaker claims that he has solved the "what someone brings but does not bring" riddle,[16] but his (possibly fumbled) solution is not of interest here.[17] Rather, it is the opposition he creates, the two ways of engaging with the phrase "what someone brings but does not bring": either

---

[15] Although Gulick (1927–41) and Rusten et al. (2011) translate the phrase λέγειν γρίφους as "to tell riddles," the collocation is rare. "To tell riddles" is usually προβάλλειν γρίφους or, less often, ποιεῖν γρίφους. If one considers the sense of the passage, as well as the use of εἰπεῖν in line four, it seems possible that riddles are not being demanded here but rather their explanations (and thus the rareness of the collocation). It may even be a shorthand, colloquial way of saying "to say what a riddle [is]," i.e., "guess its answer." Thus "to bid someone to say [what] a riddle [is]" may simply be "pose a riddle." Cf. Olson's (2006–12) v, 147 "to get others to respond to riddles."

[16] It should be noted that he uses here *griphos* not *ainigma* as Aristotle had. For a list of Greek riddle terms (including *problema*) see Pütz (2007) 192–3. At 193, regarding *griphos* versus *ainigma*: "In antiquity, these nouns [meaning "riddle"] were already used without distinction, and several other words could bear the same meaning." Cf. Suetonius, who defines *griphos* as a sympotic *ainigma* (*On Greek Games* 3.1).

[17] It seems that "something brought not brought" refers to the contributions of a dining club, playing on two senses of *pherō* (roughly "we bring contributions but do not carry them"); cf. Olson (2006–12) v, 147 who distinguishes between "bearing the cost of a dinner party" and "carrying his share of the burden"; Pütz (2007) 203–4 thinks the speaker "snobbish" and "not experienced" with riddles which "is why he now (wrongly) assumes the riddle to refer to his club" at 204; Gulick (1927–41) ad loc. translates the difference as contributing to a club versus contributing to the meal; cf. Amouroux (1999) ad loc.

the phrase is a proper riddle (i.e., it has an answer) or it is nonsense (i.e., it has no answer). The first way of listening to the phrase "what someone brings but does not bring" – that is, hearing it as a proper, soluble riddle – is active, aggressive, and inquisitive. The listener searches the words closely, searches *around* the words, stepping back to see the phrase in different ways in order to "solve" it and find the meaning (perhaps, for example, there is more than one sense of "bring," or a particular usage of "someone"). It is that active aspect of interpretation that the fourth-century Clearchus of Soli (who, among other things,[18] wrote a book on riddles) emphasizes in his definition of the popular pastime: a riddle's solution must be "discovered by the mind" by "searching" (διὰ ζητήσεως εὑρεῖν τῇ διανοίᾳ).[19] If Antiphanes' riddle is received as a proper riddle, one will search all the possible meanings to "what someone brings but does not bring," and observe it from various angles in order to find possible allusions or double entendres. This active "searching" or interpretation, then, is the first type of reaction to an obscure phrase.

The second type of reaction, however, is altogether different. Here one finds a more passive or simpler response: not to examine or to "search" the phrase further at all. Rather, the riddlee reclines on the couch, and considers the phrase not as some obscure sentence which must be creatively interpreted (or perhaps emended or corrected in some way) in order to mean properly, but precisely as a sentence which is insoluble, one that has no answer, no outside reference. He calls this riddle without an answer "nonsense" (λῆρος), and what is more, he laughs – not because the phrase is a joke, but apparently because the statement is meaningless, that is, a nonsense phrase, an insoluble object.

So, then, two choices: to interpret a phrase as an (obscure) riddle, or to interpret a phrase as unworthy of interpretation: that is, to realize the phrase as nonsense, a riddle without an answer. Unlike Aristotle, whose instrumental view of language renders invisible the concept of an answer-less riddle, Antiphanes brings the concept into the light. Such riddles or obscure statements, for Antiphanes' speaker, resemble the language of the mentally ill (λῆρος) – there is no true object of interpretation, no reference to be sought (the "reference" is one "which could not possibly be" οὐκ ἂν γενόμενον οὐδέποτέ ... πρᾶγμα παντελῶς). This vision of nonsense,

---

[18] For Clearchus of Soli, see Wehrli (1969). He, as an itinerant philosopher also wrote a book on different Eastern philosophies, and epigraphic evidence in Ai-Khanoum, Afghanistan suggests that he was responsible for bringing Delphic gnomai there (see Robert (1968) 416–57).

[19] Ath. 10.448c, Clearchus of Soli (fr. 86 Wehrli; FHG 2.321), γρῖφος πρόβλημά ἐστι παιστικόν, προστακτικὸν τοῦ διὰ ζητήσεως εὑρεῖν τῇ διανοίᾳ τὸ προβληθὲν τιμῆς ἢ ἐπιζημίου χάριν εἰρημένον.

however, is only for a passing moment: the speaker continues by announcing that the solution to the riddle has suddenly occurred to him. Although the solution itself may be unsatisfactory, the return to the Aristotelian sphere is complete: language has its reference, and nonsense is mere obscurity which can be interpreted after all. But what is important to emphasize here is the moment before the speaker's enlightenment: he dismisses the phrase not as obscure (i.e., the solution exists, but is difficult to find), but as nonsense (there is no solution – it is language without reference). Comedy creates the context for a different type of signification.

In *Gut*, the speaker eventually "solves" the riddle, but in another play of Antiphanes, actually entitled *Riddle* (*Problēma* 192 KA = Ath. 450c–e), the enigmas remain unsolved. Here Antiphanes again explores the possibility of riddles without answers, and again labels such phenomena "nonsense." But the fragment is more ingenious than the first, since the transition from active interpretation to nonsense-realization is actually depicted, frustrating the persistent desire for meaning. Unlike the fragment from *Gut*, it is not laughter which accompanies the realization of nonsense, but rather irritation, almost rage. Antiphanes effects this reaction through a series of "false" answers: that is, answers as obscure as the riddle itself. Through the course of the interchange no solution or outside real-world reference is ever found, and, as such, the language remains in a state of "something that can never be" (οὐκ ἂν γενόμενον οὐδέποτέ . . . πρᾶγμα παντελῶς), a state of a riddle without an answer, or to use Antiphanes' term, a state of nonsense.

Here is the beginning of the fragment:

(A.) ἰχθύσιν ἀμφίβληστρον ἀνὴρ πολλοῖς περιβάλλειν
οἰηθεὶς μεγάλῃ δαπάνῃ μίαν εἵλκυσε πέρκην·
καὶ ταύτην ψευσθεὶς ἄλλην κεστρεὺς †ἴσον αὐτὴν[20]
ἦγεν. βουλομένη δ' ἔπεται πέρκη μελανούρῳ.
(B.) κεστρεύς, ἀνήρ, μελάνουρος, οὐκ οἶδ' ὅ τι λέγεις·
οὐδὲν λέγεις γάρ.

(A.) A man expecting to throw his net around a number of fish pulled in a single perch at great expense; and cheated in this one, the grey mullet brought him another †equal it. For a perch willingly follows a black-tail.
(B.) Grey mullet, man, black-tail! I don't know what you're talking about. You are really talking nonsense.

From Speaker B's view a perfectly sensible first clause is presented: "A man expecting to throw his net around a number of fish pulled in a single perch

---

[20] For the textual issues here and new conjecture, see Kostantakos (2000a) 190.

at great expense." Fair enough, and nothing particularly nonsensical here. Perhaps the "expense" of the perch is simply conveying the fact that so small and so singular a fish required so much effort. But the haze falls over the language in the following sentence: "cheated in this one, the grey mullet brought him another . . ." A signal goes off, a discomfort arises. This is the moment when suspicions grow either about the state of the language (is this a riddle? an allegory?) or about the speaker (is this person a little funny in the head?).[21] Maybe it is a slip of the tongue, since, to state the obvious, there is no way that a grey mullet can "bring" a perch. But all hope is crushed in the following sentence with the explanatory δέ: "For a perch willingly follows a black-tail."[22] It is that expectancy of a clear explanation which aggravates the discomfort to the point of unbearability, since nothing is explained and the obscurity has only worsened. Exasperation: it is "nonsense," Speaker B says.

Like the speaker of the *Gut* fragment, Speaker B has rejected the active interpretive response, the "searching" that Clearchus describes as central to the riddle's hermeneutic process, and does not, like a proper riddlee, simply ask for the answer at the moment of intellectual defeat. Here, like the first fragment, a more physical or emotional response usurps the place of the intellectual, interpretive one: instead of unraveling the words or awaiting the unraveling of the words, the speaker, in frustration, cannot bear to listen to the language any further and declares it nonsense. When Speaker A attempts to assuage the aggravated Speaker B by "explaining" the riddle to her, she ends up using language just as riddling as the riddle itself. Speaker A says: "OK: I'll show you clearly: there is someone who gives his possessions but does not know that he's given them to the people to whom he's given them, nor that he has what he didn't ask for" ἀλλ' ἐγὼ σαφῶς φράσω. / ἔστι τις ὃς τὰ μὲν ὄντα διδοὺς οὐκ οἶδε δεδωκώς / οἷσι δέδωκ' οὐδ' αὐτὸς ἔχων ὧν οὐδὲν ἐδεῖτο.[23] This obscure "explanation" is met with

---

[21] Of course, the riddle is in dactylic hexameter which already frames it as a riddle, or a deviant type of language. Whether Speaker B perceives meter in the same way that the audience does, however, is another question. For the compelling argument that this fragment contains three speakers rather than two, cf. Kostantakos (2000a) 183–4.

[22] Proverbial at Ath. 7.319c with Olson (2006–12) ad loc (n. 349: glossing "i.e. 'Every cloud has a silver lining' *vel sim.*") and ad 10.450c (n. 223); Rusten *et al.* (2011) 507 n. 27: "A proverb for inseparable companions. The point of this whole parable (and the text of line 3) are unclear." Cf. Kostantakos (2000a) 193–6.

[23] Pütz (2007) 201, 203 spots a nice parallel here in the Heraclitus [22] fragment (56 DK) which describes the riddle that vexed Homer: "what we saw and caught, this we leave behind, but what we did not see and did not catch, this we bring" ὅσα εἴδομεν καὶ ἐλάβομεν, ταῦτα ἀπολείπομεν, ὅσα δὲ οὔτε εἴδομεν οὔτ'ἐλάβομεν, ταῦτα φέρομεν. Cf. also Crates *Samians* fr. 32 KA with Rusten *et al.* (2011) 140 n.4: "an assortment of absurdities and paradoxes" and Ar. fr. 347 KA.

further exasperation on B's part (διδούς τις οὐκ ἔδωκεν οὐδ' ἔχων ἔχει; / οὐκ οἶδα τούτων οὐδέν), to the point where A must switch to ordinary speech (that is, from dactylic hexameter to iambic trimeter) in order to explain things apologetically in a climactic fumble: "Well, that's what the riddle said. For what you know, you don't know now, nor what you've given nor what you have in return for that [what you've given]. Something like that." οὐκοῦν ταῦτα καὶ / ὁ γρῖφος ἔλεγεν. ὅσα γὰρ οἶσθ' οὐκ οἶσθα νῦν / οὐδ' ὅσα δέδωκας οὐδ' ὅσ' ἀντ' αὐτῶν ἔχεις. / τοιοῦτο τοῦτ' ἦν. It is a masterful moment of Antiphanes' comic technique, and Speaker B's exasperation (or perhaps that of a third speaker) in the lines that follow is particularly pleasing.[24]

Unlike Antiphanes' first fragment, it seems that these riddles are never solved but remain nonsense to the end. But the question then is: to what extent ought these riddles be perceived as nonsense (i.e., reference-free language), not just by Speaker B, but by the audience as well? Here clearly the riddlee has made the choice to reject interpretation, but can one push further and actually agree with Speaker B? Solutions have been discovered regarding the blacktail-mullet riddle. Zacher, for example, writes that the *kestreus* stands for a "mama's boy" (*Muttersöhnchen*),[25] while Gulick later expounds that the "perch" of the riddle represents a prostitute and the "grey mullet" a pimp.[26] Pütz rejects Gulick's interpretation as "too far-fetched and hypothetical," suggesting that the real solution may involve the proverbial use of "mullet" (*kestreus*) for "people who are too honest to make gains."[27] However, it seems that these scholars are likely missing the point: a proper riddle is what Antiphanes here is trying to avoid, as Kostantakos has observed.[28] Two different types of speakers are being presented: the flighty, blustering riddler, and the sensible, level-headed

---

[24] The exasperated response riddle of Speaker B (see note 29 below) – or possibly a third speaker – is vexed enough that Nesselrath (1990) 320 n. 100 posits a lacuna. Pütz (2007) 202 argues for no change since, as it stands, it would sound "like a tongue-twister to the audience" and that Speaker B's riddle "might not have been intended to have a clear solution." I would make the latter argument about all three of Speaker A's riddles as well.

[25] Zacher (1902) 1221 n. 3: "Wenn meine Emendation richtig ist, so wäre bei Antiphanes unter κεστρεύς vielleicht ein 'Muttersönchen' zu verstehen."

[26] Ath. 10.450c–e: Gulick's translation reflects this interpretation which is why I would translate e.g., ἄλλην ... ἴσον αὐτῇ as "another like it" rather than Gulick's "another like her" since although both senses are in the Greek, the latter pushes the English ear too much in Gulick's direction. Both translations may be wrong: Olson (2006–12) ad loc. keeps the daggers at †ἴσον αὐτήν.

[27] Pütz (2007) 201 n. 191. Olson (2006–12) ad loc. and Rusten *et al.* (2011) 507 n. 27 refrain from "solving" the riddles.

[28] See Kostantakos (2000a) 197: "the riddle has in fact no solution" which "is supported by the second riddle (7f), which also seems to be a piece of nonsense without solution, a series of contradictions leading nowhere." His connection of the "fishing" of the riddle's subject and the "fishing" in a *griphos* (lit. "fishing net") without solution is excellent.

riddlee. It is clear from the riddlee's abusive rant (at the end of the fragment) who the "Butt" of the comic situation is: it is, of course, the blustering riddler, since she is the one who receives the final abuse for her blathering nonsense.[29] But would this scenario be effective if the blusterer's riddles actually made sense to the audience? This would create a completely different dynamic, one relying on dramatic irony. If the audience understands what the riddlee cannot, the effectiveness (and humor) of the poor riddlee's final rant would be diminished, almost pointless. Instead, what appears to make the series of irritating riddles so effective is that their solutions are likely no clearer to the audience than to the speakers. The reason that the riddles' solutions are uncertain to later scholars is because no solutions, I would suggest, were intended (as the scene's dynamics make manifest). What is instead offered are riddles without solutions and language without reference, goading and irritating rather than signifying.

Antiphanes' *Riddle* stages the interpretive refusal that nonsense requires as language is prised from its references. If the audience were stroking their beards trying to "solve" these riddles, they would be missing the scene's point: when the language is left as meaningless and reference-free, the scene attains its particular effect. It is interesting to note here how far removed Antiphanes' treatment of language is from the options set out by Aristotle in the *Poetics*, regarding this subject of riddles. While Aristotle in the *Poetics* envisions riddles as a form of obscurity (like the solecism), the existence of the language's reference is not questioned.[30] Antiphanes, however, not only stages characters who refuse to interpret each other's language (thereby engaging the possibilities of meaninglessness), but actually seems to elicit the audience's refusal to interpret as well.

Similar examples of reference-free language in the riddling mode can be seen elsewhere in comedy, although never quite so successfully as in Antiphanes. The riddled oracles of *Knights* (ἠνιγμένος, 196) and their often equally riddling interpretations operate with similar effect to Antiphanes'

---

[29] The interchange continues with Speaker B's (as KA edits it), or perhaps a third speaker's response (13–19, with note 24): (B.) τοιγαροῦν κἀγώ τινα / εἰπεῖν πρὸς ὑμᾶς βούλομαι γρῖφον. (A.) λέγε. / (B.) πίννη καὶ τρίγλη φωνὰς ἰχθῦ δύ᾽ ἔχουσαι / πόλλ᾽ ἐλάλουν, περὶ ὦν δὲ πρὸς ὃν τ᾽ᾤοντο λέγειν τι, / οὐκ ἐλάλουν· οὐδὲν γὰρ ἐμάνθανεν, ὥστε πρὸς ὃν μὲν / ἦν αὐταῖς ὁ λόγος, πρὸς δ᾽ αὐτὰς πολλὰ λαλούσας / αὐτὰς ἀμφοτέρας ἡ Δημήτηρ ἐπιτρίψαι. (B.) "That's why I also want to tell you a certain riddle. (A.) OK. (B.) A pinna and mullet, two fish having voices, were gabbing a lot, but about the things and to whom they thought they spoke, gabbed they not. For she did not understand anything, consequently while their words were for him, they were gabbing a lot to themselves, and may Demeter destroy them both."

[30] See also Arist. *Metaph.* 991a21–2 (regarding Plato's forms), which suggests that speaking metaphorically is nonsensical (*kenologein*), along with *Top.* 139b34 which explains that metaphorical language is too obscure for precise philosophy.

riddles.[31] Although much of the oracular language bears clear references (e.g., either to Cleon or the Sausage-Seller), much of the parodic effect (as with Antiphanes) relies on language that does not. So too, the riddled dithyrambic language of comedy that skewers both song and singer runs parallel to Antiphanes' riddles: while much of the dithyrambic language can be interpreted, at its headiest and flightiest and most climactic, the language's references seem to disintegrate.[32] What Antiphanes' fragments illustrate is that continued interpretation at such moments is to miss the intended effect: not only does language-without-reference galvanize the parody, but the parody's most climactic moments rely on these brief attempts or attainments of reference-free language. Such language is to be processed not as obscurity – which demands a redoubled hermeneutic effort – but as nonsense, which demands the surrender of the interpretive urge.

How to make sense of beetles and dung

Antiphanes' *Riddle* suggests that searching for references seems to be something of a fool's errand, since, as the speaker of Antiphanes' *Gut* explained, the reference does not exist (οὐκ ἂν γενόμενον οὐδέποτέ ... πρᾶγμα παντελῶς) and, thus, any attempted interpretation would expose one as a dupe (the nonsense-riddle being spoken "just to catch us" ἐνέδρας δ' ἕνεκα). In Aristophanes' *Peace*, a similar game is played with references, and in this section, I would like to examine this well-known opening in light of Antiphanes' terminology. Here the interpretation of comedy is staged but the whole interpretive enterprise is ridiculed and scorned. There are no outside references to be sought, the *Peace* opening insists, and this insistence, I will argue, creates a certain effect: the potential meanings of comedy, those desiderata which the interpretive mode peddles, are rendered valueless.

At the opening of *Peace*, the audience is presented with a rather obscure spectacle of on-stage action: two slaves rushing to knead cakes. Owing to their complaints about the stench of the raw materials, it gradually becomes clear that these are no ordinary cakes. This is not unlike other Aristophanic openings, for example, *Knights* or *Wasps*, which also begin with two slaves in dialogue, and also play with the fact that the audience does not yet know

---

[31] See *Eq.* 195–210 and 997–1110 with Pütz (2007) 193 n. 154 for their riddling aspect. Cf. the oracles of Hierocles in *Pax* 1045–1126, and the oracle-monger at *Av.* 959–91.

[32] See Nesselrath (1990) 241–66 for the development of dithyrambic parody, and Pütz (2007) 192–210 for its riddling effect.

what the play is about (the "logos").[33] But here Aristophanes draws particular attention to the audience's quandary over the dung and the beetle, and
imagines the spectators guessing at what the "idea" is behind the obscurity
before them (43–8):

οὐκοῦν ἂν ἤδη τῶν θεατῶν τις λέγοι
νεανίας δοκησίσοφος· "τὸ δὲ πρᾶγμα τί;
ὁ κάνθαρος δὲ πρὸς τί;" κᾆτ' αὐτῷ γ' ἀνὴρ
Ἰωνικός τίς φησι παρακαθήμενος·
"δοκέω μὲν ἐς Κλέωνα τοῦτ' αἰνίσσεται,
ὡς κεῖνος ἐν Ἅιδεω[34] σπατίλην ἐσθίει."

I bet some young know-it-all spectator
would say: "what's going on?
The beetle stands for what?"[35] And then some
Ionian man says sitting next to him:
"I think he's making a riddle [or 'allegory'] about Cleon,
how he eats shit in Hades."

Scholars interpret this interchange between the young know-it-all and
the Ionian differently: Struck, for example, reads the lines as a very specific
(almost erudite) allusion to a small group of allegorists ("professional
interpreters," 41) in Athens: the audience will have been aware of this
eccentric mode of literary criticism, and will have identified these profes-
sionals as marginal, deviant, and thus laughable.[36] Casting the net more
broadly, Hubbard argues that interpreting drama in "symbolic and allegorical terms" was a more general tendency of contemporary audiences,[37]
while, broader still, Lefkowitz describes the opening as "present[ing] the

---

[33] For the "idea" or the "plot" of the play, cf. *Eq.* 36 "do you want me to tell the theme (*pragma*) to the
spectators?"; *Vesp.* begins with the guessing game over the play's theme, called *logos* at 54 ; *Pax* 44
"what is the *pragma*?" and "I will tell the *logos*" at 50; Lefkowitz (2009) 44–5 connects Peisthetairos'
idea (*gnōmē* or pragma) with the comic plot. Regarding "logos" as "plot," see Pickard-Cambridge
(1968) 67 n. 8. Cf. Zimmermann (2010) 460.

[34] I follow van Leeuwen's (1968 [1906]) conjecture with Platnauer (1964), Sommerstein (1985), Olson
(1998), Wilson (2007); but cf. Cassio (1985) 105 n. 1 with Bain (1986) 203 for arguments for the more
conservative ἀναιδέως.

[35] Olson (1998) ad loc. points to a similar passage of interpretation in *Eq.* 206 ὁ δράκων δὲ πρὸς τί;
although πρὸς τί; could mean simply "for what purpose?" (Henderson (1998b) ad loc. translates it as
"what's the point of the beetle?"), my "stands for" need not conflict with "purpose" or "point."

[36] Struck (2004) 41, although mentioning Rosen (1984) (who argues for the iambic *ainos* as a background to this scene), overlooks the importance of the *ainos* form lying behind his *ainigma* project
(24: "*ainigma*, the centerpiece of allegorical poetics.") Likewise Lefkowitz's (2009) extensive study of
the *ainos* form overlooks Struck (2004). This is because "fable" and "allegory" have become far more
separated in modern thought than they were in antiquity (see, e.g., Hegel's separation above): the
word *ainos* often seems to incorporate both terms.

[37] Hubbard (1991) 141 n. 6.

audience with a kind of mystery in need of solution"; the know-it-all's question "what is the *pragma?*," for Lefkowitz, is "imagined to be on *everyone*'s mind."[38]

Considering the moment at which this interchange is voiced – after nearly fifty lines of unsolved obscurity – this last opinion appears to be the most compelling. After all, directly following the interpreters' imagined interchange, one of the slaves breaks from the silliness with a serious, exegetical line: "I'll tell the gist of the play (*logon*) to the spectators" (50) – signaling that the unresolved obscurity had reached the critical moment.[39] Nothing is yet known, and, as the opening of *Knights* had demonstrated three years before – where Cleon really was being "riddled" behind a symbolic Paphlagonian – the Ionian's hermeneutic paranoia is not entirely unjustified. Although the first line of *Peace* is self-explanatory from hindsight αἶρ' αἶρε μᾶζαν ὡς τάχος τῷ κανθάρωι "grab the cake for the 'beetle' as quickly as possible," it is no different from the opening of *Wasps* where the two slaves reveal that they, too, are guarding a "monster" (v. 4: ἆρ' οἶσθά γ' οἷον κνώδαλον φυλάττομεν; "don't you know what kind of monster we're guarding?"). However, in neither case is there anything like full disclosure. Just as there are many possibilities for *knōdalon* besides some gargantuan monster (which, in *Wasps*, it is not), there are many possibilities for the *kantharos* besides some gargantuan monster (which, in *Peace*, it is). As Sommerstein has pointed out, the first hearing of "*kantharos*" may have confused some as referring to Kantharos the comic poet;[40] and it is not out of the question that the continued discussion of the beetle's dung-eating habits could have represented a continued extravagance of metaphor – after all, *skatophagos* was a usual term of abuse and familiar territory for *onomasti kōmōidein*.[41] Yet, despite all this, and despite the fact that the Ionian's conjectures arrive at a moment of exegetical need,[42] the two interpreters are presented as objects of ridicule. The descriptive δοκησίσοφος is

---

[38] Lefkowitz (2009) 47, my italics.

[39] Too little is known about the Proagon to gauge how much audience members knew before entering a performance (for which, see Pickard-Cambridge, 1968, 67–8), although it must be admitted the openings of these comedies (often guessing games about plot) would be dreadfully boring if everything were clear ahead of time – which is its own evidence against a simply explanatory Proagon.

[40] See Sommerstein 1985. Olson (1998) ad loc. detracts from this view, noting that Aristophanes does not follow up the Kantharos reference at either 143–5 (where there is wordplay on *kantharos*) or 695–703 (where comic poets are attacked). This makes little difference to how the first word was received in the audience.

[41] See Henderson (1991[1975]) 192–4.

[42] Olson (1998) ad 43–5 notes that the δὲ of ὁ κάνθαρος δὲ πρὸς τί; reflects "a note of surprise, impatience or indignation" (GP 173) – in this case, the latter two are most applicable.

pejorative, the Ionian's language is laughable,[43] and, thus, the critical response is unanimous: the beetle does *not* represent Cleon at all, and the idea is absurd.[44] If anyone had been considering interpreting the opening along the lines of the know-it-all and the Ionian, they have been duly chastised.

The effect of this brief interchange is suggestive: no one wants to be included in that social out-group along with the two disparaged interpreters.[45] While initially obscure lines from the opening of *Knights*, such as the slave Demosthenes' "when I was kneading a Spartan barley cake at Pylos" (v. 55), are easily resolved by discovering the line's "riddled" political reference, no such resolution of the obscure spectacle of two slaves kneading dung-cakes seems to be allowed. In order not to be identified with the ridiculed Ionian and know-it-all, this type of interpretation must be avoided. It is as if the implicit understanding assumed in Antiphanes' *Riddle* (that the obscure language has no reference) were being explicitly thematized: the only answer that is available to the question ὁ κάνθαρος δὲ πρὸς τί; is "nothing" – neither beetle nor dung refers to anything at all.[46]

What, then, ought one do as a spectator if interpretation has been prohibited? Within the next thirty lines, clear references to Euripides' *Bellerophon* will have been established, and the "logos" of the play will entice with the possibility of clear political messages (it is entitled *Peace*, after all: a fable/*ainos* of sorts).[47] Yet those two miscreant connoisseurs, derided for their reference-seeking, do not wholly disappear. By skewering the two imagined interpreters who discover hidden references behind a puzzling spectacle, Aristophanes creates an atmosphere in which

---

43 For the history of the question "why is the interlocutor Ionian?" see especially Rosen (1984) 389–90. Van Herwerdens' (1897) 48 suggests that the exuberant Ionian word σπατίλη is the reason for the speaker's being Ionian (and not vice versa). For *dokesisophos*, cf. Pherecrates fr. 163 KA, Callias fr. 34 KA with Wright (2012) 28.

44 See, e.g., Rosen (1984) 391: "part of its humor lies in the fact that . . . the dung beetle does not function as a cipher for a scatophagous Cleon in the context of the play as a whole."

45 For the "out-group" which is central to the social/superiority strand of humor research (most famously developed by Bergson in 1901), see, most recently, Stark (2004). For bibliography on the social/superiority strand of humor research (the other two being psychological/release and incongruity), see Martin (1998) 28–9.

46 Note the parallel regarding the *Knights* riddled oracle (206): ὁ δράκων δὲ πρὸς τί;: although Demosthenes is quick to give a reply (τοῦτο περιφανέστατον), the explanation is unsound since the sausage which the snake is supposed to "stand for" already has its own place in the oracle.

47 Later, Trygaeus says that his idea was based on one of Aesop's fables (129–30), with a scholiast providing the fable. A year earlier in *Wasps*, Aristophanes alludes to this same fable at 1448–9, with Hubbard (1991) 194 n. 102, 151 n. 35. For the relationship between the fable and Aristophanic poetry, see Adrados (1999) 243: "Yet above all the fable is of major importance in Aristophanes . . . whole comedies are written on the model of fables" and Lefkowitz (2009) 10–82.

interpretation itself is suspect. This is not to say interpretation is completely abandoned – after all, the play's language still functions properly (unlike Antiphanes' empty riddles), jokes still register, and the "logos" explains itself – but the meanings one might discover in interpretation are devalued. The extent to which one "searches" (to use Clearchus' term) has undergone an attack, and must retreat before it can advance again with habitual self-confidence. When the questions "what is the reference?" (τὸ δὲ πρᾶγμα τί;) and "what does this stand for?" (τοῦτο δὲ πρὸς τί;) occur again, the answer that there is no reference at all may become the more effortless response, since that more active, intense pursuit for meaning has drawn such scorn. In the next section, I will be considering the know-it-all's question "what does x stand for?" (τοῦτο δὲ πρὸς τί;') in terms of allegory, rather than riddles. The difference between these two forms is that riddles function by concealing their references, while allegories operate by making their underlying references manifest. Unlike riddles, allegories function through clarity: they are presented almost as riddles-already-solved, even though the framework of the veiled reference operates similarly.[48] For that reason, the comic exertions to separate language from allegorical reference will differ from those efforts studied here in this section on riddles. Comic allegories are generally *not* obscure and their references are clear; but as I will argue, a number of elements are added in order to destabilize that clear meaning-structure.

Allegory without allegorized

Allegory, like any word which receives a variety of uses through a long history, tends to create anxiety whenever critics attempt to employ it as an objective label. Although scholars have been using "allegory" to describe certain features of comedy for centuries (for example, the characterization of Demos in *Knights*), others have demanded a more constricted usage of

---

[48] But such a conception of allegory-*qua*-poetic form must be distinguished from allegoresis which often prides itself on discovering allegorical meaning in non-obvious sources. See Obbink (2003, 2010); Most (2010). For allegorical clarity (for allegory the poetic form), see, e.g., Hegel (1975 [1835]) 398–9: "The opposite of the riddle, in this sphere which begins from the universality of the meaning, is allegory. It too does try to bring the specific qualities of a universal idea nearer to our vision through cognate qualities of sensuously concrete objects; yet it does so not by way of the semi-veiling and the enigmas of the riddle, but precisely with the converse aim of producing the most complete clarity, so that the external thing of which the allegory avails itself must be as transparent as possible for the meaning which is to appear in it." Because of its long history (for which, see Menke (2000), "allegory" attains many conflicting meanings, and this distinction between allegory the poetic form ("transparent as possible," according to Hegel) and allegory (that which allegoresis discovers a text to be through anagnostic spelunking) is not an ancient one.

the term. Peter Struck, for example, in his recent study of allegoresis (i.e., *reading* a text allegorically), dates allegory (i.e., the poetic form) to the early medieval period, insisting that no earlier example exists.[49] This is not the first time someone has called for a more limited usage of the term – the only surprise is his disregard of the centuries of (modern) scholarship which discusses the "allegories" of ancient literature from Alcaeus' ship of state to the hoards of abstractions walking and talking in Greek comedy,[50] something which has been a point of criticism in reviews of Struck's book.[51] Regarding Greek comedy, Dover summed up the situation nicely half a century ago:

> Few people have been so ingenious, or so rash, as to find ἀλληγορία in Aristophanes. On the other hand, if "allegory" is used, as it has commonly been used since the eighteenth century, to mean simply the personification of qualities, acts, and situations, Aristophanes is pre-eminently an allegorical dramatist.[52]

Although, to his eloquent dismay, Dover *would* encounter such a study of ἀλληγορία in Aristophanes some fifty years later,[53] what ought to be noted here is his second sentence: that the term has been used (and continues to be used) to cover a feature of Old Comedy wherein abstractions are personified (e.g., Demos in *Knights*, Lady Comedy in Cratinus's *Pytine*) and political figures are represented by other characters ("Paphlagon-the-slave" is Cleon, "Labes-the-dog" is Laches). In what follows, I will be using allegory roughly in Dover's second sense, and I have no qualms if the reader wishes to replace "allegory" with another term – whether it be personification (but can Paphlagon be called a "personification" of Cleon?), or, like Newiger, following Hegel, a *Bild*, or some other term, like metaphor or fable (*ainos*).

---

[49] Struck (2004) 3 n.1, allegory being where "a writer personifies abstract ideas and encodes a formulaic, one-to-one correspondence between each character and some concept . . ."

[50] Newiger (1957), in his study of Aristophanes, also limits a perceived over-extension of the term "allegory" in his predecessors, favoring instead Hegel's term *Bild* (roughly an extended metaphor: cf. Taillardat's (1965) 6–8 definition of "image"), but still finds place for allegory, e.g., in *Wealth*. Despite Newiger's limitations, scholars still prefer the term "allegory" to Hegel's term, see e.g., Dover (2004), Rosen (1997), Rochefort-Guillouet (2002) 6; cf. Ruffell (2011) 62–5. See Bakola (2010) 181–203 for the problems with applying the term "allegory" to Cratinus' *Dionysalexandros*, compared with "true allegory" in comedy (at 203).

[51] See especially Porter (2007), focusing specifically on Struck's omission of comedy: "Aristophanes is frequently allegorical, as is Old Comedy in general, but its allegoresis is this-worldly and comic, not other-worldly and spiritual, as when Athens and Sparta have each lost their pestles, Kleon and Brasidas (*Peace*), or when Dame Poetry appears, injured and abused, on the stage in Cratinus' *Pytine*."

[52] Dover (1958) 235.

[53] See Dover (2004) 241–5 regarding Vickers (1997). At 242: "I must confess that in reading *Pericles on Stage* I feel that I am being borne by a tidal wave of 'if . . .' and 'may/might/could have . . .' into a region which I can only describe as being beyond the reach of parody."

The feature of allegory that I will be examining here is one that is often noted regarding allegory in Old Comedy: as soon as an allegory is adopted (e.g., Laches-the-general is Labes-the-dog in *Wasps*) it is, to use the terms of other scholars, "broken" or "comically confused."[54] Certain language refers to the signifier (i.e., Labes the dog), certain language refers to the signified (Laches the general), and some sentences contain elements of both. Although this feature of comic allegory is often noted, here I would like to pursue this broken signification process a bit more. I will argue, focusing on two texts (the dog trial of *Wasps*, and the *Cities* of Eupolis), that allegory creates a situation in which audiences seek references or meaning (rather like the "seeking" in Clearchus' riddle definition), finding double entendres and allusions to the allegorized level; and that, by breaking that meaning-structure, the comedian pushes in the direction *opposite* to allegory. Broken allegory forces an audience to be in a temporary state of non-interpretation, a state which allows language to exist without "deeper" or "further" significance. In a word, while allegory creates a context for meaning, broken allegory creates a context for surrender: it forfeits the act of interpretation and allows for a brief indulgence in meaningless experience.

Dogs on trial and broken allegories

Wasps, produced at the Lenaia of 422 BCE, contains a much-loved scene which begins roughly two-thirds of the way through the play (lines 891–1001).[55] The young Bdelycleon has contrived a brilliant device to prevent his jury-addicted father Philocleon from further aggravation: he creates a law court at home. The first and final trial of this homemade law court consists of a dispute between two dogs over stolen cheese, with kitchen utensils as witnesses. This is the fantastic stuff of fables and (modern-day) children's theater, but the story attains its serious, adult aspect through political allegory: the prosecuting dog "Dog" (Cyon) represents Cleon, the defendant dog "Labes" represents the general Laches. Although Philocleon briefly relaxes from his usual aggressive,

---

[54] See Süss (1954) 116–22 for the "'Durchbrechung der allegorischen Einkleidung" (defined at 116) and MacDowell (1971) 253 for allegory being "comically confused;" also Sommerstein (1981) 147 for "mixture of allegory and allegorized." Cf. Silk (2000) 142–8.

[55] See, e.g., MacDowell (1995) 165: "This scene is the best in the play"; Staples (1978) 51, calling the scene "perhaps the most hilarious moment in antiquity," although he finds the "true" brilliance at deeper, more allegorical/metaphorical levels.

pro-Cleon stance, it is only through Bdelycleon's trickery that Labes is acquitted, and the allegory as a whole quickly fades from view.[56]

As with other allegories in comedy (for example, *Knights*), absolute allegorical clarity is not of the essence for this dogs-on-trial scene: rather sentences often consist of mixed signifiers, some referring to the surface action, others applying to the allegorized, political level. MacDowell in his commentary speaks of this phenomenon in two ways – on the one hand, the device provides clarity for the spectators, on the other, it creates comic confusion:

> Ar. is very careful to ensure that even the dullest members of the audience do not fail to follow the political allegory throughout the trial. Sometimes the accuser and the accused are actually called "men" (918, 923, 933, 1000), and constantly, among all the talk of dogs and cheese, words like "the state" (917), "the soldiers" (965), "sailing round" (924), and "make out his accounts" (961) are slipped in to remind us to think also of the politician and the general.[57]

Later in the commentary, however, he views this same phenomenon from a different perspective: that the broken allegory is not for the sake of allegorical clarity, but for the comic. He writes: "The literal and allegorical aspects of the trial are comically confused. Some words in the sentence apply to Laches (ἄνδρα, περιπλεύσας, πόλεων), others only to Labes (κυνῶν, μονοφαγίστατον, θυείαν, σκῖρον, ἐξεδήδοκεν)."[58] He is correct with both analyses, of course, since the two (clarity and the comic) need not be mutually exclusive. But it seems fair to conclude that once someone has understood the invitation into the allegorical game (perhaps, for example, the prosecuting dog's introduction as "the dog of Cydathenaion" at 895), these later slippages have the effect not of didactic recapitulations, but rather something more along the lines of MacDowell's second point, that of "comic confusion."

Here are some of the confused lines from Dog/Cleon's accusation of Labes/Laches (922–5):

μή νυν ἀφῆτε γ' αὐτόν, ὡς ὄντ' αὖ πολὺ
κυνῶν ἁπάντων ἄνδρα μονοφαγίστατον,
ὅστις περιπλεύσας τὴν θυείαν ἐν κύκλῳ
ἐκ τῶν πόλεων τὸ σκῖρον ἐξεδήδοκεν.

---

[56] MacDowell (1971) 250 suggests that the scene's consequence lies in the fact that "the plot of the play is forwarded . . . for the domestic trial, and especially the involuntary experience of voting for an acquittal, is a further stage in the process of curing Philocleon of his disease." For readings of the scene, see Slater (2002) 95–8; Reckford (1987) 252, Russo (1994) 128 for the "play within a play" motif. Cf. Mastromarco (1974) 55–64, 85–96; MacDowell (1995) 165–70 for the political background; see Sidwell (2009) 188–91 for the idea that Aristophanes is actually here parodying an earlier Cleon-in-court allegory of Eupolis in *Chrysoun Genos*; Ruffell (2011) 133–53 for analysis and diagrams of the scene's structure.

[57] MacDowell (1971) 249–50.   [58] MacDowell (1971) 253.

Don't let him off the hook! He's, again, by far the most lone-eatingest
[Somm.] man of all dogs, who sailed around the mortar in a circle and ate
the rind off the cities.

If one were not aware of the allegorical context, this sentence, with its
"lone-eatingest man of all dogs" and "sailed around the mortar," would
verge on nonsense. Within the context of political allegory, however, the
problem is easily resolved by showing (as commentators do) that certain
elements of the sentence simply refer to the surface level, while other elements
refer to the political allegorized level.[59] The general Laches had served in
Sicily from 427 to 425, so the accusation here clearly indicates some alleged
misbehavior (probably embezzlement) during his tenure there.[60] Thus,
"sailing around" and "from cities," while meaningless for the domestic surface
story, attain meaning through the allegorized reference; so too, the rind and
the mortar, although meaningless to the allegorized level, rest perfectly
content in the domestic setting. The sentence thus resolves itself.

This is the way the "comic confusion" of allegory *should* work, anyway,
but the allegorical mechanism is rarely so objective and manageable as one
might hope. In the sentence above, "he sailed around the mortar," for
example, this word "mortar" becomes something like a blunt object within
the sentence: it is not soluble within the allegorical context but protrudes as
a meaningless, domestic object. It refers, as MacDowell suggests, to the
literal not the allegorical level; but within the allegory, it is a signifier
without signified. The question that always must follow such analysis is
"for whom is this the case?" For whom does the "mortar" *not* refer to the
allegorized level? The Laurentianus scholiast, for example, reports a discovered wordplay which connects the surface to the allegorized level: *thueian*
(mortar) is a pun for *thalassan* (sea), and thus the mortar "stands for" the sea
on which Laches sailed. Others have connected the mortar to Sicily, due to
the triangular shape of its profile view, i.e., wide on top and narrow at
the bottom – a more visual relationship whereby the blunt object of "the
mortar" can be resolved.[61] This, of course, applies to other parts of the
speech as well. When Cleon accuses Labes of "running off into a corner,
ensicilizing and gorging himself on a piece of cheese" (910–11), another

---

[59] See, e.g., Sommerstein (1983) ad 924–5: "a blend of two accusations one appropriate to Labes and one
to Laches: (i) 'he went round the mortar . . . and ate the rind off the cheese'; (ii) 'he sailed round Sicily
and embezzled the money paid by the cities.'"

[60] See MacDowell (1971) 163–5. There is no evidence that there was a trial, though the trial scene "shows
that Kleon was hostile to Lakhes, was threatening to prosecute him, and said that he had made money
out of his command in Sicily" at 164.

[61] See MacDowell (1971) 254.

rather blunt allegorical object emerges: the "corner." Yet this too can be "solved" by showing that Sicily is in a "corner" of the Greek world and therefore the corner "stands for" Sicily.[62] The allegory, then, is not broken or "confused" after all.

More ingenious still is the solution for the testimony of the cheese-grater, who comes to bear witness in the trial. If the Dog stands for Cleon, and Labes-the-dog stands for Laches, who does the cheese-grater "stand for"? It would seem that this too is an insoluble object within the allegory, that it does not stand for anything in particular. But L. A. Post has argued that the cheese-grater represents the Sicilian city Catana (which apparently in Sicilian dialect means cheese-grater),[63] and that, in this way, the cheese-grater's testimony still directly refers to Laches' trial.[64] The allegory has not been loosened or broken at all: signifiers are still properly mapping on to signifieds. What appear to some as blunt objects within allegory (i.e., referring only to the surface domestic situation), become, to others, soluble and allegorical to the highest degree.

This is rather familiar territory, considering Chapter 1, where I empha-sized the problems with an objective approach to nonsense: such an approach must fail since nonsense is always ultimately subjective (i.e., nonsense for one person is sense to another). So too, here, one finds nonsense's opposite, where that same objective approach must fail: what has allegorical meaning to one person, is devoid of such meaning to another. This subjective aspect of allegory is often stressed, but it becomes a much more urgent problem with comedy, where "comic confusion" and allego-rical meaning seem to be mutually exclusive. One would wish to demarcate lines around comic meaning and draw the "limits of allegory" as though something other than meaning ought to be saved in meaning's place.

Dover considers precisely this problem of comic interpretation in a 2004 article entitled "The limits of allegory and allusion in Aristophanes."[65] The way that he attempts to pose limits to the (hyper-)interpretive act of allegory

---

[62] MacDowell (1971) 253 ad 910: "Attempts to show that Sicily is in a corner of the Greek world are far-fetched and misguided." So too see the scholiast's explanation of eating in the dark referring to the fact that Sicily is in the west (i.e., where the sun sets).

[63] At Plut. *Dion* 58, Callipus, upon losing Syracuse and winning Catana, remarked "that he lost a city and won a cheese-grater" (ὅτι πόλιν ἀπολωλεκὼς τυρόκνηστιν εἴληφεν). This has been traditionally explained as a pun, i.e., that Catana meant "cheese-grater" in Sicilian. Post (1932) 265 suggests the city was named this owing to some topographical feature (cf. Zancle, "sickle").

[64] Post (1932) 265: "It may be doubted whether an Athenian audience would all have known that Catana meant cheese-grater in the Sicilian dialect. Still there must have been many old soldiers who would have grasped the allusion at once and would have been glad to explain the joke to the rest." See MacDowell (1971) 257.

[65] Dover (2004).

is by asking what the average Athenian would have been able to understand as allegorical – that is, how obvious does an allusion need to be (quite obvious) and how sophisticated was the original audience (not very). He writes: "It cannot have been at all easy for the original audience to discern what was intended as an allusion to a fellow-citizen and what was not, but it seems peculiarly easy for a modern interpreter to decide on allusions to one or other individual in that small fraction of the citizen-body containing those about whom posterity knew something."[66] His point is well noted and his reconstruction of the original audience via the far-from-subtle Aristophanic allusions he enumerates should certainly be a starting point for anyone looking for allegories in Greek comedy. The treatment of the allegorical elements in *Wasps* can be approached in this same way – for example, how many Athenians would have heard a phonetic resemblance between *thuian* and *thalassan*?

But this is not my interest here regarding the "limits of allegory." Rather, I would like to look at the problem from a different angle, not by asking whether the allegory "was there" or not, but by asking what would be *lost* by treating sentence elements like the "mortar" or the "cheese-grater" as allegorical rather than the "blunt objects" that I have been describing them as. In this passage of *Wasps*, just as in other passages of confused allegory such as in *Knights* (e.g., the slave Demosthenes' quip about kneading barley cakes at Pylos),[67] a structure has been created wherein one understands that specific domestic items refer to certain allegorized referents (e.g., the dog Laches, the stolen cheese), and one can thus map the relationships. But then certain objects appear in this signifying process that do not solve themselves, such as the mortar (τὴν θυείαν), which resists solution into the allegorical game. To put it another way: the comedian has constructed a meaning-structure wherein he asks the audience to interpret in a certain fashion, but then, by adding these elements, he is asking the audience *not* to interpret, to surrender that level of concentration for the moment and accept the dull object (the mortar) without further interpretation. To return to the imagined spectator of *Peace* who asks τοῦτο δὲ πρὸς τί; ("what does *x* stand for?"), here again, for each broken element of the allegory the answer is nothing, it is not significant within the allegorical framework.

To interpret these blunt objects as soluble within the allegorical context, however, creates an entirely different sentence. It causes the allegory to run smoothly, and the audience never to abandon its concentrated act of interpretation. The loss, then, I would like to argue, is in this particular

---

[66] Dover (2004) 241–2.   [67] *Eq.* 54–7.

result wherein the audience is invited into a position *not* to interpret. The "mortar," "the corner," "the cheese-grater," do not "stand for" anything: these are objects without further signification, and so, at each roadblock or speedbump, that active, interpretive drive must decelerate. The effect of not searching for references recalls the indolent behavior of Antiphanes' character, who rejects (and laughs at) a possibly meaningful phrase by calling it "nonsense" – not because he does not "get it" but because it seems to him that the language has nothing "to get."

Thus, although the "limits of allegory" are often discussed in terms of plausibility or audience reconstruction, it is the loss incurred by the comic text that may be the strongest critique against uninhibited allegorizing (a loss analogous to the reactionary sentiments discussed in the introduction to this book). While it is not easy to cause an audience *not* to interpret, this is one of the rare methods by which it can be effected: to create, through a highly artificial meaning-structure (allegory), elements that are meaningless within that structure. But, it may be asked, isn't this just "poetic license"? That is, if one considers, for example, Homeric similes, or metaphors such as Heraclitus' famous "time is a boy playing, playing checkers" (αἰὼν παῖς ἐστι παίζων, πεσσεύων fr. 52 DK), it can be argued that questions like "what do Heraclitus' checkers 'stand for?'" are also, in a sense, "missing the point." Silk writes well about this: "Heraclitus' *pessoi*... work[s] rather like some Homeric similes, in which the extended vehicle creates a compelling vignette of such interest that the immediate analogy is overshadowed (even though it is only and precisely the knowledge that there *is* an analogy that gives the vehicle its license to act)" (2003) 129. The same point could be made regarding *ainos* as well ("fable," the form behind the later *ainigmos*): there is no expectation of a one-to-one correspondence between the elements of an *ainos* and the conclusion to which it seems to be pointing. For example, in *Phaedo* (60c), one finds an *ainos* explaining why pain tends to follow pleasure: the gods must have joined the "heads" of pain and pleasure so that when one comes the other follows, it is explained. Like the question regarding Heraclitus' checkers, the question what does the "head" of pleasure or the "head" of pain "stand for" seems to be perverse (except to the strictest allegorists).

However, the "comic confusion" of Aristophanic allegory is different, and here "poetic license" is not exactly the operative term. While both the Homeric simile and the *ainos* present sealed-off images (the image is a closed equation, as it were, and the reader can accept the image as a whole without unbearable pressure on its parts), the Aristophanic line, in its fragmented state (with signifiers at times pointing to image or allegorized) is constantly invaded by what is being allegorized. It is applying recurrent cognitive pressures to interpret only to reveal that there is nothing to interpret: which, as I argued in the introduction, is what differentiates nonsense from other meaningless phenomena like noise. While "poetic license" is an agreement between poet and reader that an element is not "defective," it is that very acknowledgment of "defectiveness" that these broken allegories are trying to elicit.[68]

The fragmented state of these allegories applies certain points of pressure on each element: some soluble, some jarringly insoluble, as if the effect of non-meaning were a desideratum almost as valuable as meaning itself. In the next section, I will continue this analysis of broken allegories in comedy, not at the level of the sentence, but, more broadly, that of the comic action. The effect of the allegorical action, however, is the same as that of the allegorical language. While in other genres allegories are usually tropes generative of meaning, in comedy they play a second role as well: forcing elements upon the spectator which have no reference, and thus, are impossible objects of thought.

Having sex with abstractions

One of Newiger's complaints about the usage of "allegory" for a number of comedy's personifications is that characterization in (proper) allegory never extends beyond the abstract attributes of the allegorized. Allegorical abstractions, according to Newiger and his theoretical source Hegel, are "cold" because they never attain the level of individuals, that is, they never bear individualistic traits. Conversely, once these abstractions attain such individual elements, they can no longer be called true allegory.[69] This is, again, a rather strict view of allegory, and may be one difficult, in fact, to achieve. Nevertheless, it is useful here since, as Newiger points out, comedy is certainly susceptible to this allegorical over-extension which often neglects the boundaries of abstract attributes for the sake of individual characterization.

But even this is an understatement, for, often in (Old) comedy, abstract figures extend even beyond what might be called individualization.[70] Take the personified "Right" from *Clouds*, for example. Although, often enough,

---

[68] Cf. Philocleon's broken *ainoi* at *Vesp.* 1401–5, 1435–40.

[69] Newiger (1957) 7. For Hegel's discussion of allegory see Hegel (1975[1835]) 398–403, especially at 399: "the allegorical being must make subjectivity so hollow that all specific individuality vanishes from it. . . It is therefore rightly said of allegory that it is frosty and cold and that, owing to the intellectual abstractness of its meanings, it is even in its invention rather an affair of the intellect than of concrete intuition and the heartfelt depth of imagination."

[70] I stress Old Comedy here, since, as Newiger (1957) 1–2 emphasizes, comic allegory/personification changes with time, and it is with *Wealth* that Aristophanes comes closest to true allegory, i.e., Wealth is characterized much more strictly according to the abstraction "wealth" than earlier personifications (178).

his views seem to represent the abstraction he embodies, when he begins
to linger on the exposure of young boys' genitalia as being the central feature
of past virtues, the abstraction "Right" undergoes a certain stress beyond
that of individualization (977–8). Dover describes Right's indulgent fetish
aptly: "it is as if a modern preacher, having thundered 'No girl ever wore
trousers in those days!' continued 'And sometimes you glimpsed the satiny
flesh on the inside of her thighs.'"[71] Right's verbal incontinence is not just
an addition for the sake of characterization, but rather a complete departure
from the characteristics one might expect from such an abstraction of
"Right" – it does not extend the abstraction, it (temporarily) *breaks* the
abstraction. No such tensions exist in other genres: for example, with
personifications of Force (Bia, a mute female character) and Power
(Kratos, a speaking male character) at the opening of *Prometheus Bound*,
the language and action of these characters are as one-dimensional as the
abstractions they represent.[72] But such referential tensions are a hallmark of
Aristophanic personified figures – e.g., Diallage in *Lysistrata*, War and Din
in *Peace*, Demos in *Knights* – and doubtless played a role in personified
choruses like those of Cratinus' *Nomoi* (Laws), Plato Comicus' *Nikai*
(Victories), Crates' *Paidiai* (Games), and Aristophanes' *Nesoi* (Islands),
although such can only be conjecture.[73] But, in this section, I would like
to consider a particular subset of these personifications, specifically, female
abstractions which arouse sexual desire. I will primarily be discussing the
female chorus of Eupolis' *Cities*, but mention will also be given to Opora
and Theoria (Harvest and Festival) in *Peace*, Diallage (Reconciliation) in
Lysistrata, and the Spondae (Treaty Libations) at the end of *Knights*.
As abstractions of positive desiderata, it is perfectly intelligible that these
females be desired – if one desires reconciliation, one will desire
Reconciliation. But comedy increases this analogic traffic to an unbearable
point, forcing one to consider not the desire itself (which works at both
levels) but the actual sexual intercourse as well (which, of course, is impossible at the level of the allegorized abstraction). Just as with the "comic
confusion" of allegory above, I argue, this is more than just poetic license –
it produces an aggressive form of insignificance. Sexuality's violent act

---

[71] Dover (1989[1968]) ad 977. Although the pursuit of boys was certainly an old-fashioned, upper-class
pursuit and one which need not compromise morality, textual evidence supports his view: e.g., that
the mention of the genitalia comes at the end of the lines (precisely where one expects comic jolts to
arise). This *aprosdoketon* is completely in line with the complicated nature of Greek erotic morals and
issues of self-control.

[72] Introductory discussion of personified figures in different genres in Lever (1953).

[73] For chorus members representing "allegorically inanimate abstractions or institutions," see Rosen
(1997) 149–50.

against allegorical meaning induces in the audience that same surrender which was discussed in the previous section regarding the confused references of comic allegory: the "sex" is insoluble within the allegorical framework, and must be enjoyed without being understood.

In the late 420s, perhaps at the Dionysia of 422,[74] Eupolis produced a play that examined, at least in passing, Athens' treatment of its allied city-states. The chorus, like that of Aristophanes' *Birds* and Ameipsias' *Connus*, was individualized by means of different costumes (representing different states of the Athenian League),[75] and they were all female (since, of course, *polis* is of feminine gender).[76] Cyzicus, Tenos, and Chios all make appearances in the fragments, and the descriptions of their costumes fulfill (roughly) the role that one would expect staged abstractions to fulfill: namely, each woman represents attributes of her represented city. When Chios is introduced she is called (fr. 246 KA) "a fair city" (καλὴ πόλις) who "sends warships and men whenever there is need, and obeys well in all situations, like a horse that does not need a whip." Tenos is introduced (fr. 245 KA) as having many scorpions and sycophants, while Cyzicus is described as being full of (gold) staters (fr. 247 KA). It is possible to imagine perhaps a costume of gold coins for Cyzicus, but considerably more difficult to imagine what effect "scorpions and sycophants" would have had on Tenos' costume and bearing.[77] Nevertheless, the situation is clear: each city can be described through this particular meaning-structure (personification) wherein the woman who represents (or "is") each city acts as a physical object to anchor each described feature.

Sex infiltrates this meaning-structure from the beginning. The horse and ship imagery describing Chios' willing obedience emits sexual signals,[78] and the sight of the female Cyzicus reminds one of the characters of the time he "in this city[79]" screwed a woman, a boy, and an old man, on the cheap"

---

[74] For the issues of dating see Storey (2003) 216–17, (2011) 180–1.

[75] For individualized choruses, see Storey (2003) 218 who lists only these three as "likely" individualized choruses; cf. Whittaker (1935) and Wilson (1977).

[76] But see Rosen's (1997) comment that casting the cities as female was not entirely dependent on the noun's gender. He cites the male citizens in the chorus of *Peace* representing the city; a valid point, but it suggests more that Eupolis did not have to use personification than that these personifications did not have to be female.

[77] Storey (2003) 218: "They may have been costumed accordingly to match the text – Tenos with scorpions, Chios in naval gear, and Kyzikos with gold coins – but this is not essential for the presentations." Cf. Norwood (1931) 193–4; Whittaker (1935) 183; Wilson (1977) 282; Rosen (1997) 161.

[78] See Henderson (1991[1975]) 162–4 for ships, 164–5 for horses. Rosen (1997) 157 for a more thorough reading of the sexual double entendres of fr. 246.

[79] The speaker's discussion of his sexual exploits begins with ἐν τῇδε τοίνυν τῇ πόλει, the deictic suffix creating logical confusion with the city and the female character standing on-stage as Cyzicus.

and "could have spent the whole day cleaning out cunts." Of another city it is asked whether she has been properly depilated or not (fr. 244 KA, via double entendre: πεφυτευμένη δ᾽ αὕτη ᾽στίν, ἢ ψιλὴ μόνον;), and things become more aggressive still as an audience member (or perhaps an on-stage character) cannot restrain himself from gawking at one of the sexy cities, and must be reproached by another character (fr. 223 KA).[80] But sex is not just hinted at via double entendres but brought into full view as one character says that he has the perfect man for one of the cities – whether marriage or pimping is being suggested is of little difference, since the image foisted upon the spectator is clear: a man will have sex with this woman, who is a city. The meaning-structure of the personified cities has sex everywhere, and it is this interrelationship of meaning and sexual desire that must be looked at further.

Rosen, in his study of *Cities*, writes: "[T]he presence of an allegorical chorus on the Athenian stage *demands* that the audience (ancient and modern) tries to ascribe meaning to the allegory."[81] This is certainly true, but the question, as I have posed it in the previous section, is where does the allegorical meaning stop, and, particularly, what is gained and what is lost through such ascription of meaning? Athens' exploitation of its allies being compared to a man sexually exploiting a woman is a rich metaphor. It can continually be explored as a tool to consider the nature of power, both political and sexual, not only in the specifics of the Peloponnesian war, but in a more timeless, abstract fashion as well. It raises a number of questions: for example, what is the nature of the Athenian relationship with its allies? Is it that between a man and a wife, a man and a courtesan, a man and a prostitute? To what extent do all power structures follow these different (sexual) relationships, and to what extent do all (sexual) relationships follow these power structures? The political messages of the play have been read in a number of different ways, from an (imagined) marriage scene at the end (with each city married off to a different Athenian, apparently) showing Eupolis' pro-ally stance, to the degradation of the women, showing Eupolis' complicit acceptance of Athenian hegemony.[82] Whatever the view, much of this political information about the nature of Athenian power is extracted

---

[80] ὁ Φιλῖνος οὗτος, τί ἄρα πρὸς ταύτην βλέπεις; Storey (2003) 218–19 and Rosen (1997) 158–9 for discussion. Identification of ταύτην with one of the cities begins with Raspe (1832) 91 and is largely followed since that time. Opinion is divided on whether Philinus was an audience member or a character – both Rosen and Storey choose the former.

[81] Rosen (1997) 169, my italics.

[82] Especially Norwood (1931) 94 sees in *Poleis* "a plea for better treatment of the subject-allies" and Bonnano (1979) 331 that it is "hostile . . . to the despotic behavior of the *polis tyrannos* to the faithful allies, too much treated in the same way as subjects." Lesky (1966) 423; "the basic problem of . . . the

through that rich metaphor (an allied state is [like] a woman) of exploitation. Thus, for one following the hermeneutic path, the sexual attraction of the personifications is not *outside* the metaphor as some blunt, insoluble object, but entirely soluble within the allegory itself.

This, then, is the route of interpretation, that of "solving" the riddle of *sex with cities* via Clearchus' "searching." But as I have stressed throughout this chapter, for all the opulence of meaning that such interpretation brings to a text, it occludes that other effect of comic allegory which is that of potential meaninglessness. Just like the cheese-grater of *Wasps* or Antiphanes' perch–mullet riddle, "solving" the riddle or allegorical object creates a smooth plain of language, a clear series of relationships. But through that very process, the jagged geography of insoluble riddles and allegories is lost. To have sex with a city is the point at which thought yields at the literal level, it is nonsense; and when an audience is faced with such an idea, that is, having sex with abstractions, two options present themselves: the surrender involved in not interpreting further (i.e., the realization of nonsense), or the serious, ponderous, beard-stroking inquiry of the allegorist considering the nature of power. When one interprets a (comic) text to its full extent, one loses comedy's blunt objects of meaninglessness; when one accepts comedy's blunt objects of meaninglessness (e.g., having sex with cities), one loses the serious, philosophical potentials of the text. The relationship between these two responses – nonsense-realization and interpretation – is not one of surface and depth (e.g., seriousness "beneath" the foolery) or one of counterpoint (e.g., seriousness "amidst" the foolery), but one of mutual exclusivity. If this is so, it may provide a first clue as to why serious readings of comic texts so often encounter expressions of loss in comedy's reception.[83] One of the reasons that the "foolery" and "fun" of comedy are so difficult to locate is no doubt due to this mutual exclusivity: unlike humor which often relies on serious judgments, nonsense (here: language without reference) relies on interpretation's absence. This impulse to reject what might be interpreted appears to be not just an arbitrary choice, but a consequence of certain, recurrent comic features. In this case, that impulse

---

relation between central power and the subject allies"; for discussion, see Storey (2003) 219–224. For the supposed marriage scene, an idea of Norwood (1931) 196 based on fr. 243, see Storey (2003) 230; Rosen (1997) 160.

[83] For discussion, see the introduction. A good example is the reception of *Birds* where this "seriousness" vs. "foolery" opposition has centered on allegory itself. The modern spark of the debate is in Süvern's (1827) allegorism versus Schlegel's (1809) flight-of-fancy approach. There is discussion in Konstan (1995) 31–2; Vickers (1997) xix–xx; Dobrov (1995) 98–9. For a modern allegorical reading of *Birds*, see Vickers (1997) 154–89; for a more recent reading in the "flight-of-fancy" approach, see Whitman's (1964) reading of the whole play as "nonsense" (in the sense of Victorian nonsense poetry and, later, Dadaism); then Dobrov (1988, 1995) who argues that deconstruction is meta-poetically thematized in *Birds*.

is both the production and producer of the "blunt" objects of comic allegory, which, in Eupolis' *Cities*, is sex itself.[84]

Sex functions as an insoluble allegorical object not only in Eupolis' *Cities*, but in other comedies as well: Theoria and Opora (played by mute actors), who accompany Peace (represented by a statue), are naturally to be desired as abstractions of positive goods like the fruits of harvest and the joy of festivals. But comedy pushes this correlation further, much further: Opora will become Trygaeus's wife (706); they even kiss (for quite a while) on stage (which Trygaeus fears will give him the indigestions of consuming too much fruit); it is suggested that their sexual act will produce an offspring of grapes (706); those who await Theoria and Opora's return have erections for them (726); indeed, Opora will perform fellatio on one of the characters (855) and Theoria will engage in group sex.[85] So too, at the end of *Knights*, when it is time to bring out the treaty libations, and suddenly – jarringly – these treaty libations appear on-stage as two naked females, the Spondae (which, by thrusting a third element between signifier and signified, muddles the *verba–res* relationship), it is immediately to sex that thought turns: the abstractions must be penetrated, and Demos will be the one to have sex with them.[86] So too, the naked Diallage, at the end of *Lysistrata*, is told to grab the men by their phalloi (1119), has an "unspeakably beautiful ass" and "pussy" (1148, 1158–9), and is divided up between the men for which parts of her will be enjoyed.[87] Is the sex in these examples contributing to meaning or taking away from it? One can add to this Pherecrates' Lady Music, as well as the male sexual abstraction of Cratinus' *Pytine*.[88] There is a point where sexuality is a natural aspect of desire (or in Pherecrates' case, abuse), but

---

[84] For the opposition of sex to meaning, see Copjec (1994) 204: "Sex is the stumbling block of sense . . . It is only there where discursive practices falter – and not at all where they succeed in producing meaning – that sex comes to be."

[85] Henderson (1991[1975]) 64–6. For the sexual treatment of Theoria and Opora, see also Taaffe (1993) 38–40; Zweig (1992) 78. Whitman (1964) 111–12 nicely articulates their "allegorical significance" and how the two "waver tantalizingly between the abstractions which they represent and the attractions of the way they are represented." For the history of the discussion of whether these female abstractions were played by *hetaerae* or by men dressed as women see Stone (1981) 149: "in general, the older scholars tend to favor the use of *hetaerae*, while more modern critics either suggest that men were padded to look like women, or else that the evidence is insufficient for a firm conclusion," Zweig (1992) being an exception to the rule.

[86] For Spondae as sex objects, see Taaffe (1993) 31; Henderson (1991[1975]) 88, Stone (1981) 147–50; Zweig (1992).

[87] For Diallage, see Stroup (2004) 62–8; Zweig (1992).

[88] Although Süss (1954) does not focus on the sexual aspects so much as the "breaking" of the allegory, it is worth registering his surprise (at 119) that, especially regarding Pherecrates' Music, everyone's interest lies entirely at the allegorized level, with little interest in the "obscene depiction" of the woman's treatment itself. For a non-female abstraction who is also a sex-object, see the young wine of *Pytine* (a boy) in Süss (1954).

these comic abstractions drive that relationship further to its breaking point: the allegory cannot hold, and thought abandons the impossible details of sexual intercourse with abstractions. This, I would like to argue – if one accepts that there is a certain phenomenon which is lost through interpretation – is not just an interpretive choice but an interpretive choice which comedy invites the audience to make. In the surrender of (further) interpretation and the goods that such interpretation might yield, audiences instead experience those less rational moments of comedy where joy is found outside of interpretation's reasons for that joy.

Metaphors without Tenors, chapter conclusions

In this chapter, I have been examining two types of related meaning-structures – the riddle and the allegory – paying particular attention to their references. While a riddle is solved when its reference is located, the detection of an allegory's reference is what activates the allegory. The purpose of studying these reference-structures was to find examples where a word or statement's reference never materializes, thereby leaving behind a signifier without a signified. In the first section, I examined two passages from Antiphanes which present riddles without solutions. In both passages, it will be recalled, Antiphanes' characters referred to such phenomena as "nonsense." This nonsense (*qua* no-reference) caused the listeners to forswear the usual response that language induces, namely, interpretation, which was then supplanted by reactions of a more emotional nature: in the first passage, laughter, in the second, exasperation. It was this surrendering of the act of interpretation in the face of perceived nonsense that both passages shared, and this observation was applied to the opening of *Peace*, where I argued that Aristophanes thematizes that very surrender.

In the second section, I pursued this interpretive choice as it pertains to comic allegory. I argued that once an allegorical meaning-structure is activated, its ruptures begin to appear, and the allegory becomes tarnished and destabilized by reference-free elements. I first examined the dog trial from *Wasps* and then the personified Chorus from Eupolis' *Cities*. While a number of allegorical elements map on to their references (e.g., allegorized politicians or abstractions), certain elements were seen to be insoluble within the allegorical framework – whether they be the domestic objects of the dog trial or the unrelenting desire to have sex with abstractions.

The difference between the two related nonsense techniques should be noted: regarding riddles, an obscurity that is posed with an expectant answer reveals that there is no answer to be found: it is nonsense. Regarding allegories, the equation is already clearly drafted, as it were, but within that equation certain elements prove to be nonsensical. The effect of both techniques, however, is the same: both cause the audience (with the exception of the Ionian and the "know-it-all") temporarily to surrender the habitual act of interpretation.

Somewhere between these two nonsense techniques of allegories and riddles lies the nonsense technique of metaphor. The relationship of metaphor to its reference is a particularly vexed one, and rather too complex to consider in depth here.[89] But, in a sense, the topic has been considered all along: a thorough treatment of reference-free metaphors would repeat much of what I have already discussed in this chapter about the related tropes. But one last example will do, which unifies the thematic material of this chapter by combining elements from both riddles and allegories. The example is an extended metaphor from *Peace* which begins lucidly enough (like the allegories), but eventually devolves into nonsense (like the riddled language of the first section). After the personified Theoria (Festival) has been presented to the Athenian council, the men eagerly discuss how she ought to be enjoyed. This wild orgy adopts an extended metaphor from sports. Henderson, who would certainly be the authority to spot the metaphor's sexual references, at a certain point admits defeat: the text becomes "a wild mélange of metaphors behind which it is impossible to discern the actual act of love."[90]

Here is the passage (894–904):

> ἔπειτ' ἀγῶνά γ' εὐθὺς ἐξέσται ποιεῖν
> ταύτην ἔχουσιν αὔριον καλὸν πάνυ,
> ἐπὶ γῆς παλαίειν, τετραποδηδὸν ἑστάναι,
> [πλαγίαν καταβάλλειν, εἰς γόνατα κύβδ' ἱστάναι,]
> καὶ παγκράτιόν γ' ὑπαλειψαμένοις νεανικῶς
> παίειν, ὀρύττειν, πὺξ ὁμοῦ καὶ τῷ πέει.
> τρίτῃ δὲ μετὰ ταῦθ' ἱπποδρομίαν ἄξετε,
> ἵνα δὴ κέλης κέλητα παρακελητιεῖ,
> ἅρματα δ' ἐπ' ἀλλήλοισιν ἀνατετραμμένα
> φυσῶντα καὶ πνέοντα προσκινήσεται,
> ἕτεροι δὲ κείσονται γ' ἀπεψωλημένοι
> περὶ ταῖσι καμπαῖς ἡνίοχοι πεπτωκότες.

Then tomorrow you can all straightaway celebrate a very pretty athletic contest, now that you have her: *wrestle* her on the ground, *get on all fours,*

---

[89] See Silk (2003) for review and critique of Aristotle, Jakobson, and Ricœur regarding metaphors. For a thorough overview of the history of metaphorical theories, see Ricœur (1977).
[90] Henderson (1991[1975]) 169. Cf. Taillardat (1965) 102.

[*throw her down on the flank*, push her *to her knees, bent over,*] then, *oiled up* for the pancration, *strike* at her manfully and *dig* her with fist and – *cock*! On the third day, you shall have a *horse-race*, and *horse* will *ride side-by-side* with *horse*, and the *chariots*, all overturned in a heap, will *mingle together* puffing and panting. Others will *lie down*, their *foreskins pulled back*: the drivers, having *fallen* about the *turning-posts.*[91]

Like comic allegories, this extended metaphor begins in a straightforward fashion in order that its reference be clear (the tenor/reference is sex, the vehicle is sports): "wrestling on the ground" and "getting on all fours" function well in both contexts. Although the sports metaphor becomes slightly confused with "strike at her manfully and dig her with fist and cock (πὺξ ὁμοῦ καὶ τῷ πέει)," the meaning as a whole might be left unharmed. Even the riding of horses (κέλης κέλητι παρακελητιεῖ)[92] is not completely insoluble, and some semblance of visual terrain may endure; but then, who or what exactly are the chariots that suddenly arrive upon the scene (901)? With the drivers, horses, turning-posts, and chariots all mingled in the dust together, the image is brilliantly confused and question marks lie scattered about everywhere. As Henderson writes, it is "impossible to discern the actual act of love," that is, the reference (tenor) "behind" this metaphor – one must abandon that inquisitive searching for who's doing what to whom, who's riding whom, etc., and like so many of the phenomena discussed in this chapter, one must deny that interpretive urge altogether.[93]

What, then, ought these reference-free phenomena be called? As I have argued, the descriptive "obscure" does not adequately explain the operation of these phenomena, since "obscurity" suggests that there is still a reference to be discovered behind the dark filter of overly metaphorical language. Not a surrender of interpretation but a heightened focus is the effect of "obscurity." Nor can the phenomena of this chapter be adequately described as a failure of interpretation from reception's end, for many of the same reasons. To find the "solutions," for example, of Antiphanes' riddles, or the *Wasps* cheese-grater, or the confused metaphor of *Peace*, would be to miss the point, I have argued. Certainly the phenomena cannot be described as artistic mistakes or shortcomings on the part of the comedians, as if the authors had somehow momentarily lost control of their pens. Rather, these

---

[91] Henderson (1991[1975]) 169 for text (slightly modified here) and translation with double-entendres in italics. I bracket line 897 of his translation for the reasons explained by Sommerstein and Olson ad loc. in their editions.

[92] For the sexual language behind κέλης, see Henderson (1991[1975]) 164–6.

[93] Cf. Wright (2012) 115 regarding metaphors at *Nub.* 260: "Such odd combinations of images are memorable but hard to interpret precisely: no doubt that is precisely the point."

reference-free moments of language seem to be positive techniques aiming at a particular effect – an effect altogether different from meaning.

One final observation ought to be added about these phenomena. In the extended metaphor of sexual intercourse at *Peace* 894–904, the moment that the images' references are shattered seems to be at the climax: it occurs at the end of the description, it has been gradually built to, and, as the poetic/sexual climax of the passage, it is as if this moment of reference-free language had been the goal of the metaphor all along. But the simultaneous occurrence of poetic climax and broken references is not just a feature of this particular metaphor, but a general characteristic of the phenomena discussed in this chapter: the cheese-grater's testimony in *Wasps*, the levitating dung-beetle of *Peace*, the exasperation over Antiphanes' riddles, those headiest moments of oracular and dithyrambic language, and that ever-present desire for sex that overwhelms cerebral abstractions. Nonsense often seems to appear at the climaxes of comic language, and this will be one of its distinguishing traits discussed in Chapter 4, where I distinguish nonsense from jokes. Unlike jokes, which can occur at the dullest of moments, these climactic moments of perceived nonsense often require a pre-existing, heightened mood to make their (usually unbearable) presence a source of pleasure.[94] Whether it be the heat of sexual energy that evaporates language's references, or the brightness of the spectacle, or the increasing absurdity of the comic context, nonsense requires a certain atmosphere which allows language to exist without meaning – the same atmosphere that is also, in turn, one of nonsense's greatest effects.

---

[94] This is fundamentally a notion of Freud's – discussed in Chapter 4.

CHAPTER 3

Nonsense as "no-serious sense": the case of Cinesias

καὶ διθυράμβων νοῦν ἔχεις ἐλάττονα   Proverb quoted by Σ.*Birds* 1392[1]

In the previous chapter, I examined some comic tropes like allegories and metaphors and argued that in the discovery of these tropes' references often something seems to go missing, which, I argued, was the perception of nonsense. The problem with this argument is that such tropes comprise only a small part of comedy, while perceptions of nonsense seem to occur not just in the face of a handful of metaphors or "broken" allegories, but during much broader stretches of comic action. Even whole comedies, at times, are referred to as "nonsense."[2] It is not enough to search for potentially malfunctioning tropes or even formal incongruity in such moments of perceived nonsense, since the nonsense does not necessarily arise from some detected indecipherability.[3] Instead, in the great majority of cases the perception of "nonsense" seems to mean something much closer to "no serious sense" rather than "no decipherable sense." It will be recalled from the introduction, that this was the "nonsense" (*phluaria*) that Socrates had in mind when describing his characterization in Aristophanes' *Clouds*.

This chapter will focus on the discovery of nonsense in that broader context, namely, the nonsense which arises via the rejection of "serious" meaning. The central line of inquiry regards the interpretive choice of "not taking something seriously" which, I argue, is the central act behind this

---

[1] "You make even less sense than dithyrambs."
[2] For various perceptions of "nonsense" in comedy, see Whitman (1964) on *Birds*; Dobrov (1988, 1995) *passim*; Borthwick (1968a) 134 on "nonsense expressions"; Olson (1998) 102 on Agathon's "wordy nonsense"; Sommerstein (1981) 166–7 on "nonsensical" arguments; Austin and Olson (2004) lv on Euripides' "nonsense"; Reckford (1987) 61 and *passim* (although most often in the sense of Victorian nonsense); Parker (1997) 503 on "emending deliberate nonsense"; Rogers (1906) 183 on "empty nonsense"; Platter (2007) 56; Hamilton (1993[1930]) on "Aristophanes' maddest nonsense"; O'Regan (1992) 42 on Socrates' "nonsense"; Wright (2012) 17: "we are very often confronted with nonsense..."; Dover (1989[1968]) lxiii "There is a good deal of nonsense in Right's argument."
[3] There is further discussion of the relationship between nonsense and incongruity in Chapter 4.

more pervasive form of nonsense. Ultimately, I will argue that in not taking something seriously one adopts a form of interpretation similar to those Hippocratic doctors from Chapter 1, who often described patients' delirious speech as "nonsense." It is a symptomatic form of interpretation always returning to the same diagnosis, "this is nonsense," which, in the case of comedy, is identical to the diagnosis "this is play." But before this argument can be fully articulated, a thorough investigation is needed regarding this interpretive process of "not taking seriously" and why nonsense might arise when doing so.

The word "serious" notoriously haunts comic scholarship. Some scholars rise to the challenge of its definition with dictionary in hand, others retreat, believing the word to be of little value after all.[4] Silk, for example, provides a fine overview of the different meanings of "serious," but then proceeds to limit the valence of the word to purely aesthetic terrain (i.e., that Aristophanes makes "serious" claims for his art).[5] For the purposes of his general argument, this is a natural conclusion, but for most scholars, the fundamental opposition invoked with the word "serious" is the very one he dismisses: that between "seriousness" and "play."[6] That is, the questions scholars usually pose are "is Aristophanes being serious when he says Cleon is a scoundrel, or is he just playing?" "When is Aristophanes being serious? When playful?" "Does Aristophanes *mean* it, or is it 'just' a joke, 'just' nonsense?" and so forth.[7] The usual resolutions to these troubling problems are highly nuanced, with recipes concocting various alloys of seriousness and play: the comedian is being serious in his play or playful in his serious-ness; he is more or less serious in more or less serious passages; there is seriousness to be found beneath/behind the play, as I discussed in the introduction.

---

[4] E.g., Heath (2007), although far from retreating (see his important response to Silk 2000 at 37–42), feels his own use of the word in discussing the Aristophanes' politics "was a convenience, not an essential" (37). Cf. Olson (2002b), 108–9 (quoted in Heath (2007) 42 n. 123: "Comedy has not gone astray over confusion about the significance of the English word 'serious'"; Rosen (1988) 5 n. 21; Ruffell (2011) 41 on Searle's (1975) sense of "serious" illocutionary acts.

[5] Silk (2000) 302–16 for three meanings of the word. The third meaning "substantial" (315) is the one he finds useful for Aristophanes (quoting J. M. Synge: "Drama is made serious by the degree in which it gives the nourishment . . . on which our imaginations live"). So, e.g., "Aristophanes lays claim to sophistication, to originality, above all to seriousness. He does so, not despite his humour . . . but on the strength of his humour" (350) and "Aristophanes can, after all, be credited with one consistent, sustained, 'serious interest' in every sense of the word: his own medium" (417).

[6] Silk (2000) 81 on problems with play versus seriousness (which I discuss more at the end of this chapter); rejection of the pretence/serious dichotomy at 313–14.

[7] See the introduction. It is instructive to note that the statement "I wasn't being serious: it was just a joke" makes no formal pronouncements whatsoever on the statement in question being an actual "joke" (with, e.g., punchline, trigger, incongruity, etc.).

Despite this rich variety of nuance that other scholars have applied to this question of comedy's seriousness, nuance will not be a virtue of this chapter.[8] Instead what I believe is needed is a sustained focus on that one elusive end of the spectrum: the not-serious. What does it mean and how is it possible? It is a large question, so I will grasp it initially with a singular hold: namely, the context of a *komoidoumenos* being mocked. How was it possible for a *komoidoumenos* to be mocked and *not* take it seriously? What does this process of interpretation look like? I will argue that a better understanding of this particular hermeneutic process will allow for extrapolation into other contexts of Greek comic interpretation. Although today's readers are by no means *komoidoumenoi*, they are the agents of interest who succeed in taking these texts seriously or rejecting that seriousness – or to put it another way, finding these texts meaningful or finding them nonsense.

I begin with Cinesias. Mocked on the comic stage continuously for decades for being too thin, too sickly, for having bowel issues, for writing lousy poetry and even worse music, one would like to know what options were available to this poor *komoidoumenos* who suffered from such an annual stream of abuse. Was it possible not to take offense, or not to take such mockery seriously? And if so, how can one account for such behavior? This leads to a review of scholarship which has dealt with this central problem of mockery, namely, how (or whether) members of a society so sensitive to shame and status managed to endure the hubris implicit in comedy's abuse. Typical solutions to this problem range from the Dionysiac context, the law, religious ritual, to the fictional and conventional aspects of the mockery itself. But these answers, I argue, do not fully account for the basic process of how mockery might be heard, understood, yet rejected as something not "serious." Turning to Aristotle and different Greek models, I will sketch the cognitive process in Greek terms of receiving comic abuse, and develop an argument of what "taking seriously" might mean for Cinesias and his contemporaries. The conclusion that I will draw is that "not taking seriously" is a different sort of interpretation from "taking seriously" altogether, and that this helps to understand why nonsense can only arise in the former scenario. While "serious" interpretation is interpretation focused on a passage's content, "non-serious" interpretation,

---

[8] Cf. Silk's (2000) observation on degrees of seriousness: "seriousness is not some easily encapsulated commodity; it does have something to do with evaluation; but it is variable, in terms both of its nature and its degree. We can distinguish between the seriousness of a Jane Austen and a Brecht . . . just as in ordinary parlance we can, and do, speak of someone or something as *more* or *less* serious than someone or something else" (311–12).

I argue, is exclusively symptomatic. Such interpretation reduces a statement to a one and singular symptom.

Skinny Cinesias and his bowel complaints

In the early fourth century,[9] the dithyrambic poet and minor politician Cinesias, son of the kitharodist Meles, was prosecuting a certain Phanias for moving an illegal decree.[10] Phanias' defense speech, written by Lysias, depicts his prosecutor as a godless and impious man, physically and morally sick, and justly deserving an unending battle with what appears to be a terminal illness. The defendant claims that Cinesias was a member of an impious social club, the *Kakodaimonistai*, all members of which had died terribly as a result of their transgressions against the gods.[11] Cinesias, however, the sole surviving member of the impious gang, is suffering a fate worse than death:

> τὸ μὲν γὰρ ἀποθανεῖν ἢ καμεῖν νομίμως κοινὸν ἡμῖν ἅπασίν ἐστι, τὸ δ' οὕτως ἔχοντα τοσοῦτον χρόνον διατελεῖν καὶ καθ' ἑκάστην ἡμέραν ἀποθνῄσκοντα μὴ δύνασθαι τελευτῆσαι τὸν βίον τούτοις μόνοις προσήκει τοῖς τὰ τοιαῦτα ἅπερ οὗτος ἐξημαρτηκόσιν.

> For dying or being sick is common and customary to us all, but to continue being in such a state for such a long time, and to be dying day-by-day, unable finally to die, befits only those who have committed the sorts of crimes that he has. (Lys. fr. 195 Carey).

Insult to injury, it seems: it was not enough for Cinesias to be dying day-by-day; he had to endure abuse by an adversary about his illness as well.

This, however, was not all the sickly Cinesias had to endure. As Phanias claims, year after year, Cinesias' shameful actions – too shameful, in fact, even to mention in a law court – were a subject for comedians.[12] The nature of his impious actions remains somewhat obscure, but his being mocked year after year by the comedians is not. Described as one of the poets ruining

---

[9] Lysias begins writing speeches after 403 BCE and Sommerstein (ad *Av.* 1372–1409) suggests a probable date of Cinesias' death between 391 (the date of *Eccl.*) and 386 (the date of Plato's *Gorgias* where Cinesias is mentioned at 501e–502a). For the dating of *Gorgias*, see Dodds (1959) 18–30.

[10] For Cinesias' (PA 8438) political career outside of "sycophantic" prosecutions such as this one (so Ath. 12.551d–552b who quotes this fragment), see IG ii2 18, a decree in honor of Dionysius, the tyrant of Syracuse in 394/3. Sommerstein ad *Av.* 1372–1409.

[11] 195.2 Carey: ἀντὶ δὲ νουμηνιαστῶν κακοδαιμονιστὰς σφίσιν αὐτοῖς τοὔνομα θέμενοι, πρέπον μὲν ταῖς αὑτῶν τύχαις· … ἐκείνων μὲν οὖν ἕκαστος ἀπώλετο ὥσπερ εἰκὸς τοὺς τοιούτους.

[12] 195.1 Carey: ἃ τοῖς μὲν ἄλλοις αἰσχρόν ἐστι καὶ λέγειν, τῶν κωμῳδοδιδασκάλων <δ'> ἀκούετε καθ' ἕκαστον ἐνιαυτόν…

music in Pherecrates' *Mousikē*,[13] and constantly disparaged as an airy-fairy dithyrambist,[14] he seemed to have been something like the Euripides of the dithyrambic genre: that is, popular, innovative, and so, an irresistible target for the comedians. The comic poet Strattis devoted his *Cinesias* entirely to him,[15] and a dithyrambist named Cinesias also appears on stage in both Aristophanes' *Birds* and, probably, *Gerytades*.

Nor was Cinesias mocked merely for his poetry and music, but rather, in similar terms to that of Phanias' attack, for his frail and sickly physical appearance. In Aristophanes' *Gerytades*, an embassy of poets is sent down to Hades, perhaps in order to determine who the best living poet is.[16] Cinesias is selected as the representative from the dithyrambists, Meletus from the tragedians, and Sannyrion from the comedians.[17] The basis of this selection, however, is not the superior poetic skill of these three artists; rather they are chosen because they are all "Hades-visitors" (ἀιδοφοῖται) – "skinny," "frail," or, in the English idiom, those with "one foot in the grave."[18] Cinesias the Hades-visitor was no stranger to disease, and his cauterized pustules caused Galen to preserve the following fragment of Plato Comicus (200 KA): Κινησίας / σκελετός, ἄπυγος, καλάμινα σκέλη φορῶν, / φθόης προφήτης, ἐσχάρας κεκαυμένος / πλείστας ὑπ' Εὐρυφῶντος ἐν τῶι σώματι "Cinesias, skeletal, flat-bottomed,[19] with reed-thin legs, prophet of decay, cauterized with multiple burn-scars on his body by [the doctor] Euryphon." Skinny and scarred, this "prophet of decay" already appears to be decomposing in comedy, long before Phanias' attack.

As Phanias' speech claims, Cinesias had to listen to these shameless taunts about his illness and physical characteristics (not to mention his poetry) year after year. But the shamelessness of the mockery extends further still: perhaps related to his chronic illness which left him so thin, Cinesias seemed to have at some point (or perhaps more than once) suffered an unfortunate

---

[13] Pherecrates 155.8–13 KA. Described as "chorus-killing" at Strattis, *Cinesias* fr. 16 KA (τοῦ χοροκτόνου Κινησίου).

[14] *Av.* 1372–1409; *Ran.* 1437. Cf. dithyrambic descriptions at *Nub.* 333–9, *Pax* 827–31, *Av.* 918. For a study of depiction of Cinesias' poetry in comedy, see Kugelmeier (1996) 208–48.

[15] For a possible (and clever) reconstruction of the plot, see Orth (2009) 100–29. He suggests a date of not long after 408–405 (on the basis of the mocking of Sannyrion who is only heard of securely in the last decade of the fifth century). Cf. Sommerstein ad *Ran.* 153 who dates it to 414–411.

[16] So Kaibel (quoted in KA ii.2.101): "ipsi poetae legatos de suo numero electos ad inferos misisse finguntur, non tam opinor de emendanda arte Aeschylum aliosve antiquiores consulturi quam quaesituri quis inter vivos principem locum tenere videatur vel recentiores num antiquis poetis inferiores putandi sint."

[17] Sannyrion is apparently not above throwing stones from his apparently glass house: Sannyrion fr. 2 KA calls Meletus a corpse.

[18] So Hesychius interprets the word: α 1793 οἱ λεπτοὶ καὶ ἰσχνοὶ καὶ ἐγγὺς θανάτου ὄντες.

[19] ἄπυγος is Meineke's conjecture from the ἄπυος of the codd.

bowel incident. In *Gerytades*, it is said of the thin and sickly troika of poets that, "if it increases by a lot, the river of diarrhea will snatch them up and be off with them" (τούτους γάρ, ἢν πολλῶι ξυνέλθηι, ξυλλαβὼν / ὁ τῆς διαρροίας ποταμὸς οἰχήσεται, 156 KA). This can only refer to Cinesias,[20] I believe, since, whatever the particular nature of Cinesias' bowel incident was, these diarrhea jokes (especially the "purros" color of his offspring) pursued him throughout the late fifth and early fourth century.[21]

In *Ecclesiazusae* when Blepyrus is caught by his neighbor wearing the saffron gown of his wife, the neighbor asks: εἰπέ μοι, / τί τοῦτό σοι τὸ πυρρόν ἐστιν; οὐ τί που / Κινησίας σοι κατατετίληκεν; "tell me, why do you have this yellow thing on? Has Cinesias shit on you?" (328–30). The *purros* color of this passage recalls another passage from *Knights* where jurors fart themselves "brown" (*purros*) binging on silphium stalks, a trick which Demos punningly suggests was devised by "Pyrrhander" (Mr. Brown).[22] At *Frogs* 308, Dionysus' robe is described as *purros* after he takes fright,[23] and regarding the people found in the underworld's dung, Dionysus makes the following reference to Cinesias (152–3): νὴ τοὺς θεοὺς ἐχρῆν γε πρὸς τούτοισι κεἰ / τὴν πυρρίχην τις ἔμαθε τὴν Κινησίου. "By golly, in addition to these people should be anyone who learned the *purrikhen* of Cinesias." As Bliquez rightly interprets the passage: the "pyrriche's movements [e.g., crouching] suggest . . . not the lively steps and gestures of battle, but rather the contortions one would expect of a person beset with the discomfort of diarrhoea."[24] Even in a corrupt passage from Strattis' *Cinesias*, one finds the misspelling of πυρῶν (wheat), to πυρρῶν (yellowish-brown): although the passage is corrupt probably beyond repair, I would suggest that this misspelling is no scribal error.[25]

Like many a *komoidoumenos*, Cinesias had to endure this mockery year after year at Athens' festivals. His sickliness, frailty, and perhaps occasional

---

[20] At *Ran.* 146, one also finds "dung" (σκῶρ) in the underworld – but this also leads up to a joke about Cinesias at 153. See Dover ad loc. for the notion of mud in the underworld (with Pl. *Resp.* 363e).

[21] Scholiasts ad *Ran.* 366 (ἢ κατατιλᾷ τῶν Ἑκαταίων κυκλίοισι χοροῖσιν ὑπᾴδων) claim that the line refers to Cinesias (in the Ravenna, Venetus Marcianus mss., etc.); cf. Dunbar ad *Av.* 1372–1409 who suggests that it is "probable that on some occasion before 405 BC (*Frogs*) Kin. had an embarrassing public attack of diarrhoea, which his reputation for impiety enabled Ar. to treat as deliberate sacrilege." Dover ad *Ran.* 366 suggests that Cinesias "seems on some occasion to have been seized with diarrhoea and left his mark conspicuously."

[22] *Eq.* 896–901 with the last two lines being Αλ. οὐ γὰρ τόθ' ὑμεῖς βδεόμενοι δήπου 'γένεσθε πυρροί; / Δη. καὶ νὴ Δί' ἦν γε τοῦτο Πυρράνδρου τὸ μηχάνημα. Sommerstein ad loc. compares *Ran.* 308, *Eccl.* 329, 1061–2 for such a reading.

[23] So Dover's interpretation of this passage ad loc. regarding ὑπερεπυρρίασε.

[24] Bliquez (2008) 326. Cf. Borthwick's reading, discussed below.

[25] Strattis *Cinesias* fr. 14. Orth (2009) 106 already explains the line as containing fecal humor ("Das Erstaunen von Sprecher A und der Witz der Stelle dürfte besonders auf der für ein attisches

incontinence were not private troubles, but matters of public laughter and amusement. By the time of the *Ecclesiazusae* a character could make, with slightest effort, a joke about Cinesias' bowel incident, a joke surely linked to countless past jabs from comedy. But what, then, of Cinesias? There is no evidence that he ever brought a lawsuit against one of these poets for slander, and there is no evidence that he ever took recourse to violence or revenge. Indeed, there is scarce evidence that any *komoidoumenos* ever did.[26] This need not preclude the possibility that Cinesias was enraged and upset each and every time he was mocked on stage – perhaps he was. But it raises the question: what options were available to Cinesias? In particular, was it possible for an Athenian like Cinesias not to take offense or not to take such mockery "seriously"? And, if so, what would such a process of interpretation entail?

How could he not take it seriously? Some modern solutions

Onomasti komoidein (mocking by name) is one of Old Comedy's most tantalizing features. It appears to be so direct and its negative opinions so easily articulated – Cinesias is a hack, Cleon a crook, Cleonymus a glutton, etc. – that it often appears to be a virtual conveyor belt between stage and reality. The scholarship is vast on the subject, and at times mockery is treated as if it were no different from any other form of abusive speech, whether it be slander, insult, or threat. The utterance is leveled and the effect – whether it be offense, retaliation, or prosecution – is irrevocable. In some ways, this is a natural way to treat mockery, especially by those who are interested in Athenian legal history: if ever there were laws which prohibited comic mockery, such laws too must have treated mockery as roughly equivalent to straightforward abuse.[27] In other ways, however, such a view of comedy's mockery (i.e., only offensive) is surely too limited. It is hard to believe that mockery was always distilled into personal offense, party aggression, and political opinion, whether prosecutable or not – in short, that mockery was always "taken seriously." But if this is the case, it only raises the question of how it was possible for such mockery to be interpreted

---

Publikum nahe liegenden Assoziation mit dem für Kot verwendeten κόφινος κοπροφόρος (Xen. Mem. 3.8.6; cf Ar. fr. 680 KA κοπρολογεῖ κόφινον λαβών)") but does not know Bliquez (2008). Kaibel emends to the metrical πυρῶν which Orth (2009) 105 writes is "die ökonomischste Lösung."

[26] Regarding Aristophanes and Cleon, see Rosen (2010) 229–35; Sommerstein (2004a); Halliwell (1991) 65, Rosen (1988) 59–82.

[27] See the distinction in Arist. *EN* 4.14, 1128a30–1 between *loidorēma* and *skōmma* (τὸ γὰρ σκῶμμα λοιδόρημά τι ἐστίν, οἱ δὲ νομοθέται ἔνια λοιδορεῖν κωλύουσιν). For discussion of Athenian laws in these and other contexts, Halliwell (1991); Sommerstein (1986, 2004b); Wallace (2005). Discussion of Aristophanes and Cleon with textual evidence in appendix in Sommerstein (2004a).

differently from more straightforward forms of abuse or attack. To state the abstract question in its most concrete form: how would it have been possible for Cinesias to hear a joke like εἰπέ μοι, / τί τοῦτό σοι τὸ πυρρόν ἐστιν; οὔ τί που / Κινησίας σοι κατατετίληκεν; "tell me, why do you have this yellow thing on? Did Cinesias shit on you?" and not take offense?

Foremost among solutions to this problem of mockery-not-taken-seriously is the context of the Dionysiac festival. Unlike day-to-day street interactions where abuse could quickly escalate and lead to legal action (or worse), the context of the festival was something special, a place where mockery could be indulged in without the targets of that mockery seeking reprisal. Some articulate this Dionysiac difference in terms of the law: namely, that comedy enjoyed either a virtual or actual license to abuse citizens. One scholar writes, "the comic poets . . . enjoyed, in practice at least, a special license to abuse,"[28] while another observes, "the freedom of comedy entailed a virtual, though not a legally defined, immunity to the law of slander."[29] The festival, in short, provided a circumscribed context wherein comic abuse was permitted and generally free from prosecution's reach.

But can such legal or quasi-legal reasons explain the hermeneutic phenomenon of not taking comic mockery seriously? Surely not, and I doubt either scholar would suggest as much. The reason is that such a legalistic view cannot distinguish genuine personal offense from the ability to act on that offense: one might imagine Cinesias, for example, taking offense each and every time he was mocked, but simply being unable to retaliate owing to the context in which the mockery was delivered. Far from not taking mockery seriously, Cinesias could have taken it very seriously indeed, but simply would have been impotent to retaliate thanks to those quasi-legal restraints. If not-taking-seriously were reduced to some sort of legal prohibition, one could only assume a rather unpleasant festival: a continuous flood of injury, generating a great deal of anger in injured parties and their friends, only to be coupled with a helplessness to do anything about it.[30] Although the legalistic view can help to explain a number of phenomena (e.g., why there is so little evidence for prosecutions of comic slander), it cannot explain the phenomenon of not taking mockery seriously.

---

[28] Heath (1987) 27.

[29] Halliwell (1991) 70. Cf. at 54: "This, I stress, is not to claim that comedy was ever granted a technical exemption, only that its culturally determined position placed its festival performances outside the framework in which defamatory or vilificatory utterances could readily be perceived as actionable." Cf. Halliwell (2008) 244 n. 70.

[30] Aristotle locates a pleasure following anger being the hope for revenge (*Rh.* 2.2, 1378b). Such a festival would remove even that pleasure.

Other scholars explain the possibility of inoffensive mockery in terms of ritual practice rather than prohibition or legal restraint. As one scholar has articulated the process, in this ritual context, where daily norms are inverted, the perception of mockery marks the transition into the upside-down world of ritual and *rite de passage*.[31] This is why, when audience members are mocked:

> instead of being injured in their sense of honor, they endure it, indeed, they are amused by it. The breaking of norms is fun. In such liminal relationships there is no above and below, all is made ambiguous. The fallback into the atavistic-barbaric is frightful and wonderful at the same time, but by the end, one is happy that the amusing nightmare is over.[32]

For those who feel that not-taking-mockery-seriously is rather intuitive and obvious, this passage is certainly remarkable for defamiliarizing the experience. Within such a view, the phenomenon of not-taking-mockery-seriously is exclusively ritualistic, at least when occurring in the context of comedy. Cinesias, then, perhaps on hearing yet another joke about his incontinence, did not perceive himself to be mocked in the way that he would on the street or at a symposium, but felt that he was undergoing some sort of liminal ritual experience or *rite de passage*. Such a solution, however, only raises more questions: if the *komoidoumenos* is able to enjoy mockery, or at the very least not be offended by it, owing to the "atavistic" ritual nature of the Dionysia, how then should one treat ancient mockery in its other contexts, for example, at the symposium or even jocular daily intercourse with friends?[33] Aristotle, after all, lists the festival as only one of a number of contexts in which a person, thanks to a heightened mood, does not take offense and get angry at perceived belittlement.[34] Either all such

---

[31] Bierl (2002) 171: "Die verbalen Attacken markieren meist den Übertritt in eine solche verkehrte Welt."

[32] Bierl (2002) 171: "Anstatt in ihrem Ehrgefühl verletzt zu sein, dulden sie dies, ja freuen sich heiter darüber. Der Normbruch macht Spaß. In solchen liminalen Verhältnissen gibt es kein Oben und Unten, alles ist ambiguisiert. Der Rückfall ins Atavistisch-Barbarische ist furchtbar und wunderbar zugleich, doch am Ende ist man froh, daß der heitere Spuck wieder ein Ende findet."

[33] See Lucian's symposiasts who laugh at the jester's mockery of them: οἱ μὲν οὖν ἄλλοι ἐγέλων ὁπότε σκωφθεῖεν (Lucian, *Symp.* 19); cf. Antiph. fr. 80 KA (=Ath. 6.238b) and Eub. fr. 25 KA (=Ath. 6.260d) on the positive quality of being able to laugh when mocked; for the anecdote of Socrates shrugging off his depiction in *Clouds* feeling that in the theater he is mocked "as if in a giant symposium," see [Plut.] *Mor.* 10c–d (cf. Ael. *VH* 5.8). For the religious aspects of the symposium, Murray (1990) 10–11 formulates it well; cf. Ath. 5.192b–e.

[34] *Rhet.* 2.3.12, 1380b1: καὶ ἔχοντες δὲ ἐναντίως τῷ ὀργίζεσθαι δῆλον ὅτι πρᾶοί εἰσίν, οἷον ἐν παιδιᾷ, ἐν γέλωτι, ἐν ἑορτῇ, ἐν εὐημερίᾳ, ἐν κατορθώσει, ἐν πληρώσει, ὅλως ἐν ἀλυπίᾳ καὶ ἡδονῇ μὴ ὑβριστικῇ καὶ ἐν ἐλπίδι ἐπιεικεῖ. Cf. *Pol.* 7.17, 1336b16–23, with Halliwell (2008) 319 regarding the connection between festival scurrility and sympotic scurrility.

contexts are fall-backs to "atavistic-barbaric" experiences, or such contexts are altogether different from festival mockery. Neither of these is a particularly appealing option.

This possibility of continuity into other contexts suggests that it may not necessarily be the circumscribed space of the festival which regulates how mockery was received, but rather the form of the on-stage comedy itself. Unlike a direct attack (abuse, threat, etc.), fiction and convention blur the referentiality of the *onomasti komoidein*. Stark argues, for example, that those mocked by name are really mere character types being mocked, not actual people.[35] Thus, one might suppose that Cinesias or some other *komoidoumenos* is enabled not to take offense because, in effect, he realizes that *he* is not actually being mocked at all, but rather a character type, and that everyone else realizes this as well. Other scholars stress the impossible complications of referentiality involved in fictional scenarios: both fictional and non-fictional characters are being mocked, after all, and fictional characters, not real people, are the ones mocking.[36] Cinesias is being mocked but *at whom* is he to get offended?[37] Others remind that it is too simplistic to consider comedy's "real" characters (e.g., Cinesias in Strattis' play) as non-fictional, since such "real-life" characters are very much entangled in the multiple levels of fictionality.[38] In such scenarios, Cinesias, owing to the levels of fictionality, perhaps through the very confusion of the various levels of fictionality, cannot even articulate what the abuse is. Or perhaps, as with Stark's character-type model, Cinesias recognizes that the person being mocked is not really him, but a sort of fictional construct, like Helen's *eidōlon*.

Closely connected to these realms of fictionality is consideration of mockery's conventionality. What appears at first glance to be a direct attack should be instead recognized as conventional and generic. A great deal of comic mockery is orchestrated by cues already conventionalized in archaic iamb.[39] Thus, many of the features of mockery, inasmuch as they are generic and prefabricated, render the very act of literary mockery more of an elegant, regulated dance than a straightforward attack. Cinesias, in such a view, through the very recognition of such convention (and the recognition that others recognize this convention), has the opportunity not to take such mockery seriously. Such a view would seem to suggest that it is not so much that the on-stage depiction of Cinesias is fictional (that is, not recognized

---

[35] A central argument of Stark (2004).   [36] A central argument of Saetta Cottone (2005).
[37] An important point made by Halliwell (1991) 53.   [38] Ruffell (2011) 29–53.
[39] Rosen (1988); for expansion on this role of convention in mockery see Rosen (2007).

"as" Cinesias), but that somehow the attack *itself* is not a real one, being instead recognized as something conventional, artistic.[40]

There is much to be appreciated in these views of the fictionality and convention of comic mockery, especially in the way they grasp at a certain difference between "real" abuse and to the unreal aspects of mockery, and I will return to some of these views later. For now, however, they fall short in answering the question at hand (how does one not take mockery seriously?) for much the same reason that the ritual explanation falls short: it is difficult to extend these accounts to other contexts – for example, jocular day-to-day interactions with friends, sympotic banter – in which mockery might not be taken seriously. There are certainly ways in which sympotic banter, for example, might be considered "fictional" or "conventional" inasmuch as the abuse in such contexts is not "real," but this would be an extension of these terms beyond their normal usage, and beyond that which the above scholars seem to intend (e.g., pre-existing literary genres, fictional characters, etc.). What is needed is a more basic account of "not taking mockery seriously" – one which describes that interpretive process, central to comedy but not exclusive to it, in general terms. Although a variety of solutions have been considered, what needs to be determined is the interpretive process of not-taking-seriously itself, what it means to do so, and how it is achieved. Otherwise, this process which seems so intuitive will continue to be invoked as a mere token of faith.

"Taking seriously" and "serious content"

To begin, it may be useful to draw a distinction between two forms of "taking seriously." When Malcolm Heath, for example, writes, "Aristophanes does not encourage us to take the claim seriously" or when Zachary Biles writes of Aeschylus in *Frogs*, "the central point of his argument was far more likely to be taken seriously by the audience than anything Euripides said,"[41] this may be a different usage of the idiom than Cinesias' hypothetical interpretive act. Instead, Cinesias' act of "taking seriously" more closely resembles, for example, Halliwell's usage of the idiom in contexts of mockery and banter, where one Socratic disciple

---

[40] Cf. Halliwell's (2008) 256–63 description of the slanging match in *Knights*.

[41] Heath (2007) 10 n. 31; Biles (2011) 247. For this usage of the idiom, see, e.g., Carey (1993) 253: "That Aristophanes can create two such absurd accounts of the same events suggests that neither was intended to be taken seriously as an explanation of the origin of the war." Rosen (2007) 83: "Aristophanes, however, never allows the audience to take any of the Paphlagonian's indignation seriously." Cf. Brockmann's (2003) x "ernst gemeinte Kritik" and Mastromarco's (2002) 220 "valenza seria."

takes Socrates' "'banter' too seriously" or another "appears to treat [banter] seriously by taking offense."[42] Although the idiom "take seriously" may cover a variety of interpretive contexts, only in the context of mockery does the act of "taking seriously" seem to involve offense and negative emotions.

Offense, however, is not the only difference. Related is the question of "content." As I argued earlier, a common notion about comedy is that "serious content" is often said to lie "beneath" or "behind" comic foolery (e.g., Aristophanes' opinions about Cleon's policies, Strattis' opinions about Cinesias' choruses, etc.).[43] The first usage of "taking seriously" appears to be directly related to that "serious content": if one "takes seriously" Aristophanes' claim to be a political advisor, one has arrived, I would suggest, at comedy's "serious content."[44] If one "takes seriously" Aeschylus' claim in *Frogs* about the poet's role, so too one has arrived at that comedy's "serious content." This connection between "taking seriously" and "content" is a usage found in humor theorists as well.[45]

But to what extent is Cinesias' form of "taking seriously" concerned with "content"? It will help to turn to an example. In Pherecrates' *Cheiron* (quoted in Ps.-Plutarch's *On Music*), Music appears on stage and complains to Justice about the violent treatment she has received from contemporary poets. Among these abusive innovators is Cinesias, about whom she claims the following (fr. 155 KA, 8–12):

Κινησίας δέ <μ'> ὁ κατάρατος Ἀττικός
ἐξαρμονίους καμπὰς ποιῶν ἐν ταῖς στροφαῖς
ἀπολώλεκέ μ' οὕτως, ὥστε τῆς ποιήσεως
τῶν διθυράμβων, καθάπερ ἐν ταῖς ἀσπίσιν,
ἀριστέρ' αὐτοῦ φαίνεται τὰ δεξιά.

Accursed Attican Cinesias, making ex-harmonic bends in his strophies, has destroyed me to such an extent that in his dithyrambic poetry, just as in his shields, his right appears to be his left.

---

[42] Halliwell (2008) 150 and 289 n. 59. For this usage of the idiom, see Storey and Allan (2005) 65–6: "If the expectation of the festival was that people were free to 'insult' other people, even when some serious issues lay beneath the comments made, they did not need to be taken seriously, because of the context of the festival"; cf. Sommerstein (2009) 42 n. 36: "A jesting mock-insult will only produce its desired effect if the addressee is, or can be assumed to be, sufficiently familiar with the speaker to be confident that the insult was not seriously meant."

[43] See the introduction.

[44] For "serious content," see, e.g., Lowe (2008) 10: "This is not to say that comedy is primarily interesting for its serious content. . ."

[45] E.g., Emerson (1969) 170–1, my italics: "One person makes a joke and the second person, acknowledging that the first person intended a joke, responds with a serious comment on the *content* of the joke as though the first person had spoken seriously . . . [T]he transposer acknowledges the joke, but evidently *takes the topic so seriously* that he does not want to leave it in the joking realm."

Interpretation of this passage usually involves a mapping of these alleged Cinesian innovations on to a fifth-century history of music.[46] E. K. Borthwick, for example, rejecting the hitherto claimed mirror-like properties of shields (which would make "the left the right"), outlines what he believes to be the historical innovations Cinesias was introducing to the dithyramb. After some ingenious connections regarding shields in the *pyrrhic* dance and Cinesias' alterations of dithyrambic choreography, he concludes with a fairly typical reading of the passage: "Pherecrates' criticism of Cinesias is directed at the medley of separate styles of music and dance which he has jumbled together, and in this he might be said to anticipate strictures made on the same formal grounds by Plato (*Leg.* 700) when he complains about the degraded taste of contemporary music."[47] Here Borthwick can be seen connecting the passage to the historical events of the period and articulating Pherecrates' central criticism.[48] If such articulation can be labeled the "serious content" of the passage, might it be said that Borthwick takes the passage seriously? He certainly is aware of Pherecrates' humor, yet he simultaneously discerns enough value in the text to connect it to contemporary events and extract an opinion. What is more, he articulates that opinion: a specific criticism about the "degraded taste of contemporary music" which is similar, as he says, to the criticism found in Plato's *Laws*.[49] To this extent, I would suggest, Borthwick may be said to take the passage seriously: it is not that he misses the joke, but rather is able to arrive at the humorous passage's "serious content" by connecting the passage to a contemporary reality.[50]

In Gregory Dobrov and Eduardo Urios-Aparisi's article on this Pherecrates passage, the authors explicitly state what remains implicit in other scholarship, namely the passage's playfulness: "the poet assumes a moral posture ... that *playfully* engages ideas asserted more *earnestly*

---

[46] Schönewolf (1938) 64–9; Düring (1945) 176–97; Süss (1954) 118–22, (1967) 26–31; Pianko (1963) 56–62, Restaini (1983) 139–92; Zimmermann (1993) 39–50; Kugelmeier (1996) 243–6; Lauriola (2010) 133–41; Roselli (2011) 188. For the dating of Pherecrates' death, see Olson (2010b).

[47] Borthwick (1968b) 67.

[48] For the historicist "serious" reading as the connecting of the text to real events, see Ruffell on Searle's serious/non-serious distinction (which roughly correlates to non-fiction/fiction). Ruffell (2011) 41: "historicist critics take an approach very similar to Searle and isolate and separate 'non-fictional' and 'fictional' elements. . ."

[49] This assertion of value from which textual analysis seems often to proceed seems both a natural and unavoidable first step: what would one do with the text otherwise? To see the text as valueless – for example, in the case of Borthwick, valueless for shedding light on contemporary events – yields analytic silence. In such scenarios of perceived textual valuelessness terms like "nonsense" or "rubbish" arise.

[50] A long history here: for studies on the scholia's discussion of different *komoidoumenoi* and *onomasti komoidein*, see Halliwell (1984) and Chronopoulos (2011) who discusses the "translation" of jokes into the "critical idiom."

elsewhere" and cites for that "elsewhere," among others, Plato's *Laws* as Borthwick does above.[51] Taking Lady Music as a hetaera and reading the text against the grain, Dobrov and Urios-Aparisi arrive at a different conclusion than most, claiming not that a negative opinion is being voiced about musical innovation but rather a positive one: "Traditional music is . . . revealed to be a sphere in which *innovation is fundamental*, just as sex is the basis of a hetaira's 'business'. The humor . . . playfully exploits the problem of degree, implying that some clients are more 'kinky' than others."[52] For these scholars, the passage is not criticizing musical innovation but championing it, reminding that such innovation has always been a part of music/Music's livelihood. Although they emphasize the playful mode of the passage adverbially, one might say that they ultimately take this text no less "seriously" than Borthwick: a certain serious meaning or content is extracted or "revealed" (to use their word), namely that "innovation is fundamental" in music. Like Borthwick, they are aware of the "playfulness" of the passage, yet (again, like Borthwick) they, by connecting the passage to a contemporary reality, have arrived at a certain serious content amidst that passage's playfulness.

Cinesias himself, however, as I have suggested above, enters into a different process of interpretation when he takes a passage like this "seriously." While it may be imagined that he responds to a line like "he has made the left his right" by standing up, shaking his fist, and storming out of the theater, one can anticipate no such offense from these scholars. Only in contexts of mockery does "take seriously" seem to involve offense and negative emotions. The question of interest here, however, regards the "serious content" in Cinesias' interpretation. If one can be said to take a passage seriously by arriving at some "serious content," what would be the "serious content" that Cinesias arrives at? Is it the same that Borthwick articulates, namely that Cinesias has jumbled musical forms together and thereby degraded contemporary music? If so, one might conclude that upon registering that "content," Cinesias takes offense. On the other hand, if such a criticism of jumbled forms were not actually true, would this deprive Cinesias of the opportunity to take such mockery "seriously" (as it might, e.g., the above scholars)? To return to the line "did Cinesias shit on you?," it does not seem to be a prerequisite that there be something "true" about the line in order for Cinesias to take offense, but then this calls into question the "serious content" he arrives at when he takes the line seriously. The nature of mockery's "content" needs a further look.

[51] Dobrov and Urios-Aparisi (1995) 154, my italics.
[52] Dobrov and Urios-Aparisi (1995) 162, their italics.

Although ancient Greek has no comparable idiom to the modern European "take seriously,"[53] the closest it comes to dealing with this question of mockery is a passage in Aristotle's *Rhetoric*. In Book II of the *Rhetoric*, Aristotle explains negative responses to mockery in terms of hubris: the reason people take offense at mockery, he claims, is because it is a hubristic act: ὀργίζονται δὲ τοῖς τε καταγελῶσι καὶ χλευάζουσι καὶ σκώπτουσιν· ὑβρίζουσι γάρ. "People get angry at those who laugh at, deride, and mock them: for they are committing hubris"[54] (and he famously defines "hubris" a little earlier[55]). *Orgē*, "anger," for Aristotle, is specifically a negative response to a perceived belittlement (*oligōria*), and one might imagine that such perceived belittlement (of his music, of his person) would be the source of Cinesian offense.[56]

This central idea – that to take offense at mockery is to register that mockery as a hubristic act – may be more important than the discussion of truth-values that follows. Aristotle proceeds to claim, for example, that the offense may be greatly aggravated if there is something true in the mockery ("But this angry feeling is much aggravated, if he suspect that this, whatever it may be, on which he prides himself, does not really belong to him"[57]). Thus, Cinesias, who may have prided himself on improving music, according to Aristotle, would take even greater offense if, upon hearing Pherecrates' remarks, he had the lingering premonition that perhaps he really was ruining music after all. Or, as Aristotle continues, if Cinesias believed in his own musical genius, but feared that others did not, buying into the Pherecratean critique, his offense also could be heightened ("or that if it *does*, at all events other people don't think so (*lit.* it does not appear so, μὴ δοκεῖν.)"[58]). However, these lingering truth-values do not seem to be

---

[53] For the common idiom outside of English, see modern Greek "παίρνω στα σοβαρά," French "prendre au sérieux," German "ernst nehmen," Russian "принимать серьёзно."

[54] 2.2.12, 1379a30–2 from the section on anger, *orgē*, 2.2.

[55] 2.2.5, 1378b23–5 ἔστι γὰρ ὕβρις τὸ βλάπτειν καὶ λυπεῖν ἐφ' οἷς αἰσχύνη ἐστὶ τῷ πάσχοντι, μὴ ἵνα τι γένηται αὐτῷ ἄλλο ἢ ὅτι ἐγένετο, ἀλλ' ὅπως ἡσθῇ "For hubris is injury and harm involving shame to the one suffering it, done not for some benefit beyond the act itself, but for the pleasure of it."

[56] Definition of *orgē* at 2.2.1, 1378a30–1: ἔστω δὴ ὀργὴ ὄρεξις μετὰ λύπης τιμωρίας φαινομένης διὰ φαινομένην ὀλιγωρίαν ... Cf. Konstan (2006) 39–76.

[57] Cope's (1973[1877]) translation (up to αὐτοῖς) ad Arist. *Rh.* 2.2.14, 1379a38–9 ταῦτα δὲ πολλῷ μᾶλλον, ἐὰν ὑποπτεύσωσι μὴ ὑπάρχειν αὐτοῖς, ἢ ὅλως ἢ μὴ ἰσχυρῶς, ἢ μὴ δοκεῖν.

[58] Cope's (1973[1877]) unpacked translation of the last three words of Arist. *Rh.* 2.2.14, 1379a38–9 (quoted above). Alternatively, if Cinesias were truly confident in his musical genius, the mockery against his music would not cause offense at all (i.e., an English-speaker might say "he would not take it seriously"): Arist. *Rh.* 2.2.14, 1379b1–2, ἐπειδὰν γὰρ σφόδρα οἴωνται ὑπάρχειν ἐν οἷς σκώπτονται, οὐ φροντίζουσιν. "For whenever people have a strong conviction that they really possess the assumed advantage ... in those particular things ... at which the taunt is levelled ... they care nothing about it" (Cope's translation).

prerequisites for offense, since it is hubris, not truth, that is the central focus of that offense. That is, one might imagine Cinesias taking offense at a line like "did Cinesias shit on you?" even if there were nothing at all "true" in the statement (for example, no past bowel incident either actual or believed). In such a scenario what would generate the offense, according to Aristotle, would be the belittlement (*oligōria*) implicit in the hubristic act itself.

If "taking seriously" is arriving at some "serious" content, I would suggest that this is the "serious content" arrived at in mockery "taken seriously." It is not necessarily "he is accusing me of jumbling musical forms" or "he is accusing me of defecating in improper places," although these are not excluded; it seems rather to be "he is belittling me in front of my peers" or "he is committing hubris against me by this act" (Aristotle's γάρ in ὑβρίζουσι γάρ being salient here). Of course, it may be objected that this is extending the notion of "content," already a slippery term, past its comfortable limits. After all, if the interpretive act in response to mockery is centered on hubris rather than truth-values, mockery can be related to a number of other hubristic acts that are not verbal at all. Although one might "take it seriously" (in the sense of "get upset") when laughed at, as so many Greek tragic figures do,[59] it may seem awkward to insist that there is some "content" in this laughter which one "takes seriously." Similarly, although one might "take it seriously" (again, "get upset") when playfully slapped, it is questionable whether there is some "content" in that playful abuse. Demosthenes' public slap by Meidias during the festival of Dionysus is usually a *locus classicus* for hubris, and there can be no doubt that he took it seriously, but is there some sort of true "content" in that slap which is the offended party's interpretive focus?[60] Another person publicly slapped at a festival did not seem to "take" it so "seriously": in *Frogs*, a certain chubby (perhaps fictional) runner was losing a festival race, and in response the people of the deme "hit him on the belly, the sides, the flanks, the butt, and as he fled, being slapped repeatedly, he was farting and blowing on his torch."[61] There is no mention of offense here in the midst of such physical abuse and it even seems that, given the context, such offense would be incongruous. But does one slap have a "serious content" while the other

---

[59] See Eur. *Med.* 383, Soph. *Aj.* 367, etc. See Dillon (1991); Catto (1991); Halliwell (2008) 26 n. 63 for more citations.

[60] Dem. *Meid.* 74 with MacDowell ad loc. and 7–9; Fisher (1992) 44–50 counts 124 uses of *hubris* in the speech (at 44).

[61] *Ran.* 1095–98: γαστέρα, πλευράς, λαγόνας, πυγήν, / ὁ δὲ τυπτόμενος ταῖσι πλατείαις / ὑποπερδόμενος / φυσῶν τὴν λαμπάδ᾽ ἔφευγεν. For this "evidently customary" treatment of slow torch-racers, see Dover ad *Ran.* 1096.

does not? One might compare the soldiers in Xenophon's *Cyropaedia* who consider (2.18–20) the physical abuse of a mock battle to be a most wonderful *paidia* (play, game) while perpetrating it, but not particularly fun while suffering it.[62] The physical abuse itself has not changed, of course, only, it seems, the mode of interpreting it (e.g., is it a "play" fight or is it "real" fight?). To what extent these hubristic acts may be said to have a "content" when offended parties take such acts seriously, I suppose, will depend on the comfortable usage of the reader.

To sum up thus far: I have been defining the idiom "take seriously" which, as an idiom, pervades the scholarship on Greek comedy and, as an interpretive act, appears to be central for offended *komoidoumenoi*.[63] While usage suggests that an interpreter who takes a passage "seriously" arrives at some sort of "serious content" in that passage, in the contexts of mockery the nature of this "content" is somewhat different. It is tempting to summarize it thus: "take seriously" in the scholarly or propositional sense tilts on a fulcrum of truth-values (e.g., "did Cinesias introduce these innovations?" "was there really a bowel incident?"), but in the context of mockery, "take seriously" tilts on a fulcrum of hubris (e.g., "am I being belittled in front of my peers?" "am I a victim of hubris by this act?"). Whether the latter scenario constitutes its own sort of "serious content" is debatable, but the relationship between mockery and other perceived hubristic acts, suggestive in Aristotle's description, is fairly clear. If Cinesias were to take a line like "did Cinesias shit on you?" seriously, he would be doing so in much the same way that he would take offense at derisive laughter or a playful slap. In all such cases the recognition he would arrive at is "I am a victim of hubris by this act" (ὑβρίζουσι γάρ).

"Taking seriously" in Greek

The question about Cinesias' interpretive choice still remains unsolved, although the question itself has become more refined. How would it have been possible for Cinesias to hear a line like "did Cinesias shit on you?" and not take it seriously? Ancient Greek does not observe the modern idiom "take seriously/not take seriously," but this absence need not occlude the possibility of an interpretive choice between serious and playful modes of

---

[62] Some play beatings become even more serious than in Xenophon: see Hippoc. *Epid.* 5.1.50.2: ἡ παρθένος ἡ καλὴ ἡ τοῦ Νερίου ἦν μὲν εἰκοσαέτης, ὑπὸ δὲ γυναίου φίλης παιζούσης πλατέῃ τῇ χειρὶ ἐπλήγη τὸ κατὰ τὸ βρέγμα, καὶ τότε μὲν ἐσκοτώθη. . .

[63] At least as moderns would describe it. More below on ancient Greek usage.

communication. Interlocutors often ask upon hearing an utterance "are you playing (*paizeis*)?" (with the implied or stated contrast, "or being serious, *spoudazeis*?")[64] and Plato at one point comes very close to the modern idiom when Socrates urges his conversation partner not to "take" him as one "playing" (μήτ' αὖ τὰ παρ' ἐμοῦ οὕτως ἀποδέχου ὡς παίζοντος)[65] – a turn of thought which becomes more frequent in later writers.[66] One might also think of the interpretive choice made by Cleon before his Pylos expedition: when Nicias first offers him the command at Pylos, Cleon first thinks it is "not in earnest" (so it is translated) until he understands that the general "really" means it (the distinction being between τῷ λόγῳ and τῷ ὄντι).[67] This does not necessarily imply that Cleon thought Nicias to be "playing," but rather probably engaged in some related mode, like "bluffing."[68]

All of these interpretive choices of "taking seriously/not seriously," however, occur in response to propositions, not mockery. Speakers make a statement, an offer, a proposition, and the interlocutor asks, "are you being serious/playing?" This opposition does not occur so readily in contexts of mockery where verbs of emotional reaction like *akhthomai*,[69] *duskheraino*[70] replace the modern idiom, and even *spoudazo* is suggestive of an intransitive emotional shift.[71] More importantly, whatever this distinction is between mockery taken seriously/not seriously, it certainly

---

[64] LSJ s.v. σπουδάζω 1.3 citing the opposition at Pl. Grg. 510c; παίζω 11.1 citing the opposition at Xen. Mem. 4.1.1. Cf. e.g. Pl. *Euthphr.* 283b6–7 πότερον παίζετε ταῦτα λέγοντες ἢ ὡς ἀληθῶς...σπουδάζετε; *Grg.* 481b6: εἰπέ μοι,... σπουδάζει ταῦτα Σωκράτης ἢ παίζει; Lys. 24.18 Carey. For the question *paizeis*?, see Pl. *Meno* 79a7, Men. *Dis Ex.* 60, Achill. Tat. 6.13.1.1; cf. Pl. *Grg.* 481c1–2, Plut. 20c4.

[65] Pl. *Grg.* 500c1.

[66] See Strabo *Geog.* 14.5.14.35 ἐπεὶ δ' ἐκεῖνος ἐν παιδιᾶς μέρει δεξάμενος, Plut. *Brut.* 34.5 μετὰ παιδιᾶς δεχομένων, Diod. Sic. 20.33.4.2 ἀποδεχόμενος τὸν ἄνδρα τῇ παιδιᾷ. But cf. the phrase οὐ ἐκ παρέργου ... ποιεῖται (with Woodhouse s.v. "seriously" translating "took ... seriously") and Sandbach and Gomme ad *Samia* 638: "to do anything παρέργως is not to take it seriously."

[67] Thuc. 4.28: ὁ δὲ τὸ μὲν πρῶτον οἰόμενος αὐτὸν λόγῳ μόνον ἀφιέναι ἑτοῖμος ἦν, γνοὺς δὲ τῷ ὄντι παραδωσείοντα ἀνεχώρει καὶ οὐκ ἔφη αὐτὸς ἀλλ' ἐκεῖνον στρατηγεῖν... Classen's (1963[1869]) note ad loc: "'nur mit Worten,' nicht im Ernste."

[68] "Pretense" being Graves' (1958) word of choice ad loc.: "λόγῳ μόνον ἀφιέναι 'only pretended to give up'. λόγῳ is opposed to ἔργῳ or τῷ ὄντι; i.128, 'τῷ δὲ λόγῳ ἀπέδρασαν αὐτόν,' 'he pretended that they had escaped from him.'"

[69] When Socrates teases Antisthenes as a "pimp" (Xen. *Symp.* 4.61), the latter "gets really upset" (μάλα ἀχθεσθείς); when the Old Oligarch describes the reaction of the *demos* to certain undesirable members of the lower class being mocked in comedy, ἄχθομαι is the verb of choice: ὥστε οὐδὲ τοὺς τοιούτους ἄχθονται κωμῳδουμένους "consequently they don't get upset when these sorts of people get mocked" (2.18).

[70] The word in Arist. *EN* that describes the boor's reaction to play and mockery is *duskheraino* "to get upset" or "to be disgusted," "to take it seriously" (4.8.3, 1128a7–9; 4.8.10–11, 1128b2–3).

[71] LSJ s.v. *spoudazo* 1.3 translates the ἐσπούδακας of Pl. *Phdr.* 236b5–7 as "*Did you take it seriously*, that I...?" But note that this is listed as an intransitive usage (1.3 "to be serious or earnest"). In the context of this banter with Phaedrus, Socrates' sense of ἐσπούδακας seems to be "have you gotten upset/

does not occur along the lines of the familiar *spoudazein/paizein* opposition. One reason for the difficulty of such a desired opposition is, of course, that the verb *paizein* itself can mean both "play" and "tease."[72] Through the very act of "playing" (*paizein* in the sense of "tease"), one might create offense in an interlocutor who takes that teasing seriously ("gets upset"), even though the hypothetical recipient is perfectly aware that the speaker is "playing."[73] Utterances spoken in play can be "taken seriously" for the very reason that they are spoken in play: the listener senses a certain denigration implicit in the banter and does not appreciate it.[74] A clear dichotomy like "are you *really* insulting me/or just playing?" is not readily available and one can only catch glimpses of such an opposition in Platonic distinctions like mockery deployed "without force," *aneu thumou.*[75] What remains to be seen, however, is what exactly changes when one chooses to take a mocking utterance (or any utterance) seriously/not seriously. Does the "content" of the lines remain the same, or are the two forms of interpretation radically different?

Cinesias in *birds* and hearing "in play"

Among the many visitors to *Nephylococcygia* at the end of Aristophanes' *Birds* is a dithyrambic poet named Cinesias. Like the visitors before him, Cinesias asks for a pair of wings and like other such unwelcome guests in comedy, Cinesias gets a beating. What leads to this physical abuse is Cinesias' singing and song itself. After explaining that he requires wings in order to snatch "new air-whirled and snow-clad preludes from the clouds,"[76] he turns to an example of one such song (1390–1400):

serious?" or as W. H. Thompson (1973[1868]) translates it ad loc.: "you are seriously annoyed" (citing *Ran.* 812, ὡς ὅταν γ᾽ οἱ δεσπόται / ἐσπουδάκωσι, κλαύμαθ᾽ ἡμῖν γίγνεται "whenever the masters get seriously annoyed, we get a beating"). Cf. Gomme and Sandbach ad *Dysc.* 148, Austin and Olson (2004) ad *Thesm.* 571–3; Rowe (1986) and Yunis (2011) ad *Phdr.* 236b5–7 seem to take the verb transitively.

[72] See, e.g., Ischomachus' *paizeis* to Socrates at Xen. *Oec.* 11.7; Pomeroy (1994) 165 ad loc.: "Although you're teasing me, Socrates. . ."

[73] Consider again Antisthenes' reaction at Xen. *Symp.* 4.61 (μάλα ἀχθεσθεὶς) at Socrates' teasing. Cf. Halliwell (2008) 41–2.

[74] Mockery/teasing being a form of hubris, which in turn is a form of *oligōria* (belittlement). Cf. Arist. 2.2.3–4, 1378b11–15 and the difference between being thought ἄξιος σπουδῆς and ἄξιος οὐδενός; 2.2.6, 1378b30–1, τὸ γὰρ μηδενὸς ἄξιον οὐδεμίαν ἔχει τιμήν, οὔτε ἀγαθοῦ οὔτε κακοῦ.

[75] Pl. *Leg.* 935c–936a on the difficulty of distinguishing between playful mockery and the more offensive sort (e.g., ἢ διαλάβωμεν δίχα τῷ παίζειν καὶ μή, καὶ παίζοντι μὲν ἐξέστω τινὶ περί του λέγειν γελοῖον ἄνευ θυμοῦ, συντεταμένῳ δὲ καὶ μετὰ θυμοῦ, καθάπερ εἴπομεν, μὴ ἐξέστω μηδενί;). England (1921) ad loc. reminds that at Pl. *Euthyd.* 288d3, συντεταμένον and σπουδάζοντα are used to describe the same state of mind. Cf. Halliwell (1991) 67–8; Morrow (1993) 372–4; Jouet-Pastre (2006) 94–6; Halliwell (2008) 24–5, 300–1.

[76] ἐκ τῶν νεφελῶν καινὰς λαβεῖν / ἀεροδονήτους καὶ νιφοβόλους ἀναβολάς. (1384–5).

K. σὺ δὲ κλύων εἴσει τάχα.

Π. οὐ δῆτ' ἔγωγε.

K. νὴ τὸν Ἡρακλέα σύ γε.

ἅπαντα γὰρ δίειμί σοι τὸν ἀέρα.

εἴδωλα πετηνῶν

αἰθεροδρόμων

οἰωνῶν ταναοδείρων –

Π. ὢ ὄπ.

K. ἁλίδρομον ἁλάμενος

ἅμ' ἀνέμων πνοαῖσι βαίην.

Π. νὴ τὸν Δί' ἢ 'γώ σου καταπαύσω τὰς πνοάς.

K. τοτὲ μὲν νοτίαν στείχων πρὸς ὁδόν,

τοτὲ δ' αὖ βορέᾳ σῶμα πελάζων

ἀλίμενον αἰθέρος αὔλακα τέμνων.

C. After you listen, you'll soon know.

P. I don't think so.

C. By Heracles, you will!

I will go through the whole air for you [*sings*]:

Mirages of winged,

air-travelling,

neck-extending birds

P. Hey now!

C. . . . having leapt on a seaward run, may I go on gusts of winds . . .

P. By Zeus! I'll stop your gusts! [*starts chasing Cinesias*]

C. [*Running away*] . . . now proceeding the way of the North-Wind,

now bringing myself southerly,

cleaving a harborless furrow of ether.

The nature of the mockery of Cinesias' music here need not be subtle, and at some level the passage is little different from the depiction of Cinesias' music in Pherecrates or depictions of dithyrambic poets elsewhere. He is an airy-fairy dithyrambist, his music is laughable, scarcely endurable, and the mockery only need be negative in order to initiate the delight of chasing the poet around the orchestra.

Matthew Wright analyses this passage in much the same terms as Borthwick, and Dobrov and Urios-Aparisi above, linking the passage to what is known of contemporary innovations in music and Cinesias' role in those developments. But he presents this reading – what I was calling above for Borthwick, and Dobrov and Urios-Aparisi "taking the text seriously" – as an analysis of how the "joke" of the passage "works." Regarding the view that Cinesias used avian imagery, Wright explains, "in fact it [i.e., that Cinesias used avian imagery] is not necessary in order for the joke to work."[77] Instead, he suggests, "it is just as likely that the parody depends on style alone – in other words, that 'airiness' is primarily a stylistic metaphor, and that compound words and pretentious content were generally thought to be 'airy' or 'high-flown', irrespective of the specific subject-matter of the poetry."[78] No less than the scholars above, Wright sets the text in a context or contemporary reality (τῷ ὄντι, to borrow from Thucydides above) of what was "generally thought" rather than dismissing the text as just words (τῷ λόγῳ). In so doing, I suggest, like the above scholars, Wright takes the text seriously. However, what is interesting to see is that, by taking the text seriously, he is able to explain the "joke" of the passage. That is, through those very connections to contemporary reality the joke is explained.[79]

Similarly, Kugelmeier explains the *Birds* passage in these terms: "The physical lightness of flight becomes a metaphor for mental 'light-weight,' which should be attributed to Cinesias' poetry. Only in this way does the scene attain its special wit."[80] Like Wright, Kugelmeier does not dismiss the passage as non-referential, but connects it to contemporary thought and music, and in so doing, as I am suggesting, takes the text seriously. So too, like Wright, he does this in the context of explaining the passage's "joke" (*Witz*), which appears to be streamlined with the negative opinions about Cinesias. Like the scholars above, both scholars here recognize the playfulness of the passage, yet, in order to explain the joke of the passage, especially its referential aspects, it seems a prerequisite, oddly enough, to take the text seriously.

But what of Cinesias? As I have been arguing, the hypothetical audience member named Cinesias had an interpretive choice on his hands: he could take this mockery seriously (i.e., get upset) or he could not. Aristotle, in the *Nicomachean Ethics*, spells out two extremes of behavior that might apply to Cinesias in this situation. Although Aristotle is specifically describing behaviors in the context of "play" (*paidia*), the passage has everything to do with mockery, teasing, and playful banter. The extremes for Aristotle are the *bomolokhos* (buffoon) who says and treats everything as a joke and the *agroikos* (boor) who

---

[77] Wright (2012) 111.   [78] Wright (2012) 111.
[79] This important feature of jokes will be discussed further in Chapter 4.
[80] Kugelmeier (1996) 221–2: "Die physische Leichtigkeit des Fliegens wird zur Metapher für geistiges 'Leichtgewicht', das der Kunst des Kinesias unterstellt werden soll. Nur so nämlich erhält die Szene ihren eigentlichen Witz."

says and treats nothing as a joke. The *agroikos* is said to "get upset" (*duskherainei*) – one might say "take it seriously" – whenever such playful banter is engaged in. The *bomolokhos*, however, who presumably has the opposite reaction to the *agroikos*, never "gets upset" at mockery and never "takes it seriously."

Halliwell rightly notes, regarding this and other such passages in Aristotle, that the philosopher emphasizes the roles of both "speaking" and "listening" in playful banter. The key word that appears is *emmeles*, "harmonious" or "well-tuned": "Aristotle seems to conceptualise playfulness as a kind of mutually pleasurable interchange, somewhat like a coordinated musical performance," discerning a "quasi-musical harmoniousness of reciprocal banter."[81] This harmonious relationship in the context of play (ὁμιλία τις ἐμμελής)[82] applies to both speaking and listening (καὶ οἷα δεῖ λέγειν, καὶ ὥς, ὁμοίως δὲ καὶ ἀκούειν;)[83] and so it would seem that those who are said to "play harmoniously" οἱ δ᾽ ἐμμελῶς παίζοντες (1128a4) are engaging in both playful "speaking" *and* playful "listening." Such "playful listening" appears again later in the passage (λέγειν ἐν παιδιᾶς μέρει καὶ ἀκούειν).[84]

Playful banter from the perspective of the speaker creates no major problems in exegesis or translation: λέγειν ἐν παιδιᾶς μέρει might be turned "joke around," "tease," "mock," and so forth. Less clear, however, is the receiving end: what exactly is "playful listening" (ἀκούειν... ἐν παιδιᾶς μέρει)? This is the Cinesias question. Elsewhere the verb for this act of listening is ostensibly supplied by the term *hypomenein*, a verb of endurance usually collocated with negative phenomena like pain (*hypomenei algones*) or labor (*hypomenei ponon*). So, for example, it is a positive quality in a person to be dexterous at both making and "taking" jokes (*hypomeinai*) (Arist. *Rhet.* 2.4, 1381a33–5 καὶ οἱ ἐπιδέξιοι καὶ τωθάσαι καὶ ὑπομεῖναι), and this verb of endurance appears in similar contexts of playful banter in the *Nicomachean Ethics*.[85] If jokes (*skōmmata*) for Aristotle are a "sort of abuse" and wit an "educated hubris," it would make sense to depict the act of listening as a sort of endurance.[86] Cinesias, one might imagine, in seeing his carefully wrought compositions trounced on stage, would have to endure the

---

[81] Halliwell (2008) 310, 328. At 328: "on not *taking* them (too) seriously."

[82] *EN* 4.14, 1127b34–1128a1   [83] 1128a1, cf. 1128a18.

[84] 1128a19–20: speaking and hearing "in part of play" seems to mean more "playfully" than "in the context of play."

[85] *EN* 1128a27, regarding the ethical norms of play (*paidia*) and what sorts of jokes or mockery one should listen to, he writes ἃ γὰρ ὑπομένει ἀκούων, ταῦτα καὶ ποιεῖν δοκεῖ. This can be taken in terms of aischrology, but mockery is certainly at the fore as well (e.g. σκώπτειν at 1128a7, 14, 25, 30–1).

[86] *Loidorēma*, *EN* 1128a30; πεπαιδουμένη ὕβρις, *Rh.* 2.12, 1389b11–12. Cf. Halliwell (2008) 307–31.

mockery in much the same way that he would endure physical pain or rainy weather.[87]

What is remarkable about equating "hearing in play" (ἀκούειν ἐν παιδιᾶς μέρει) to a sort of "endurance" (ὑπομεῖναι) is that the "content" of the mockery – if that is the right word – remains unchanged in such "play listening." That is, the realization "I am a victim of hubris by these words" would seem to be a constant in the realms of both playful teasing and more serious abuse. The only difference in the context of play is that the mocked person must endure such negative opinions about himself. This is reminiscent of the legalistic view of the Dionysia described earlier, where it was imagined that every *komoidoumenos* was offended but simply unable to retaliate: a rather grim picture. If "playful listening" is a sort of "endurance," the mocked person must endure the mockery as if it were no different from any other act of hubris. There would be little room or possibility for anything but negative emotion in either context.

Just like that depiction of the Dionysia, this depiction of "playful listening" as a sort of "endurance" disappoints, not just in its depiction of play or banter as uniformly negative in reception, but in its treatment of mockery's content as uniform. To tease Cinesias for his poetry is no different from telling him that he is a lousy poet directly. In a sense, it would seem that there is no option but to take this criticism "seriously": to *not* take the criticism seriously in this scenario simply would mean to acknowledge and accept it, but instead of reacting against it, to "endure" it. Although this may not be what Aristotle meant by the very *hypomenein*, it clearly reveals the dead-end in this line of analysis. So long as one arrives at the content of the mockery (e.g., "I am a victim of hubris by this act"), there is little difference between "taking seriously" and "not taking seriously" (or "play listening"). The interpretation is the same, only accompanied in the first scenario with anger, in the second with a bitten lip. This is an impasse, and in the next section I would like to look at a more modern view of "play listening" – specifically the concept of the "play signal" – in order to overcome this impasse.

The play signal

The idea of a "play signal" – although now common in studies of animal play – was introduced by Gregory Bateson in 1955 out of an interest in

---

[87] For the rainy weather metaphor, see Cephisodorus *Amazones* 1 KA σκώπτεις μ᾽, ἐγὼ δὲ τοῖς λόγοις ὄνος ὕομαι. The proverb ὄνος ὕεται (ἐπὶ τῶν μὴ ἐπιστρεφομένων, at Phot 337.19=Sud.394) suggests that the speaker in Cephisodorus is claiming imperviousness to the mockery. For more examples of imperviousness to mockery, see Halliwell (2008) 41–3.

different types of communication.[88] He sensed that in communication there is the "denotative" message, on the one hand, and, on the other, the "metacommunicative" one, which is to say the message about the message. He developed these ideas by studying animals at play, noting that because aggressive play was so similar to actual aggression, there needed to be some way for animals to communicate that this "aggression" was not actual aggression and "combat" not actual combat. There needed to be some exchange of signals "which would carry the message 'this is play.'"[89] Decades later these animal "play signals" have become fairly well documented by ethologists – physical signs (gestures, facial displays, nips) which both initiate a bout of play and frequently recur during the play as if reminding at certain moments of intensity "this is (still) play."[90]

In explaining this "play signal," Bateson provided an example of the animal "nip," which is particularly useful here, if one considers the earlier distinction between Demosthenes' physical abuse and the physical abuse of the flabby runner in *Frogs*. Bateson writes: "The playful nip denotes the bite, but it does not denote what would be denoted by the bite."[91] Regarding the two cases of festival slapping (Demosthenes and the flabby runner), one might say the playful slap denotes the slap, but it does not denote what would be denoted by the slap.[92] As Bateson suggests: "Not only does the playful nip not denote what would be denoted by the bite for which it stands, but, in addition, the bite itself is fictional. Not only do the playing animals not quite mean what they are saying but, also, they are usually communicating about something which does not exist."[93]

If this distinction in "play" communication is applied to the context of mockery, it is possible to offer a different type of "playful listening" than the endurance model posed above. In the "play signal" model, the conclusion that a victim of mockery arrives at – whether it be Cinesias or a sympotic

---

[88] Bateson (2000[1972]), first printed in 1955 as a "A theory of play and fantasy" in *Psychiatric Research Reports* 2; 39–51. Bateson's student Fry (1963) pursued his lead into the area of humor, but with unequal success (although occasional important insight). Cf. Raskin (1985) 35–6; Mitchell (1991).

[89] Bateson (2000[1972]) 179.

[90] See, e.g., Bekoff (1972, 1975, 1995, 1998); Pellis (1996); Palagi (2008, 2011).

[91] Bateson (2000[1972]) 179–80 explains it thus: "The next step was the examination of the message 'This is play,' and the realization that this message contains those elements which necessarily generate a paradox of the Russellian or Epimenides type – a negative statement containing an implicit negative metastatement. Expanded, the statement 'This is play' looks something like this: 'These actions in which we now engage do not denote what those actions *for which they stand* would denote'" (his italics). Later, on the same page, he expands further: "These actions, in which we now engage, do not denote what would be denoted by those actions which these actions denote."

[92] Similarly in the "mock battle" in Xenophon, which is combat, yet not "real."

[93] Bateson (2000[1972]) 182.

bomolokhos – is not "I am a victim of hubris by this mockery" which simply must be "endured" if it is to be taken "playfully." Instead, the conclusion of mockery-taken-playfully is something altogether different: namely, "this is play." The mockery does not "denote" the hubris "for which it stands" and, in the act of "playful listening," what is being communicated in that mockery "does not exist."

Robson, in his study of Aristophanic humor, has much to say about signals and the "frames" these signals initiate. He writes, for example: "By text in a 'Playful' frame I mean discourse which the speaker accompanies with certain signals or rather, in terms of my model, discourse that the listener perceives as being accompanied by certain signals, these signals suggesting that humorous mode discourse is on its way."[94] Based on Goffman's concept of "frames" (contexts for communication like "buying train tickets" or "opening a present" which drive both the terms and interpretation of that communication),[95] these frames proliferate in Robson's discussion: a signal initiates a play frame, the play frame initiates a "joke telling" frame, which, for example, is to be distinguished from a frame like "reprimanding a child."[96] Frames for Robson and Goffman are to be numbered in the thousands if they can be numbered at all, and this concept of a "frame" has certainly been successful in explaining a number of features of communication and, for Robson, in explaining certain features of humor.

But much as this proliferation of frames may provide clarity in some areas, it waters down the fundamental break in communication that Bateson was pursuing regarding the play signal and his sense of a play frame. The play frame for Bateson is not a segment of communication marked by certain words and gestures in the way that "reprimanding a child" or "buying a ticket" is. It is rather a different order of communication where any segment of communication may be engaged in with the signalled proviso that the players do not "mean what they are saying" and are "communicating about something which does not exist." What interests Bateson about play is not how it lies within communication (which is the watered-down concept of a play frame), but how it lies, in a sense, outside it (thus, his interest in "metacommunication"). It is also noteworthy that the ethological notion of a "play signal" does not just initiate a "frame," but recurs continually throughout bouts of play, particularly at moments of intensity.

---

[94] Robson (2006) 30. Nash (1985) 36 also uses play signal in this sense.   [95] Goffman (1974).
[96] Robson (2006) 31. Earlier, he outlines an incongruence theory of humor which he names "frame-abuse," where a speaker passes from one frame to another without appropriate signaling. For further discussion of this incongruence theory and its relationship to conflicting "scripts," see Chapter 4.

One might apply Cinesias as an example here. If "playful listening" is modeled along Bateson's recognition of play signals, the conclusion Cinesias arrives at is not "I am a victim of hubris," but the realization of the signal "this is play." This is quite different from Robson's sense of the word, where Cinesias would, via a "play signal," enter into a "play" frame which then leads on to a "this is a joke" frame; at which point, he would have to "get" the joke ("did Cinesias shit on you?"), and then have to decide whether or not to take that joke "seriously" (i.e., "get upset"). In Bateson's model, as I understand it, it seems that all Cinesias really has to "get" is "this is play." The very act of getting offended or "taking seriously" consists of appending a certain "content," function, or purpose to the joke (e.g., "I am a victim of hubris by this mockery"). In not taking a joke seriously, the focus is no longer on the "content" at all but rather on the play signal itself.

If there is any truth to this "play signal" position, it may shed some light on a peculiar aspect of "nonsense" left unresolved in Chapter 1 regarding the "nonsense" of sympotic play. It will be recalled that whereas verbs for nonsense like *phluarein* and *lērein* are usually pejorative or, in medical texts, symptoms of delirium, in the context of sympotic play they seemed to bear a positive connotation. Sympotic companions were said to "speak nonsense" to one another, to "blather," and so forth (*phluarein, lērein*).[97] There, I considered the formal relationships between such sympotic "nonsense" and medical "nonsense." Perhaps, for example, the sorts of the things symposiasts were saying resembled the sorts of things feverish nonsense-speakers were saying, for example, repetitive or rambling speech, punning word-salads, statements that do not reflect reality ("I am bigger than this room"), and so forth.[98]

But the connection between medical "nonsense" and sympotic "nonsense" may have more to do with modes of interpretation than these formal resemblances. It will be recalled that although the Hippocratic doctors often list "speaking nonsense" as a symptom of delirium or fever, they never once actually described the "content" of that nonsense (and so I found potential examples elsewhere, like the delirious Thrasyllus' claim that he owned all the ships in the Piraeus). The doctors did not need to describe the content of

---

[97] In the sympotic epigram, the important line was χρὴ δ', ὅταν εἰς τοιοῦτο συνέλθωμεν φίλοι ἄνδρες / πρᾶγμα, γελᾶν παίζειν χρησαμένους ἀρετῆι, / ἥδεσθαί τε συνόντας, ἐς ἀλλήλους τε φ[λ]υαρεῖν / καὶ σκώπτειν τοιαῦθ' οἷα γέλωτα φέρει. "Whenever we come together as friends for such an occasion, we should laugh and play in a good way, and take pleasure in each other's company, and talk nonsense to one another, and mock the sorts of thing that bring laughter." The fragment from Alexis was (fr. 9 KA): μετρίοισι χρωμένους ποτηρίοις / λαλεῖν τι καὶ ληρεῖν πρὸς αὑτοὺς ἡδέως "with a moderate amount of drink to chat a bit and talk nonsense with one another pleasantly."

[98] See Chapter 1 for discussion.

such "nonsense," of course: whether it be a confused mumble or a tyrannical rant, it did not matter what these patients were "babbling" about. As far as the doctors were concerned, once the patients' speech was recognized as a symptom of a certain disease, that is, when the patient was diagnosed as "speaking nonsense," the patient's speech could not be anything more than that diagnosed nonsense. Such babble appears so undifferentiated in the medical texts despite being differentiable (e.g., delirious talk "about" the Piraeus, the weather, the size of the city's gates) because the patient's nonsense is not "about" anything once it is diagnosed as nonsense. The patient's speech becomes completely reduced to a symptom in that diagnosis, and once it is, the "content" of that speech no longer matters: he is "just" speaking nonsense.

If one returns to the sympotic contexts of "nonsense," perhaps this symptomatic type of interpretation may shed some light. Just as in the medical contexts, what is spoken under the heading of sympotic "nonsense" could practically be anything, from "small-talk" about the weather, to silly propositions and less-than-serious opinions, to speech-acts like mockery or prayers, to the more babbly types of punning word-salads. What unites these, just as in the Hippocratic context, is this overarching label of "nonsense." In this way, mockery might be included after all as a potential instance of "speaking nonsense," inasmuch as mockery also might undergo that similar symptomatic interpretation which renders it "just" nonsense.

Herein lies the difference in interpretation, I would like to suggest, between taking mockery seriously (δυσχεραίνειν *vel sim.*) and hearing it playfully (ἀκούειν ἐν παιδιᾶς μέρει *vel sim.*). What differentiates mockery-not-taken-seriously from its more serious forms is that it too is interpreted, I would like to argue, exclusively as a symptom. Like the Hippocratic doctor interpreting the nonsense of a patient as nothing but a symptom, non-serious interpretation also devalues content in favor of the sympto-matic "this is play."

Extrapolation

When Cinesias sat in the theater year after year hearing his bowels and music mocked, he may have become irritated, or, to use the modern idiom, he may have "taken it seriously." But he might also have done something else, namely, not taken the mockery seriously at all. It has been the object of this chapter to describe what this process entails. I have been arguing that "not taking seriously" is a rather different form of interpretation from its more sensible counterpart and that this difference in interpretation is parallel to the difference in the ways a Hippocratic doctor might listen to a feverish patient as opposed to a healthy one. Cinesias' "non-serious" type of interpretation is symptomatic just as the doctors' interpretation of patients' "nonsense" is symptomatic: the content of the patient's speech is important only up to the point that such speech reveals the patient to be delirious. At the point of this realization, the content of the speech is (and always was) completely unimportant, and every further utterance is a mere symptom pointing to that one and the same illness. In the case of Cinesias, however, the diagnosis is not one of illness, but of play.

In some ways this is far from a surprising conclusion: surely, if one is looking for the opposite of "serious," to discover "play" is rather trivial and obvious. But what is of interest here is not that opposition of contexts ("the serious" and "play"), but rather the opposition between content-focused and symptomatic interpretation. Of interest is the signal itself, rather than the "frame" or "zone" of play which the signal is often said to initiate (for reasons I described above). For this signal, as it is often described, is not communicative in the same way content is communicative: whereas the statement "Has Cinesias shit on you?" is rich in historical allusion and potential opinions, the play signal is something impoverished to the point of being binary (either "this is play" or not). So too, such signals are not communicative but metacommunicative: that is, they are not "saying something" so much as pointing to how the communication is to be understood, and it is from this perspective that one might reconsider the "fictional" or "conventional" aspects of mockery discussed earlier.[99]

If such metacommunicative signals are at work in comedy, it would help to explain why the focus on or interpretation of comedy's content or messages – whether they be political opinions, *onomasti komoidein*, or aesthetic boasts – is at some level inextricable from the "serious." Cinesias had a bowel incident, Cinesias is a lousy poet, Cinesias is impious: one cannot articulate comedy without treating it seriously, inasmuch as "taking

---

[99] Cf., e.g., the problem well articulated by Rosen (2007) 22, n. 32: "This is not to say that it is always easy to distinguish between 'real' mockery, with its ramifications for real people and historical events, and poetic mockery, which operates in a mimetic zone marked off from everyday reality, however much its content flirts with that reality" and "The lines between these two types of mockery are often blurry... especially since the very act of mockery practically by definition implies that the mocker is interested in having a 'real' effect against a target, no matter how disingenuous this might turn out to be." I would argue that the aspects of "convention" (or "fiction") are not layers added to "real" mockery but, in a sense, are always already there (i.e., mockery-*qua*-mockery is always distanced from the "real"). This is why etymologies and usages of words like "mockery" (*OED*), "Spott" (Grimm), and *skōptein* (Halliwell (2008) 18) are just as much entangled in categories of mimetic play as they are in abuse.

seriously," as I have been arguing, is focus on the content.[100] On the other hand, the signal "this is play" is not the "content" or "message" at all, but rather a sort of metacommunication that directs how the message is to be taken. When such a play signal is recognized and accepted, it overrides the message, rendering it mere grounding for the play signal's appearance.

This is not to reject the common notion in comic scholarship that one might laugh at a comedy and then wake up the next morning thinking about the serious thoughts "behind" that comedy (or, of course, even sooner than that). The argument is rather that the moment that one does so, the moment that one begins to think about comedy's content, is the moment that that overriding play signal vanishes. It is the moment one begins to "take" comedy, like an offended *komoidoumenos*, "seriously" and thus the moment that the persistent feeling returns that not all of comedy can be reduced to its content and that some part of it lies beyond "serious meaning." To return to the Hippocratic parallel: once the Hippocratic doctor starts "taking seriously" the content of what the sick patient is saying, he is no longer treating the patient as delirious: the detected symptom and its accordant diagnosis have vanished.

Conclusions

When Silk rejected the opposition of "serious" and "play" as a useful instrument for describing Aristophanes' oeuvre, it was for good reason. Play, as pretense, as make-believe, fantasy, or fiction, is not limited to comedy, but one might say all-embracing for tragedy and the mimetic arts in general.[101] After all, everything that an audience in the theater sees is "play," is *a* "play": neither is comedy distinct in this way, nor does the

---

[100] I would suggest that this content-centered aspect of the serious also substantiates the notion that "to explain a joke kills the joke." Cf., e.g., Cooper (2010) 268: "It is said that when a joke is explained it ceases to be funny." Trahair (2007) 7: "What is intrinsically comic about the object is lost in the rational articulation of what the comic means." Giora (1991) 483: "Explaining a joke kills it by filling in the gap." White (1977) 243–4: "Humor can be dissected as a frog can, but the thing dies in the process," quoted in Wright (2012) ix. Eastman (1921) viii (quoted in Raskin (1985) 7) reports Bernard Shaw to have said, "there is no more dangerous literary symptom than a temptation to write about wit and humor. It indicates the total loss of both." Cf. Lowe (2008) 12 for the opposite position.

[101] Silk (2000) 81 on the opposition between "play" and "serious, real action" (cf. his discussion of "pretense" and "posing" at 313–14); at 81, his italics: "Once the terms of the covert analogy are spelled out, it is obvious that no true equivalence exists between 'serious' tragedy and 'serious' living: both tragedy and comedy, in or out of drama, are in this sense equally *playful*." But one might suggest in response: although "equally *playful*," tragedy is the genre that insists it is not play, while comedy is the genre that insists it is. Cf. Pirandello (1998[1988]) 63: "What's a stage? Well, look, it's a place where people play at being serious. They act plays there. And we're going to act a play. Yes, seriously, that's right!" For fantasy, cf. Ruffell (2011) 29–30.

audience need to be reminded of something so rudimentary. To argue that comedy is somehow letting the audience know that it is "play" in this sense can only be the blandest of assumptions: comedy can hardly be singled out as "play" or, in this sense, a more "playful" genre.

However, what is remarkable about non-comic genres is how quickly the freedom of play – in short, the ability to choose whatever reality one wishes at any single moment – is discarded for more calibrated instruments like probability and causation. The player exchanges play's absolute freedom and limitless power for a yoke of necessity where choices lead to inevitable consequences, where one cannot turn back time, and where death is final. All this despite the fact that the players could at any point brush aside all of these inevitabilities and erase that chosen path of suffering. In comedy, however, that ability, that freedom of play is demonstrated and championed over and over again: at any point, the player can change the nature of the play, whether it be the consequential structure of a sentence (the shit hit . . . Cratinus), the recreation of a plot (*Wasps*), or the raising of the dead (*Frogs*).[102] The possibilities of comic play are limited only by the imagined limits, and at each and every point where that freedom is reaffirmed, the irresistible reminder "this is play" is insisted upon yet again.

Despite Silk's rejection of play as a useful category for Aristophanes' art, the specific formal elements of comedy that he enumerates are precisely those which I would like to suggest give rise to this persistent play signal.[103] Elements like his "discontinuity," which resembles the "incongruity" often cited by humor theorists, instantiate comedy's insistence "this is play." After all, what may be the most important thing to get about jokes is that they *are* jokes (in the sense of "not serious"/bona-fide discourse).[104] Although some humor theorists would argue that this recognition is a first step *en route* to a joke's enjoyment, if one takes a Freudian view of jokes, this recognition *is* the joke's enjoyment.[105]

This constant, repetitive, but irresistible play signal – the one that, as metacommunication, lies outside of comedy's content and thus is so ungraspable for those who (naturally) feel that content is the source of comic joy – may help to clarify this hermeneutic problem of the "serious." The interpretations that one might apply to comedies as a whole – Aristophanes' stance on Cleon or his opinions about poetry, for example – can only favor content in all its variety over that monolithic symptom of play. Interpretation

---

[102] *Ach.* 1173; *Ran.* 173.   [103] I will discuss such formal features in Chapter 4.
[104] For "bona-fide discourse," see Raskin (1985) 140; Robson (2006) 78; Ruffell (2011) 86.
[105] I will discuss Freud's views in Chapter 4.

itself denies that repeated revelation – idiotic in its repetitiveness, really, yet irresistible – of the play signal. This favoring of content over symptom, I would argue, at the broadest level accounts for comedy's peculiar effect when it is interpreted: every literary allusion, every political opinion, every moral sentiment, every mythical background weights the text with significance beyond itself and through that very addition creates comedy's central loss. Although it has become customary to defend the significance of Old Comedy in terms of its political voice, its direct communication of values, its moral censure, such apologies may overlook that feature most central to the genre: what may be most significant about comedy is the lasting impression of its insignificance.

CHAPTER 4

Nonsense as "no-sense": jokes, puns, and language play

> – Does it mean anything, all this silliness?
> – Everything means something.
> – But where is the evil?
> – Amidst the silliness there is evil.
>
> Chorus of the Dishwashers from Lars von Trier's *The Kingdom*

To ask why something is "funny," or why something makes us laugh is probably similar to asking why babies are cute or why sex is so much fun: descriptions of formal features can only take us so far. One could say, of course, that "cuteness" lies in babies' little ears and noses, and that sexual pleasure lies in a certain form of friction (and then describe these features in minute detail), but such formal descriptions, no matter how exact, never quite capture *why* these things are pleasurable.[1] The real reason for these pleasures, it seems, is not a formal one at all: when considered in evolutionary terms, babies are perceived to be cute and sex is perceived to be pleasurable because, if they were not, humans would have been in trouble long ago. We, like many animals, are driven to the enjoyment of these things not because there is something necessarily pleasurable about them, but because they are, from nature's perspective, necessary for survival (and so the pleasures which accrete around them ensure their practice: i.e., humans continue to procreate and nurture their offspring).[2] In such evolutionary light, the formal features of babies and sex are rather arbitrary: like Xenophanes' horse-gods and cow-gods, sexual pleasure easily could

---

[1] And so, e.g., the experience of Ruffell (2011) who, after almost fifty pages of very complex formal analysis of comedy's "joke semiotics" (54–111), admits at 101: "Thus far, I have been skirting around the issue of whether there is anything specific to comedy that makes it *funny*" (his italics) and the instinct which follows: "It remains a possibility that there is something entirely non-structural which is central, or at least plays a role."

[2] Cf. Hurley, Dennett, and Adams (2011) 1–3 on the perception of sugar's "sweetness" in evolution as an analogy for humor.

have been derived from friction-free sex, and "cuteness" from babies with perfectly massive noses and ears.[3]

The same can be said of humor[4] or the comic (i.e., why some things are "funny" and this "funniness" pleasurable), especially when it is considered in terms of evolutionary play. This activity "play," which is shared by all mammals, occurs especially in the young, as though it has something to do with learning (e.g., exploring one's environment, practicing skills that one needs for "real" life, etc.).[5] If one considers, for example, play-fighting – a behavior found in many mammals – while it apparently is great fun to engage in this activity (and so the young especially are driven to it), at the same time this playful aggression appears to be somehow useful.[6] A great deal is being learned about one's own powers, the weaknesses of the body, the sensitive spots, the emotions that arise in conflict, all of which could be useful for real life, and real fighting. Nevertheless, even though an "educational" aspect of play has been noticed since Plato and Aristotle,[7] it would be a mistake to think that the pleasures of play arise *as* pleasures of education or usefulness: if one were to realize play's usefulness, it would become instantly boring. But just as with sex and babies, it can be argued, so with play: it is not that play is somehow "inherently" pleasurable, but its usefulness for animals is what has caused pleasures to accrete around the activities called "play."[8]

What does this have to do with comedy or humor? If one considers, again, playful aggression, it would seem that play has a lot to do with humor and comedy. Audiences take immense delight in playful aggression, especially

---

[3] See Lewontin (2010) for the pitfalls in arguing for evolutionary causation; cf. Laland and Brown (2002). My interests are not in tracing some evolutionary model of humor (see Veatch 1998), but rather in the theoretical shift away from formal descriptions that an evolutionary perspective allows.

[4] The term "humor" has undergone major changes in the past century. While now the term is very broad, often used as a category overarching any intentional utterance/act eliciting laughter, for earlier theorists (e.g., Freud) "humor" was very narrow. It was a category *separate* from jokes and the comic: specifically it involved those devices which replace painful emotions with laughter (e.g., self-deprecating humor, gallows humor). This is something often misunderstood – e.g., by those who think that Freud's later essay on "humor" (1927) covered and reconsidered the "comic" (cf. Hubbard (1991) 9), or the notion that early twentieth-century Japan had no concept of "humor," which can be true only in "humor's" narrowest sense. For different senses of the term "humor," see Ruch (1998).

[5] Burghardt (2005) 3–43 for review. His interests in finding "play" among non-mammals and avoidance of research on (human) infants shape his views against the common theory that play exists as instinctive practice/exploration (first in Groos (1898); see Thompson 1998 for a modern version). Other evolutionary explanations include play as a release of excess energy (first in Spencer (1872) 627–32, favored by Burghardt (2005) 30), and play as a result of sexual selection (Chick 2001).

[6] For an ancient example of play fighting (and its educational "uses"), see Chapter 3 on the mock battle in Xenophon's *Cyropaedia*.

[7] E.g., Pl. *Resp.* 7.536e–537a, Arist. *Pol.* 7.17 1336a33–4, with Halliwell (2008) 20–1.

[8] If one discerns a sort of "practice" behind "play," it is akin to the role of dreams described in recent studies (see Stickgold *et al.* 2001).

seeing on-stage victims suffer, whether it be Cinesias in *Birds* being chased around the stage, the Kinsman from *Thesmophoriazusae* being tortured in his stocks, Xanthias and Dionysus being whipped in *Frogs*, or other forms of physical abuse. If one turns to verbal forms of abuse, it would be hard to find five minutes of comedy without it – and so, many consider aggression to be a source, if not *the* source, of the "comic."[9] Like the aggression of play-fighting, this aggressive humor or aggressive behavior, whether it occurs in comedy or in conversation, often attempts to approach as close as possible to the "real" thing: a certain thrill lies in pushing toward that edge, and seeing how close one can approach "real" aggression without crossing the boundary.[10] This "educated hubris" (as Aristotle calls the right amount of play, *eutrapelia*[11]) often seems like something of a paradox in that the very things that make people uncomfortable (aggression, dangerous fighting, abuse, etc.) become in comedy (or humor) the things that they are thrilled by. But when one considers this phenomenon in terms of exploratory play, it is not so paradoxical at all: aggression *is* dangerous, and that is precisely why it needs to be explored and practiced through play. The closer one approaches the "real thing" while playing, the more thrilling the play; but the instant one crosses that boundary, all the dangers which were just being pleasurably explored become "real," and the pleasure or fun largely disappears.

Although this "play" explanation may work for some aspects of aggressive humor, what of verbal humor? A large number of jokes are not obviously aggressive, but rely purely on linguistic aberrations. Take puns, for instance: when Aristophanes writes ὑπὸ γέλωτος εἰς Γέλαν ἀφίξομαι "Conveyed by laughter, I'll go to Lafton," (fr. 629 KA) or "from this *pole* it will be called *polis*" ἐκ τοῦ πόλου τούτου κεκλήσεται πόλις (*Birds* 184), there is no trace of aggression, although everyone detects attempted humor in the lines. So, when humor theorists attempt to explain such examples, aggression theories vanish, and formal descriptions return with a vengeance. The long-familiar idea of "incongruence" becomes the consolation prize, and humor theorists dissect the punning sentence into its constituent parts, mapping the countless permutations such wordplay can involve.[12]

---

[9] Martin (1998) for overview.

[10] For the play-boundary, see the comedian Tina Fey's line "If you want to make an audience laugh, you dress a man up like an old lady and push her down the stairs. If you want to make comedy writers laugh, you push an actual old lady down the stairs" (M. Cavna, *Washington Post* 5/25/10). Cf. Lucas (1968) ad Arist. *Poet.* 1449a35.

[11] Arist. *Rh.*, 2.12, 1389b11–12: πεπαιδευμένη ὕβρις with Halliwell (2008) 322–3. Cf. Heath (2010) for a question regarding Halliwell's notion that play "transmutes" aggression.

[12] Incongruity, usually defined as contrasting ideas (but see Attardo (1994) 48 for a more expansive definition quoting McGhee (1979) 6–7), has been retranslated into numerous notions over the years

In this chapter, however, I would like to consider language play from this same perspective of exploratory play. I will do this by making the simple observation that those same verbal elements that are often marshaled as "comic techniques" (repetition, punning, rambling speech) often can produce very negative reactions as well – irritation, annoyance, disgust. This striking boundary between positive and negative reactions over the same material, or as John Morreall has recently described it "funny-ha ha" and "funny-strange" (cf. the German *komisch*), suggests something potentially negative about language play.[13] Whether this negative aspect has to do with perceived malfunctions in language and logic, or whether it is simply irritation over play which is deemed unjustified, it offers an opportunity to study an important aspect of nonsense that has not yet been discussed: not the nonsense which connotes positive experiences like play (which was the subject of Chapters 2 and 3), but the nonsense which connotes negative experiences like delirium (which will be the subject of this chapter and Chapter 5).

These two sides of nonsense – play and delirium – exhibit no clear boundary. Although I have been arguing that there is a certain pleasure found in the rejection of comic interpretation (the realization "this is nonsense"), one might imagine that, if this were in fact enjoyable, comedy could attain success by staging nothing more than Pseudartabas spouting his gibberish for hours (ἰαρταμαν ἐξαρξαν ...) or Socrates randomly playing with words like *aerobateo*.[14] In such scenarios, one is perfectly capable of realizing "this is nonsense," but such scenarios are not only foreign to comedy, but, furthermore, far from being enjoyable, would likely be irritating within the first minute, positively unbearable soon thereafter. Here it seems that the realization "this is nonsense," although available as a reaction, would not be pleasurable at all. Thus, this other connotation of nonsense from Chapter 1 – delirium – now needs a closer look.

Language play like the Aristophanic pun "Conveyed by laughter, I'll go to Lafton" is different from aggressive play like the mockery against Cinesias

---

like conflicting "frames" or "scripts." For breaking "frames," see Robson's (2006) 16–18 application of Goffman's (1974) concept of "frames" to humor (cf. the metaphor of the "frame" and "frame-breaking" already in Staiger (1946) and later applied to Aristophanic jokes in Kronauer (1954)). For opposing "scripts," see Raskin (1985); Attardo (1994); Lowe (2008) 8–11; Ruffell (2011) 86–96 (see Attardo (1994) 199 that the "notion of 'script'" is essentially that of the "frame"); Jernigan (1939) for an earlier study of incongruity in Aristophanes; Freud (1989[1905]) 6–9 for the incongruity theories current at his time.

[13] Morreall (1987); at 204: "Were we able to experience incongruity only in serious ways, our lives would be fraught with urgency. But because we can also enjoy incongruity, our lives have a certain play to them, 'play' in the obvious sense, and also in the older sense of slack or looseness." Cf. Morreall (2009) 27–68.

[14] See the introduction for discussion of these passages.

studied in the previous chapter. While the danger of aggressive play is that the play will become "real" (Cinesias will get angry, retaliate, etc.), the problem of language play is that the "real" is often nowhere to be found. Unlike aggressive play which is often rich in "sense" (e.g., "let's kill Socrates," "don't vote for Cleon"), language play often produces major obstacles to the articulation of such "sense." Although this obstructed articulation can often be irritating, as I will argue, this should not cause one to overestimate the role of sense or meaning in comedy's enjoyment: the perception of nonsense, despite its potential negative manifestations, is still a comic goal.

I will begin the chapter by considering two representative theorists who also detect a problem in language play. The first – Aristotle – argues that the pleasure of jokes (*asteia*) lies in the process of "getting" the joke, which he considers to be pleasurable learning (*manthanomai*). If one did not register such a "sense" (or "truth" as he calls it), the jokes would simply appear to be a mistake. But when Aristotle discusses this "mistake," he is clearly referring not to *any* mistake, but rather to something along the lines of Xenophon's qualification, "the type of mistake that most people never make," which, as I argued in Chapter 1, is central to the idea of "nonsense" and its connotation of delirium.

The second theorist – Freud – inverts Aristotle's belief that the pleasure of a joke lies in getting the joke's sense (or "learning" its "truth"), and argues instead that the pleasure dwells in the joke's "nonsense." The "sense" of the joke, on the other hand, acts as a mere decoy to keep the critical mind busy. The vital observation for Freud is that children do not need to discover a joke's "sense" in order to enjoy jokes, but instead take pleasure exclusively in perceiving the joke's "nonsense." This observation reveals for him the role that sense plays in jokes for adults: it is not a source of pleasure, but rather a safety-net for it.[15] There are many ways this view resembles that of Bateson discussed in the previous chapter and I will discuss these resemblances at the end.

Freud's notions offer a way forward in approaching the central question of this chapter ("if the discovery of nonsense is some central comic pleasure, why is comedy not all Pseudartaban gibberish?"). Freud's notions, however, are also rather abstract, so examples are necessary.

[15] Freud's argument about jokes and "sense" seems to be analogous to the experience of throwing a child into the air: although it is critical to catch the free-falling child, it would be a mistake to locate the child's pleasure in being caught rather than the thrill of free-fall. For Freud, "sense" is critical in the same way.

First I turn to comedy's puns and wordplay, especially so-called "bad" puns in order to approach this idea that the perception of nonsense, which can be so negative, is nevertheless a comic goal. Rather than seeing such puns as "feeble" or "failing," as they are often described, I argue that they reveal an aspect of Aristophanic poetics where the production of "sense "is not necessarily the aim. I develop this idea in the following section on comic coinages, where I locate Michael Silk's notion of comic "exuberance" in this habit of playing with words past the point of any easy articulation of sense. Considering further the idea of the "comic climaxes" discussed in Chapter 2 – namely, those moments in comedy when one does not know what one is laughing at (e.g., no discernible "punchline") – I examine the final coinage of the *Ecclesiazusae* and relate it to Freud's idea that jokes "replace high spirits" just as "high spirits replace jokes." At such points, a comedy of Pseudartaban gibberish seems the faintest possibility: it is not that such comedy would be impossible, but that the heightened mood required for such comedy would be highly difficult to achieve. I reinforce this idea by considering the resemblances between such climaxes and delirium in the following section where I study a moment of verbal repetition in the *Thesmophoriazusae*. Like the final word of *Ecclesiazusae* this moment of repetition could be indefinitely extended, but it is a dangerous game to play and a volatile material to play with. The chapter ends with a rambling speech from Antiphanes' *Cleophanes*.

So, it is true that comedy is not all Pseudartaban gibberish, not least because the perception of nonsense is often a negative experience. Nonetheless, as I argue in this chapter, such delirium is not just a problem lurking behind comedy but, paradoxically, like the aggression discussed at the beginning of this introduction, its aim. As I will argue, most of the time, potentially negative experiences are avoided through the appearance of "sense" and the assurance that meaningful communication is still occurring on the comic stage. But sometimes, when the moment and conditions are right, a long passage of repetitive language, of rambling speech or of gibberish, can create an extended comic climax. At such a point, the audience can laugh without needing something to laugh at, and like children (or other "mentally impaired" creatures), they can enjoy mastery over the meaningless, without mastering it with meaning.[16]

---

[16] Some studying the behavior of infants observe laughter first arising in situations of perceived mastery – see Schultz (1996[1976]) for different studies. One thinks of the first part of Hobbes' famous "laughter as superiority" definition: "laughter is nothing else but sudden glory arising from sudden conception of some eminency in ourselves . . ."

Aristotle on how to play with words (and still make sense)

What separates a good pun from a bad pun? Not much. Although many jokes hinge on a word used in more than one sense, such wordplay is often subtle and lies in the background of the joke.[17] Puns, on the other hand, seem to advertise their wordplay, as if the play on words is what the joke is "about." The language is slave to sound rather than sense, and, for that reason, puns are often felt to be "groaners," and the lowest class of jokes.[18] But even within the class of puns, there exists a spectrum – in fact, that same spectrum: the ones that are deemed best are not simply following the pre-existing homophony of a language's matrix, but are applying that homophony to a situation's needs: creating the senses, purposes, and forces that language is meant to create.

This is, in any case, how Aristotle treats puns. The best puns are those which create an opportunity for a new idea to be expressed. In the *Rhetoric*, Aristotle touches on wordplay briefly while discussing the broader category of "*to asteion*," a term which literally means "urbane," but, like the Latin *urbanus*, covers ideas like "witty," "lively," and "clever."[19] When used substantively, *ta asteia* can mean, as Halliwell puts it "witty remarks or *bon mots* which spring a kind of cognitive surprise, giving hearers something new to grasp or understand."[20] The pleasure of such *asteia*, for Aristotle, resides in that new understanding or learning (*mathēsis*), since "Learning easily is pleasurable for everyone by nature" (τὸ γὰρ μανθάνειν ῥαδίως ἡδὺ φύσει πᾶσιν ἐστί, 3.10.2, 1410b9–10). Following that premise, Aristotle argues that a phrase which causes the mind both "to search" (ζητεῖ τοῦτο ἡ ψυχή, 3.10.3, 1410b20) and, through that searching, to learn something quickly (ποιεῖ ἡμῖν μάθησιν ταχεῖαν, 3.10.4, 1410b21), creates pleasure – and the phrase which creates this sort of pleasure is *asteion*, "clever, lively, witty."

Although this category applies to a number of tropes and utterances – metaphors, antitheses, riddles, apothegms, etc. – its pertinence to jokes and

---

[17] Cognitive humor theorists lately refer to words used in two ways as the "connector" of a joke (Attardo (1994) *passim*). Such theorists often describe a joke as operating in two different scripts or frames, with the "connector" toggling between the two.

[18] See Redfern (1986); Culler (1988) 4: "To groan at puns, one might conjecture, is viscerally to reaffirm a distinction between essence and accident, between meaningful relations and coincidence, that has seemed fundamental for our thinking." Attardo (1994) 108–70 for further bibliography on puns.

[19] See Schenkeveld (1994) for the history of the term and further bibliography. Its obvious opposite is *agroikos* "boorish, uncultured" (lit. "of the country") – but as will be seen below, in rhetorical terms it is often opposed to *psychros* (lit. "cold"), that which "falls flat" either as a joke or as an attempt at loftiness.

[20] Halliwell (2008) 328 n. 168.

puns is what is of interest here. Puns and wordplay also can create an opportunity to "learn" something, and, owing to the brevity of such expressions, learn something "quickly."[21] After discussing metaphors, similes, and the element of "deception" in clever remarks, Aristotle briefly turns his attention to puns or wordplay (3.11.6, 1412a33–1412b3):

τὰ δὲ παρὰ γράμμα ποιεῖ οὐχ ὃ λέγει λέγειν, ἀλλ᾽ ὃ μεταστρέφει ὄνομα, οἷον τὸ Θεοδώρου εἰς Νίκωνα τὸν κιθαρῳδόν "θράττει σε·" προσποιεῖται γὰρ λέγειν τὸ "θράττει σε" καὶ ἐξαπατᾷ· ἄλλο γὰρ λέγει· διὸ μαθόντι ἡδύ, ἐπεὶ εἰ μὴ ὑπολαμβάνει Θρᾷκα εἶναι, οὐ δόξει ἀστεῖον εἶναι.

Changes of letter [as in a pun] make the speaker mean not what he says but what the word plays on, like the remark of Theodorus to Nikon the harpist, *Thrattei se*. He pretends to say "It disturbs you" and deceives, for he means something different. Thus it is pleasing to the learner, but if the latter does not understand that Nikon was a Thracian [barbarian] it will not seem urbane. (trans. Kennedy (2007))

Although the text here might be more aggressively emended,[22] I will follow Cope's emendation and explanation of this pun. Cope, who removes the first σε,[23] argues that the θραττ- pun plays on θράττει "it disturbs [you]" and Θρᾷττ᾽ εἶ "you're a Thracian (f.)." He explains: "This person is addressed by Theodorus with the word θράττει which means *apparently*, 'You are confounded' . . . It *really* means, however, Θρᾷττ᾽ εἶ, 'You are a Thracian maid-servant,' not only an out-and-out barbarian, but effeminate to boot, and a menial."[24] Other explanations have been offered, all following Aristotle's cue that the joke turns on Nicon's Thracian status,[25] but, ultimately, it makes little difference which of these emendations is followed

---

[21] For the importance of condensed form for Aristotle to make an expression "witty", see his discussion of the fourth-century comedian Anaxandrides's apothegm (3.11.8–10, 1412b15–32): he translates the line into a number of versions which are not in the same form, and thus not witty.

[22] Following Cooper (1920) 53–4, who argues for a colloquial word *θράττω meaning "thrum" a lyre (citing the lyre-imitation φλαττοθραττοφλαττόθρατ of *Ran.* 1286–95, the θρεττανελό of *Plut.* 290, 296 and especially the musical line of Mnesimachus' *Hippotrophos* (v. 57 μολπά, κλαγγά, θράττει, πνεῖται), but not following his textual conjecture θράττεις, the original pun might have been between the imperative θράττε ("Strum [the lyre]!") and Θρᾷττ᾽ εἶ ("You're a Thracian [f.]"). Perhaps the later tradition, unaware of that colloquial verb, either added the σε to fit the known verb θράττω "to disturb" or emended from a possible συ. To be added to Cooper's evidence is the lyre-maker Cleophon (known to be a lyre-maker from oratory) whom only comic poets refer to as "Thracian" (see Austin and Olson's note at *Thesm.* 805). Noteworthy too is Orpheus' dismemberment by Thracian women: perhaps, a jab at Nicon's music?

[23] Cope 133: "we must first remove from the text the first σε . . . which has been introduced from the second (where it is required) . . . the first σε must be an error of the transcriber."

[24] Cope 133.

[25] Alternatively, perhaps "Thracian" was a more generic insult, akin to something like a "boor."

here.[26] What is important is the aspect of wordplay that most interests Aristotle: that the pleasure of a pun arrives through the process of "learning" (διὸ μανθόντι ἡδύ). But what exactly is being "learned" here? It cannot be that the listener has "learned" that Nicon is a Thracian, since, as Aristotle continues to say, the witticism's "learning" effect requires a pre-existing knowledge of Nicon's origins (ἐπεὶ εἰ μὴ ὑπολαμβάνει Θρᾷκα εἶναι, οὐ δόξει ἀστεῖον εἶναι). The "learning" involved here, rather, seems to be something close to the colloquial English idea of "getting" something (a joke, an idea, etc.). If listeners know that Nicon is a Thracian ahead of time, they will be able to "get" the joke, and thus the phrase will be *asteion*. If not, the joke's recipients (using Cope's translation of οὐ δόξει ἀστεῖον εἶναι) "will see no point in it at all."

Thus, Aristotle is envisioning two possible scenarios of reception for this wordplay: in the scenario where Nicon's ethnicity is not known, the phrase presumably just seems odd – there is some sort of mispronunciation (τὰ δὲ παρὰ γράμμα) involved in the phrase "it confounds you," sounding rather like some phrase about Thracians. In the second scenario, however, there is a "point" to "get," or as Aristotle puts it, there is "learning." What precisely is being "learned," however, is uncertain. The "point" as Cope would have it seems to be some sort of (playful) negative judgment on Nicon: he is a barbarian, an effeminate, a menial, and so forth (i.e., "Thracian maid-servant"). But how that recognition of a playful judgment constitutes any "learning" or new knowledge is far from clear.[27] That it is difficult to articulate what the *mathēsis* is may correspond to the fact that it is often difficult to articulate what one has "gotten" about a joke, despite the certainty that one has indeed "got" it.[28]

---

[26] Kassel (1976), following the mss., simply prints θράττει σε twice, wherein there is, of course, no τὰ δὲ παρὰ γράμμα at all. Ross (1959) aggressively emends to θράξει σε and θρᾷξ εἶ σύ, just to make the Thracian masculine. Meineke (1970[1834]) discerns the Thracian singing with the phrase θρᾷττ᾿ ἦσε. Cooper (1920) imagines θράττεις "you strum" with a lingering sigma that becomes σε or συ to activate a Thracian pun.

[27] See Halliwell (2002) 188–93 (especially 191 n. 38 on this passage) regarding the mistake of reducing Aristotle's *manthanein* to learning "information" and missing thereby "the rich potential of the philosopher's verb" (187).

[28] In any case, as Aristotle makes clear, the *mathēsis* of a phrase ought not be confused with the subject of Chapter 2, a phrase's "reference" (of metaphors, riddles, etc.). In that chapter, I used "reference" in terms, e.g., of a metaphor's "tenor." That is, in the metaphor the "old age is a reed," the "old age" is the "reed"-metaphor's reference (tenor). But the *mathēsis*, for Aristotle, involves the *interaction* between "reed" and "old age" (3.10.2, 1410b12–14): "Metaphor especially creates this [learning]: for whenever [Homer] calls old age a reed, he creates learning and knowledge (μάθησιν καὶ γνῶσιν) through the genus: for both are things which have lost their bloom."

Another pun that is less obscure to commentators[29] is shown by Aristotle to be "witty" (*asteion*) along the same lines as the Thracian pun (3.11, 1412b11–14):

> ἐν ἅπασι δὲ τούτοις, ἐὰν προσηκόντως τὸ ὄνομα ἐνέγκῃ ὁμωνυμία ἢ μεταφορά, τότε τὸ εὖ. οἷον "Ἀνάσχετος οὐκ ἀνάσχετος"· ὁμωνυμίαν ἀπέφησεν, ἀλλὰ προσηκόντως, εἰ ἀηδής.

> In all these cases, if a word is introduced appropriately, either as a homonym or a metaphor, it is well done. For example, "Mr. Baring is unbearable". The homonym is negated, but appropriately if he is unpleasant. (trans. Kennedy)

Like the first pun which requires the listener to know that the harpist is a Thracian in order that the phrase be received as "witty," here the wordplay also requires a pre-existing understanding for that cognitive spring to be sprung – namely, a sort of contextual awareness which Aristotle glosses as saying something "appropriately" (προσηκόντως). Two scenarios again are envisioned: one where Mr. Baring is not recognizably unbearable, the other where he is. In the first scenario, since the wordplay is "inappropriate," it creates no opportunity for learning, and thus is not at all "clever." Like the Thracian wordplay where the listener does not know that the harpist is Thracian, the inappropriate phrase seems to be "pointless."[30] In the second scenario, the stage is properly set where the listener already understands that Mr. Baring is a rather vile character. Only in this scenario can there be something to "get," a "point" to it, or as Aristotle would have it, something to "learn." What exactly that *mathēsis* is, is again difficult to articulate: it again seems to be a judgment of sorts, a new knowledge (or quasi-knowledge) about Mr. Baring's character, or, perhaps, the speaker's opinion about his character.

Thus, a "witty" or "clever" pun, in Aristotle's opinion, is one where there is a "point," something to "learn," or at least, in the close English idiom, something to "get" (although what that something is often seems to be elusive). The question that is of interest here has more to do with Aristotle's former scenarios: if a wordplay is *asteion* when there is a "point," when there is some sort of cognitive sense to capture, what would Aristotle call wordplay

---

[29] An off-hand pun that comes between these two is βούλει αὐτὸν πέρσαι (3.11.7, 1412b3). Some, like Kennedy (2007), think the pun lies in *Persae*, others like Cope (1973[1877]) 133–4 that it turns on *boulē* ("may the council destroy him").

[30] This is something different from Aristotle's term *epipolaios* (lit. "on the surface"), which refers to enthymemes which are too easy, too ordinary, and thus not popular: 3.10.4, 1410b22–3: ἐπιπόλαια γὰρ λέγομεν τὰ παντὶ δῆλα, καὶ ἃ μηδὲν δεῖ ζητῆσαι "for we mean by 'superficial' the ones which are clear to everyone and there is no need at all to ponder them." A faulty pun, on the other hand, causes one to ponder but come up empty-handed in the search for sense.

where there is no "point," no *mathēsis*? That is, what is that phenomenon when the unfortunate punster implies that a (perceived-to-be) non-Thracian harpist is a Thracian, or an entirely endurable Mr. Baring is nothing of the sort? Perhaps Aristotle would call such a pun *psychron* – a negative aesthetic judgment which generally denotes any attempted rhetorical effect which "falls flat" (to use our idiom).[31] In the context of jokes, it is something like our "groaners," "lame" jokes, or "bad puns." One finds, for example, in Eupolis a joke (σκῶμμα) criticized as *psychron*,[32] and, later, in the third century, Timocles calls a pun *psychron*[33] (also in Alexis and Machon[34]); in Xenophon's *Symposium* as well, Socrates admits to forcing a "lame" pun (speaking *psychra*).[35] But even in these cases of "bad" or "strained" puns there is still something to "get," some sort of "learning": it just seems that their error lies in not creating a significant enough "learning" to warrant the wordplay.

On the other hand, regarding Aristotle's hypothetical scenarios where the "Thracian" and "unbearable" puns are *not* witty, it seems that the label "bad" or "*psychron*" does not quite do these phenomena justice. It is not just that a rhetorical effect has been attempted which leaves the audience "cold," but rather that the language containing the wordplay itself does not quite seem to make "sense." Aristotle's two imagined non-*asteion* scenarios recall something more like J. L. Austin's concept of the pragmatic "misfire" – a kind of mistake where words (in this case wordplay) do not adequately reflect the situations in which they are uttered (such "misfires," incidentally, being adopted by Stierle (1976) and Kloss (2001) as the source of comic speech/action).[36] In the first case, a person plays with the word *thrattei* even though there is no context to warrant any mention of Thracians; in the

---

[31] Aristotle discusses *ta psychra* at 3.3.1–4, 1405b34–1406b14 regarding more serious oratory, not puns (but cf. his interesting observation of the risibility of certain "frigid" metaphors at 3.3.4, 1406a32–4). Although *to psychron* is often opposed to that which is *asteion* (cf. Isoc. *Ad Nic.* 34), it should be noted that "not-*asteion*" is not necessarily *psychron* (cf., e.g., n. 21 on Anaxandrides where Aristotle rewrites the comedian's *asteion* phrase in a number of non-*asteion* ways, none of which would be *psychron*). Rather, the rhetorical effect must be *attempted*, and then fail. For useful citations and discussion of the term, see Austin and Olson (2004) 114; Kaimio and Nykopp (1997) 27–9; Van Hook (1917) 68–76; Gutzwiller (1969) 16–26; Halliwell (2008) 317 n. 145, Wright (2012) 108–10.

[32] Eup. fr. 261 KA: Ἡράκλεις, τοῦτ ἔστι σοι / τὸ σκῶμμ' ἀσελγὲς καὶ Μεγαρικὸν καὶ σφόδρα / ψυχρόν with Austin and Olson (2004) 14 glossing *psychron* here as "a vulgar childish joke."

[33] A "bad" pun on Tereus and the verb τηρεῖν (fr. 19 KA).

[34] Alexis fr. 184.3 KA regarding Araros; Machon fr. 16.281–4 Gow regarding Diphilus.

[35] *Symp.* 6.7: Socrates puns on the Syracusan's ἀνωφελεστάτων with ἄνωθεν . . . ὠφελοῦσιν.

[36] See Austin (2000[1962]) 12–24 for "infelicities" and "misfires;" Kloss (2001), who, following Stierle (1976), sees the source of the comic in the pragmatic (Austinian) "failure" of speech/action. For Aristotle the pun must *reflect* context, not fail it. Although Austin's examples of "misfires" (e.g., marrying a monkey) often strike the reader as comical, it should be noticed that he refers to these not as "comic" but as "nonsense" (4).

second case, a person plays with the word *anaskhetos* although the context, again, does not allow for it: the cognitive mind of the listener is being led to certain places (e.g., "Thracian," "unbearable") but without any particular reason. On the other hand, a proper relationship between the wordplay and the situation (something said appropriately, προσηκόντως) activates these puns' more regularized cognitive springs (and the accordant pleasures involved). Those puns that reside fully outside of appropriate context cannot create that pleasurable "learning" and the cognitive movement seems to be going in other directions.

If such a spectrum of *mathēsis* between good and bad puns does exist – to wit: a good pun has a "point," while a bad one threatens to have no "point" at all – some more examination is needed of this opposite end of the spectrum (that imagined ideal where wordplay creates no "learning" at all). Elsewhere, Aristotle treats homonymy specifically as a device by which one may reach falsehood or fallacy (which is to say words not reflecting reality). It seems that by following a language's pre-existing homophony one can produce statements wherein one's words (*lexis/verba*) do not accurately map on to reality's extra-linguistic references (*pragmata/res*). Aristotle's homonymies are very subtle indeed (thanks to the strict standards of logic), and consist of the types of mistakes *most people make* when uttering statements about the world. Aristotle insists that one should not, for example, misuse *manthanein* to mean "learn," when one means it in the sense of "know"; or the verb *dei* as "ought to be" when one means it as "must be."[37] If one misuses words in such a way, one is bound to create a falsehood (ψεῦδος) or, more precisely, "a false illusion in connection with language" (τὰ μὲν παρὰ τὴν λέξιν ἐμποιοῦντα τὴν φαντασίαν, *Soph. el.* 165b24–5, trans. Forster) – much the same way as one who miscalculates on the abacus will confuse the pebbles' result with reality.[38] This sort of homophony, however (when compared with the puns discussed above), is rather hair-splitting, since the differences between the meanings and uses of a single word generate the sorts of mistakes that most people make with

---

[37] *Soph. el.* 165b33: τὸ γὰρ μανθάνειν ὁμώνυμον, τό τε ξυνιέναι χρώμενον τῇ ἐπιστήμῃ καὶ τὸ λαμβάνειν ἐπιστήμην. . . . διττὸν γὰρ τὸ δέον, τό τ᾽ἀναγκαῖον, ὃ συμβαίνει πολλάκις καὶ ἐπὶ τῶν κακῶν (ἔστι γὰρ κακόν τι ἀναγκαῖον), καὶ τἀγαθὰ δὲ δέοντά φαμεν εἶναι. "For here 'to learn' is a homonym, meaning both 'understand by using knowledge' and 'acquire knowledge' . . . Here 'must exist' is used in two senses; it means 'what is necessary,' which is often true of evils (for some evil is necessary), and we also say that good things 'ought to be'" (trans. Forster, modified). See Janko (2002[1984]) 169–71 for more citations of Aristotle's discussions of homonyms; Barnes (1971) for his different sense of "homonym" in logic.

[38] For the exciting analogy, see *Soph. el.* 165a6–31. Cf. Fait (1996).

language.[39] With puns and wordplay, however, there is a much higher order of homophonic mistake: no speaker would *actually* confuse Mr. Anaskhetos with the adjective ἀνάσχετος, or the word for "Thracian" with the verb θράττω.

Yet, considering the homophony of wordplay in the context of such mistakes allows for a better understanding of that opposite end of the *mathēsis* spectrum, discussed above. It will be remembered from Chapter 1 that Xenophon's Socrates made the distinction between mistakes that "most people" make and those that few make in order to define mental illness (*Mem.* 3.9.6). This distinction became an important part of Chapter 1's argument distinguishing "nonsense" (*phluaria*, *lēros*) from more general "falsehood" (*pseudea*). This same distinction can be seen operating here regarding homophony: while most people might be deceived by statements relying on the kind of homophonic mistakes discussed in *Sophistici Elenchi* (e.g., the difference between *dei* "must" and *dei* "ought"), no one would be deceived by statements relying on more obvious homophonic errors, such as *arkhē* (empire) and *arkhē* (beginning). Yet, it is precisely this higher order of errors which Aristotle stresses in his discussion of *asteia* (3.11.7, 1412b4–8):

> οὕτω δὲ καὶ τὰ ἀστεῖα, οἷον τὸ φάναι Ἀθηναίοις τὴν τῆς θαλάττης ἀρχὴν μὴ ἀρχὴν εἶναι τῶν κακῶν· ὄνασθαι γάρ. ἢ ὥσπερ Ἰσοκράτης τὴν ἀρχὴν τῇ πόλει ἀρχὴν εἶναι τῶν κακῶν. ἀμφοτέρως γὰρ ὃ οὐκ ἂν ᾠήθη τις ἐρεῖν, τοῦτ᾽εἴρηται, καὶ ἐγνώσθη ὅτι ἀληθές.

> And so likewise in witticisms, pointed sayings *in general*, as to say that "to the Athenians the *command* of the sea was not the *beginning* of their misfortunes"; for they derived benefit from it. Or, as Isocrates puts it, that "the command was to the city the beginning of her calamities." For in both cases that is said which one would not suppose likely to be said by any one, and (yet, at the same time) is recognised as true. (Cope's translation with glosses abridged)

That relative clause of the last sentence is the most important here (ὃ οὐκ ἂν ᾠήθη τις ἐρεῖν): Cope explains his translation with, "*lit.* which one would not suppose that any one, τινά, would say." Just as with Xenophon's orders of mistakes, so too here, Aristotle stresses normative values and expectations: one would not expect anyone to say an *arkhē* (empire) is an *arkhē* (beginning), presumably because such confusion is the sort of homonymic error that no one would make. Yet, this initial supposition of an error is only

---

[39] Consider, e.g., the anecdote of Wittgenstein and Fania Pascal as told by Frankfurt (2005) 24–34. The higher the standard of logic, the more "non-sense" one sees in common language.

the first part of the statement's reception – the first movement, as it were. That all-important counter-movement which follows is the recognition that the statement *does* in fact correspond to reality: "it is recognized that it is true" (καὶ ἐγνώσθη ὅτι ἀληθές)[40] – a movement often described by recent humor theorists as a "resolution."[41]

It is that recognition of the ἀληθές element which also distinguishes the "witty" Thracian/Unbearable puns discussed above from the hypothetical homophonic "misfires" (where Nicon is not a Thracian, etc.). If, for example, Isocrates had said that the command of the sea (ἀρχή) was the beginning (ἀρχή) of the day (instead of "troubles"), this would be received rather like the infelicitous Thracian and Unbearable puns: there is no corresponding reality for this utterance to catch, no ἀληθές element. To put it in Aristotle's terms in the *Sophistici Elenchi*, such homonymic utterances create "a false illusion in connection with language" – only, with wordplay, the "mistake" is of a much higher order.

If the "witty" (*asteion*) pun requires a "learning" (some "point" to "get"), the opposite side would have no "learning," no "truth" element at all. It would be a homophonic mistake pure and simple – an utterance, which, through homophony, becomes unreflective of reality. But as an utterance based on a mistake which is made not by many people (e.g., *dei* ought and *dei* must) but by very few people (e.g., *arkhē* empire and *arkhē* beginning), what has been articulated here is the definition of "nonsense" as it was described in Chapter 1. Unlike jokes or "witty" puns, the pleasure of which (according to Aristotle) seems to arise from that *mathēsis* or "truth" element, the opposite side produces a "senseless" language where there seems to be nothing to "get." If one imagines the "nonsense" scenarios described in this section – the misfired Thracian/Unbearable wordplay, or the hypothetical "the rule of the sea was the beginning of the day" – one can see that none of these scenarios would be pleasurable in the way that humor is pleasurable: laughter is not the obvious response. Rather, one might expect perhaps a certain irritation to arise – the irritation of the mistake, of language produced which is not functioning properly.

When considering such puns occupying positions on Aristotle's *mathēsis* spectrum, it becomes clearer what the source of the negative reaction to a

---

[40] Aristotle introduces this section of the *Rhetoric* dealing with this deceptive element of (some) witty or clever remarks (ἐκ τοῦ προσεξαπατᾶν) with the description of the soul's reaction to such utterances (which, as I have explained it, seem to be "mistakes" but, in fact, are not): καὶ ἔοικε λέγειν ἡ ψυχὴ "ὡς ἀληθῶς, ἐγὼ δ' ἥμαρτον." "And the soul seems to say 'how true, and I was wrong'" (3.11.6).

[41] See Attardo (1994) 4–9, 143–73 for "resolution" discussion, although his argument that puns have inherent resolutions due to a Cratylist folk theory of language (152–3) seems backward.

"bad" pun consists of: there does not seem to be "point" enough, it is verging too close to that opposite side of the spectrum – where sentences are being produced *via* homophony without any recognition of the need to produce "sense."[42] This is a rather anxious prospect, and would not be particularly pleasurable to listen to. In such a case, a listener's cognitive mind is being led to places that do not reflect the context of communication (e.g., "Thracian" and "unbearable"), and, I would argue, this forced mental wandering can create certain negative responses.

Aristotle's view is representative of a common notion: namely, that the pleasure of jokes lies in "getting" them, in registering their "sense." To return to the hypothetical scenario posed at the beginning of this chapter, it is fairly clear why Pseudartabas spouting gibberish for hours on end would not be the stuff of comedy. Such comedy would not be full of witticisms (*asteia*), according to Aristotle, but full of "mistakes." Like the recognition of any mistake, "this is nonsense" would primarily be a negative reaction; positive reactions, on the other hand, would arise from registering "sense," whatever that "sense" may be.

Freud and the "nonsense" part of jokes

Aristotle explains that the pleasure of a joke lies in discovering its "sense," or, more precisely, in "learning" something. The problem, as I have suggested, is that it is not often clear what one has "gotten" or "learned" when one has "gotten" a joke, and the alleged "sense" often seems, as Nick Lowe has nicely articulated it, a "flickering illusion of a meaningful proposition."[43] So while Aristotle based his observations on the intuition that a joke's pleasure arises from "getting" the joke, Freud acknowledges that what is "gotten" about a joke is often elusive, and thus may not be the source of pleasure at all. The true pleasure, he argues, arises not from a joke's "sense" (*Sinn*), but its "nonsense" (*Unsinn*).[44] Instead of creating pleasure, the "sense" part of a joke functions simply to "conceal" the nonsense, which,

---

[42] One might expect Aristotle to discuss puns in terms of technique as he does with Anaxandrides' apothegm; e.g., the homonymic play involved in double entendres leaves something unsaid (the enthymemic core of cognitive *asteia*), while puns often are (overly) obvious because they state the homonym twice (e.g. the *anaskhetos* pun). But instead Aristotle focuses on the appropriateness of context for good and bad puns.

[43] Lowe (2008) 9.

[44] Freud (1989[1905]) chapter IV "The Mechanism of Pleasure and the Psychogenesis of Jokes" 143–70, especially 160–70. Cf. the summary of the book on 293.

on its own, would not be pleasurable.[45] This rather odd idea is based on an objective and important observation about children – one supported by later experiments – namely, that children (approximately up to age six[46]), cannot "get" jokes at all (i.e., articulate their "sense" or "point"), although they take pleasure in them.[47] Instead, it seems that children enjoy hearing and producing language that is perceived as "nonsense" (e.g., rhyming words, meaningless syllables, etc.). So, for example, if a child heard Aristophanes' rather *psychron* or "pointless" pun ὑπὸ γέλωτος εἰς Γέλαν ἀφίξομαι "I'll go to Lafton conveyed by laughter," the enjoyment would be no different than the most "pointed" of jokes, it is argued, because it is purely the meaningless *gel-* play (and no more) that is the pleasure-creator (Aristotle's *mathēsis* being a null object for children). After children – through language development – *learn* to joke (e.g., develop an ability to detect ambiguities), and appreciate the "point" of jokes, there is a sharp decrease in enjoyment of the former language play. Instead of deriving pleasure from "pointless" homophony, repetition, and general wordplay, there is a recoil against such childishness.[48]

Coupled with this important observation about children is his related observation regarding mood (155–6, my italics):

> A cheerful mood, whether it is produced endogenously or toxically, reduces the inhibiting forces, criticism among them, and makes accessible once again sources of pleasure which were under the weight of suppression. It is most instructive to observe *how the standards of joking sink as spirits rise. For high spirits replace jokes, just as jokes must try to replace high spirits* . . . Under the influence of alcohol the grown man once more becomes a child, who finds pleasure in having the course of his thoughts freely at his disposal without paying regard to the compulsion of logic.

When one is intoxicated or in high spirits, it seems, one requires much less "sense" in one's jokes: the very jokes or puns that might cause one to recoil in a sober state become somehow funny in an intoxicated or joyful one

---

[45] For "concealing," see Freud (1989[1905]) 64, 71, 253; at 160: "The two fixed points in what determines the nature of jokes . . . immediately explain why an individual joke, though it may seem senseless from one point of view, must appear sensible, or at least allowable, from another. How it does so remains the affair of the joke-work; if it fails to do so, it is simply rejected as 'nonsense.'"

[46] Schultz (1996[1976]); cf. Attardo (1994) 143 n. 1 for other studies.   [47] Freud (1989[1905]) 153–9.

[48] Freud (1989[1905]) 153–5. For an interesting theory of "silliness" (*Blödeln*) as social reaction, see Wellershoff (1976). Kloss (2001) 13 takes the heightened mood of silliness (described, e.g., in Freud (1989[1905]) 155–6) to incite *increased* cognitive activity (e.g., searching for double meanings, etc.). But this is not what Freud is referring to regarding heightened mood, where he argues that one does not *need* to discover meanings when in a heightened mood (see below).

(here too can be recalled the presence of children and the inebriated in the ancient theater audience).[49] The question that follows is: if adults require less "sense" in their jokes when intoxicated, and children (who are in some way already "mentally impaired") require none, what does this suggest about the role of "sense" in jokes? Freud's answer to this question is that jokes "conceal" nonsense with "sense" in order to make the pleasures of nonsense enjoyable. Owing to the necessary developments of language and logic which make daily interactions and communication possible, a high standard is set on functional language and a sharp devaluation on useless language (e.g., language which seems not to map on to reality, endlessly repeated phrases, phrases based on senseless rhyming, etc.).[50] For that reason, little enjoyment is created by such useless language on its own – in fact, it is usually very irritating – and, thus, that childish pleasure can only be accessed by adults via "sense" or the illusion of "sense."

Since Freud believes that there is some impulsive resistance against "useless" language, and that one therefore requires an illusion whereby language might *seem* useful, it follows for him that contemporariness (i.e., reference to surroundings or matters of immediate concern) and aggression (i.e., a clear *purpose* of the language) would be two highly useful tools in providing that illusion. Freud discusses both of these – "contemporary relevance" (*Aktualität*)[51] and (aggressive) purpose (*Tendenz*) – at length, specifically as tools for creating such an illusion of sense. As with the behavior of children, his ideas are based on an objective and important observation: that people often laugh much more intensely at contemporary jokes or aggressive jokes than ones that are purely verbal (which he

---

[49] For children in the ancient theater audience, see Olson's (1998) note ad *Peace* 50–3; Henderson (1991) 135 n. 7. For inebriated people in the audience, see Philoch. *FGrH* 328 F 171 with Bowie (1995) 113; for an interesting analogy between comedy and alcohol, see Ar. *Pol.* 7, 1336b20, where he claims that children must be exposed to such things only after they have been made immune (*apatheis*) to them by education.

[50] Freud (1989[1905]) 153: "'Pleasure in nonsense,' as we may call it for short, is concealed in serious life to a vanishing point."

[51] "Topicality" being Strachey's translation for Freud's "Aktualität." At 149: "There are jokes which are completely independent of this condition [contemporary relevance/topicalty/*Aktualität*], and in a monograph on jokes we are obliged to make almost exclusive use of examples of that kind. But we cannot forget that, in comparison with these perennial jokes, we have perhaps laughed even more heartily at others which it is difficult for us to use now because they would call for long commentaries and even with such help would not produce their original effect. These latter jokes contained allusions to people and events which at the time were 'topical', which had aroused general interest and still kept it alive. When this interest had ceased … these jokes too lost a part of their pleasurable effect and indeed a very considerable part."

differentiates as "jests").[52] I do not think this observation can be contested, whatever one makes of his analysis: a verbal joke containing aggression against Cleon or Cleonymus is likely to receive more laughs than a purely verbal joke like the *gel-* pun (a potential "groaner").[53] In such cases, according to Freud, the "nonsense" of jokes becomes hidden within the aggression: that is, the critical mind can focus on senses like "Cleon is a fool," "Cleonymus is fat," while the pleasures of nonsense are enjoyed more intensely. In Freud's view, then, the "sense" of a joke is largely an illusion: jokes function by hiding useless language (perceived nonsense) in what would seem to be useful, in this case aggressive language.

Considering how important "nonsense" is for Freud, it is unfortunate that the word has so many meanings in his book. He identifies certain illogical sentences as, objectively, "nonsense";[54] other times it seems to be something extra-linguistic, a "nonsense" which gets "liberated."[55] Sometimes nonsense is positive ("the pleasures of nonsense"),[56] sometimes it is negative (the "nonsense" which gets "rejected").[57] Sometimes "nonsense" is the result of play, other times it is virtually synonymous with "play."[58] On top of this, there are "nonsense-jokes" and "comic-nonsense" which seem to bring him to the point of *aporia* on the subject.[59] But at least one of Freud's elisions is important here: namely, that the perception of "nonsense" can be both positive and negative. To return to the question of this chapter: Freud's reason why comedy is not all Pseudartaban gibberish is very much the opposite of Aristotle's. While Aristotle locates pleasure in the process of "learning" or registering a joke's "sense," Freud would locate pleasure in the Pseudartaban gibberish itself, despite the negative reactions that arise against it. "Sense," on the other hand, merely functions to allow the pleasures of such gibberish to occur. For Freud, the negative aspects of nonsense make its perception no less of a comic goal.

---

[52] Cf. Attardo (1994) 103: "It is not clear what the reasons are for this marked preference for referential jokes. Possible factors may be a higher degree of sophistication in verbal jokes (see Raskin 1990) which would make verbal jokes hard to process and hence scarcer, or a widespread perception of verbal jokes as 'bad quality' humor . . ." This betrays the limits of the linguistic approach.

[53] See Plutarch for a list of such groaners below.

[54] E.g., Freud (1989[1905]) 8–9, 65, 68, 160, 161, 169 n. 19, 247, 254, 255–7.

[55] E.g., Freud (1989[1905]) 153, 160, 165, 168, 169 n. 19.

[56] E.g., Freud (1989[1905]) 153, 169 n. 19, 252.   [57] E.g., Freud (1989[1905]) 160, 255–7.

[58] For result of play, see, e.g., 169 n.19 "playing with *thoughts* that inevitably leads to nonsense"; for virtually synonymous with play, compare 154: "But the characteristic tendency of boys to do absurd or silly things seems to me to be directly derived from the pleasure in nonsense" with 157: "The play is now being rejected as being meaningless" and 168.

[59] Nonsense-jokes: 65–7, 169 n. 19, 252–4; comic-nonsense: 241, 257, 264–7; for the *aporia*, see 169 n. 19, the longest footnote of the book to which he adds second-thoughts in 1912.

If there is any truth to this idea – that the perception of nonsense is a comic goal in spite of being a potentially negative experience – some examples are required. Gibberish, repetition, rambling speech, and such phenomena are, after all, well-worn territories in the study of comedy. However, they tend to be studied not for their ability to obstruct communication, but for their ability to produce laughter: that is, they are studied under the rubric of "humor," not "nonsense." This is why perceived gibberish[60] – e.g., ἰαρταμαν ἐξαρξαν ἀπισσονα σατρα in *Acharnians*,[61] ναβαισατρεῦ in Birds,[62] the νοραρεττεβλο on a Greek comic vase,[63] not to mention that fourteen-syllable word from *Mary Poppins* – tend to be grouped in a far broader category of deviant but ultimately interpretable comic language: for example, the "humorous" language of foreigners[64] or the so-called "sesquipedalian" comic coinages like ὀρθοφοιτοσυκοφαντοδικοταλαιπώρον.[65] Furthermore, since the usual method for explaining the humor of such aberrant linguistic phenomena (as commentators rightly have shown) is to explain the point or

---

[60] As discussed in the book's introduction, even with "gibberish" the subjective aspect must be kept in mind. Consider too that perceived gibberish often has, e.g., religious use or divine meaning (and so, as such, is not properly "gibberish" or "nonsense"). For the *voces magicae* (where lines like ιαεωβαφρενεμουωοθιλαρικριφιαευ are part of the incantation), see Betz (2007[1986]); Preisendanz (2001[1974]). For cross-cultural examples, see Tambiah (1985) 17–59. For *glossolalia*, see Attardo (1994) 162 and Goodman (1972) for more bibliography. For an anecdote from Acts, where the disciples, after a bout of glossolalia, are asked whether they are drunk, see Chapter 1.

[61] *Ach.* 100. See Olson (2002) ad *Ach.* 100 for different attempts to extract sense from this line with the conclusion that "the more important point is that, despite the Amb[assador]'s claim to be able to understand what Pseud. is saying . . ., Dik.'s reaction in 101 leaves little doubt that this is gibberish and intended to be recognized as such." See Willi (2002) 19–20, (2003) 213–25; Kloss (2001) 34–50; Colvin (1999) 288–9 for discussion.

[62] *Av.* 1615. This "Triballian" phrase is more contentious then the "Persian" one: some (e.g., Dunbar (1995) following Bayard (1920) discern the line ναί, Βαισατρευ = ναί, Πεισέταιρε. Others (e.g., Sommerstein (1987)) prefer to see gibberish, citing the *Acharnians* Persian line as parallel. See Willi (2002) 19–20, (2003) 213–25; Kloss (2001) 34–50; Colvin (1999) 289–90 for discussion; cf. the foreign gibberish from the mime of P. Oxy. 3.413.

[63] νοραρεττεβλο is a piece of nonsense found on a vase of the Tarpoley painter (400–390 BCE) which represents a comic scene with dialogue. See Csapo (2010) 40–52; Pickard-Cambridge (1968) 217; Beazley (1952). Although Beazley suggests that the scene may represent a binding-spell (an actor has his hands over his head and speaks of being bound), no one, to my knowledge, has suggested that this νοραρεττεβλο is itself an incantation. If so, it would be the earliest dated *vox magica*. For gibberish or nonsense inscriptions on Greek vases, see Immerwahr (2006).

[64] See Kloss (2001) 34–54; Michael (1981) 113, 210; Kronauer (1954) 30–1. Dover (1987) downplays the humorous potential of foreign dialects/solecism, considering dialect more along the lines of realism. To be added along with "foreign" gibberish is the wide array of animal sounds of the comic stage (e.g., the βρεκεκεκὲξ κοὰξ κοάξ from *Ran.* 209–20 and the bird language of *Birds*). Also, consider the possible emphasis on sound (πάσας δ' ὑμῖν φωνὰς ἱείς) to describe the early comic poet Magnes at *Eq.* 520–4.

[65] *Vesp.* 505. For a list of these in Aristophanes, see Starkie (1909) 49–54; Kronauer (1954) 21; Jernigan (1939) 41–6. Spyropoulos (1974) limits his collection of coinages only to those which provide an "accumulated" sense (i.e., accumulated elements with no "new" semantic value), not a clear new one (2–13) – almost a tenth of the Aristophanic corpus (111).

meaning of the words (e.g., by translating the Scythian's Greek into Attic in *Thesmophoriazusae*, or breaking down a coinage into its components), the perception of "nonsense" (which by definition does *not* mean) tends to become lost in the shuffle. The same can be said for repetitions and rambling speech. They are studied for their ability to produce not an impression of nonsense, but laughter – for example, so-called "boomerang" jokes which are repeated by different characters,[66] or the seemingly endless culinary lists of Anaxandrides' *Protesilaus* (fr. 42.30–71 KA) or Mnesimachus' *Hippotrophos* (fr. 4.8–65 KA).[67]

In what follows, however, I would like to examine some of these typically cited comic features not as comic techniques – that is, techniques which produce laughter by tapping some comic "source"[68] – but as phenomena which can create potentially negative reactions. What I wish to discover in these examples is evidence that, although the impression of nonsense can be a negative experience, it nevertheless appears to be a comic goal. I will attempt this first by looking at wordplay – particularly the phenomenon of "bad puns" – and then turn to phenomena like repetitions, comic coinages, and rambling speech.

Comic wordplay

In Old Comedy, wordplay is everywhere. Starkie, for example, counts forty-nine instances of homonymic wordplay in the *Acharnians*[69] alone – a list which does not include wordplay based on paronymy or *paronomasia*

---

[66] For the repetition involved in a "boomerang joke," see Kloss (2001) 205; MacDowell (1971) ad *Vesp.* 989. For repetition in Greek comedy generally, see Kloss (2001) 204–237; Spyropoulos (1974) 127–9; Miller (1944), (1945); for repetition in the famous ληκύθιον scene of *Frogs*, see Sider (1992). For a stunning repetition in Roman comedy, see Plaut. *Cas.* 598–609.

[67] See Millis (2001) ad loc. for bibliography. Although they are often taken to be in the tradition of the *Deipnon* of Philoxenus of Leucas, such lists are the material of comedy before Philoxenus: e.g., *Ach.* 545–54. See Spyropoulos (1974) for more examples in Aristophanes.

[68] See e.g., Kloss (2001) 15, my italics: "Die Wiederholungsautomatik des Fehlerhaften ist bei einigen dieser Phänomene *eine wesentliche Quelle der Komik, die aber schnell versiegt*, wenn nicht fortwährend den einzelnen dadurch zustandekommenden Fehlleistungen ein Gegensinn zugesellt [sic] werden kann." The fact that alleged "sources" of the comic are also sources of negative reactions ought to dispel this persistent idea of a "comic source" – as if the "comic" were some faucet of pleasure which can only be enjoyed in tiny increments.

[69] Starkie (1909) xli–xliv, covering the *Tractatus Coislinianus'* category of laughter which arises κατ' ὁμωνυμίαν, enumerates instances for each play. Others who treat wordplay or punning more broadly than strict homonymy will find more examples (see, e.g., Kronauer (1954) 14–20; Michael (1981) 104, 236). Starkie's list is more thorough than many later treatments, but should be used with caution: many textual emendations have been made since Starkie's day (cf, e.g., his pun-explanation of "Tharraleides" with Dunbar's explanation at *Av.* 17).

(alterations of words).[70] But what is more interesting than its sheer volume is that this relentless wordplay is rarely felt to be a series of "clever" expressions, articulating a new idea, point, or "learning" (as Aristotle would say) each time. Rather, the comedians often enough seem to play with words simply for the sake of playing with words, and even the most forgiving commentators often seem to wince. Take the following pun from *Clouds*, for example, where Strepsiades laments (22–4):

> τοῦ δώδεκα μνᾶς Πασίᾳ; τί ἐχρησάμην;
> ὅτ᾽ ἐπριάμην τὸν κοππατίαν. οἴμοι τάλας,
> εἴθ᾽ ἐξεκόπην πρότερον τὸν ὀφθαλμὸν λίθῳ.

> What were the twelve minas [I owe] to Pasias for? What did I use them for?
> Because I bought a *prized* horse.[71] Man oh man!
> I'd rather have my eye *prised* out with a rock.

Dover writes regretfully on these lines, "Aristophanes' puns are seldom sophisticated, and the pun on -κοπ- is one of his feeblest." Other commentators voice similar complaints elsewhere,[72] and it leads one to wonder: why is it that most Aristophanic puns, to use Dover's word, are *not* "sophisticated"? It would be careless to conflate Dover's category of "sophisticated" with Aristotle's category of "clever" (*asteion*), but they are perhaps not so separate either. Dover does not seem to mean that Aristophanes' puns are rarely "allusive" or "literary,"[73] but rather that they often seem to be more "silly/stupid" than "clever," more "buffoonish" than "urbane." The -κοπ- pun seems to be constructed for the sake of the wordplay rather than some particular idea. Even though Strepsiades wishes to lament his debts and manages to do so, the form of his utterance contorts itself around that irresistible κόπτω verb, leaving λίθῳ to hang flaccidly at the end of the line, as if to squeeze out some last-minute sense. It feels "feeble" and unsophisticated – qualities which, as Dover suggests, are not at all rarities in Aristophanic wordplay.

If one wished for a survey of such "bad" or "feeble" puns in Aristophanes, Plutarch would be the place to start. In his *Comparison of Aristophanes and*

---

[70] The *Tractatus Coislinianus'* category of κατὰ παρωνυμίαν is treated differently by Starkie (1909) xlix–liv (who lists Aristophanes' coinages here) and, e.g., Janko (2002) 175–181, who defines it as being closer to paronomasia.

[71] Lit. branded with a *koppa*. Dover (1989[1968]) ad 23: "There existed a breed of horses which it was customary to brand, as a guarantee of pedigree, with the letter *koppa* . . ."

[72] Cf. Sommerstein (2001) ad *Plut.* 1129: "the Greek says simply *askōliaze* 'hop!' . . . with an extremely feeble pun on *kōlē.*" Cf. Ruffell (2011) 71 "laboured pun;" 72 "a further (awful) pun;" 73 "atrocious pun," etc.

[73] For different ideas on "sophisticated" humor, see Attardo (1994) 216; Raskin (1990). Cf. Dover (2004) 243 on audience "sophistication."

Menander, Plutarch expresses irritation over Aristophanic puns (παρωνυμίας), antitheses, and homoioteleuta, which, he writes, are employed too often (πολλάκις), inopportunely (οὐκ εὐκαίρως), and "feebly" (ψυχρῶς).[74] His list of eight examples provides a good survey of this phenomenon and reminds one of modern commentators' groans over Aristophanes' more "feeble" moments:

1. Fr. 724 KA[75]

   ὅτι τοὺς ταμίας ἐβάπτισεν, οὐχὶ ταμίας ἀλλὰ Λαμίας . . .

   because he doused the rich men, no, not the *rich men*, but the
   witch-men

2. *Knights* 437[76]

   οὗτος ἤτοι καικίας ἢ συκοφαντίας πνεῖ

   He gusts as a north-easter or a sycophant-er.

3. *Knights* 454[77]

   γάστριζε καὶ τοῖς ἐντέροις καὶ τοῖς κόλοις

   Stuff him one in his guts and belly.

4. Fr. 629 KA

   ὑπὸ γέλωτος εἰς Γέλαν ἀφίξομαι

   I'll go to Lafton conveyed by laughter.

5. Fr. 661 KA[78]

   τί δὲ σοὶ δράσω, κακόδαιμον, ἀμφορεὺς
   ἐξοστρακισθείς;

   What will I do to you, poor wretch, once *depotted*?

6. *Thesmophoriazusae* 455

   ἄγρια γὰρ ἡμᾶς, ὦ γυναῖκες, δρᾷ κακά,
   ἅτ' ἐν ἀγρίοισι τοῖς λαχάνοις αὐτὸς τραφείς

   Raw are the evils he does us, women, himself raised among *raw*
   vegetables.

---

[74] *Comp. Ar. et Men.* 853b1–9. Although the essay is an epitome, the passage discussed here is generally considered to be a direct quote (beginning with φησί). See Haesler (1978) x, Ziegler *RE* col. 872. For dating of the epitome, see Quadlbauer (1960).

[75] KA do not attempt to scan this line.

[76] The *-ias* endings being a suffix for names of winds (and thus the *sykophantias* a coinage). See Fowler (1936) 464.

[77] Fowler (1936) 464 explains this as a play on *gastrize* which usually means "stuff the belly" with food, but here as "punch in the belly." But cf. *Vesp.* 1529 and *Eq.* 273 which show the verb to be more likely contemporary usage than a pun. Perhaps Plutarch's gripe is simply with the quadruple repetition of *-ois*.

[78] Cf. Fowler (1936[1969]) 465 envisioning a man speaking these words before shattering a pot (and thus word play on *ostrakon*).

7. *Acharnians* 1111

ἀλλ' ἦ τριχόβρωτες τὸν λόφον μου κατέφαγον

But look, moths (lit. hair-eaters) have eaten up my crest.

8. *Acharnians* 1124–5

φέρε δεῦρο γοργόνωτον ἀσπίδος κύκλον.

κἀμοὶ πλακοῦντος γυρόνωτον[79] δὸς κύκλον.

A. Bring here my Gorgon-faced shield's orb.

B. And to me, give a gyre-faced cake orb.

Although these different plays on words or sounds can all be categorized into different groups (whether as paronomies, homoioteleuta, or both), it is more important to see that Plutarch groups them together as evidence for a single complaint: namely, that Aristophanes uses these irritating sound effects too often, and inappropriately (οὐκ εὐκαίρως). Plutarch continues by criticizing Aristophanes' shortcomings in characterization (which is the bulk of the surviving critique),[80] but here he is identifying something else.[81] Like Dryden, who scorned Ovid's "Jingles" as "nauseous" and "pour'd on the Neck of one another,"[82] Plutarch criticizes Aristophanes for his sheer addiction to wordplay. Unlike Menander, Aristophanes does not realize what a volatile substance wordplay is, and that it must be applied sparingly, if at all.[83] But what, exactly, is it that offends Plutarch so much about these puns *qua* puns?

---

[79] I print Plutarch's γυρόνωτον rather than the Aristophanes mss. τυρόνωτον because it better conveys the Γορ – γυρ sound similarity that so irritates him. For the majuscule error (Τ read Γ) in Plutarch's ms., see Olson (2002a) ad *Ach.* 1124–5.

[80] The μὲν οὖν at 853c15 introduces a new idea – the criticism of Aristophanic characterization.

[81] It is a mistake to read the first complaint as the latter one about characterization *pace* Van der Stockt (1992) 156. Although Plutarch does say that Menander occasionally takes part in such devices but rarely (ὀλιγάκις 853b7) and with care (ἐπιμελείας 853b7), this should not create the conclusion that the devices *themselves* are faultless, rather quite the opposite – that the devices themselves are generally to be avoided and if used, used cautiously (as does Menander). See Van der Stock (1992) 153–61 for Plutarch's views on comedy (this passage and *Quaest conv.* 7.711f–712D). Cf. Di Florio (2003/4); Blanchard (2007) 53–4; Teodorsson (1989) 116; Sandbach (1970) 114; Plebe (1952) 104–12. Murray (1964) 214–16 imagines a dialogue where someone else defends (and praises) Aristophanes, but he does not mention the comparable complaints at *Quaest. conv.* 7.711f–712D.

[82] Dryden's preface to *Fables, Ancient and Modern* (1700) quoted in Tissol (1997) 11: "The Vulgar Judges, which are Nine Parts in Ten of all Nations, who calls Conceits and Jingles Wit, who see *Ovid* full of them, and *Chaucer* altogether without them, will think me little less than mad, for preferring the *Englishman* to the *Roman*: Yet, with their leave, I must presume to say, that the Things they admire are only glittering Trifles, and so far from being Witty, that in a serious Poem they are nauseous, because they are unnatural. Wou'd any Man who is ready to die for Love, describe his Passion like *Narcissus*? Wou'd he think of *inopem me copia fecit*, and a Dozen more of such Expressions pour'd on the Neck of one another and signifying all the same Things?"

[83] Often described as a sort of punning "temperament": puns "are a latent resource of language, and certain temperaments simply will not resist trying to mine and exploit this rich ore, because (like Everest) it is there." Redfern (1984) 9 quoted in Tissol (1997) 6.

A pun like ὑπὸ γέλωτος εἰς Γέλαν ἀφίξομαι[84] surely is offensive to Plutarch not because it was assigned to the wrong characters, but rather because the pun itself is "feeble" (*psychron*) – Dryden's "nausea" is immediately recognizable to anyone who has ever groaned at a pun. A pun's "feebleness" seems to be interconnected with *general* questions of context, but not necessarily specific ones:[85] that is, for Aristotle, the requirement of a pun's status as "clever" was contextual in the most general sense: namely, language had to reflect reality (Mr. Baring had to be unbearable, Nicon had to be Thracian, etc.). What makes Aristophanes' ὑπὸ γέλωτος εἰς Γέλαν ἀφίξομαι offensive for Plutarch is probably similar: there is no exigent context causing the speaker to utter these lines. Like the similar line in *Acharnians* 606 ἐν Καμαρίνῃ κἂν Γέλᾳ κἂν Καταγέλᾳ, either the Sicilian city's name is causing the speaker to mention laughter, or the laughter is causing him to mention the Sicilian city – but, presumably, no situation allows (or allows enough) for both. If the pleasure of a pun is in "getting" its "point" (Aristotle), it is not difficult to explain why Plutarch feels that such "pointless" wordplay is, to use his own term, "nauseating nonsense" (φλυαρία ναυτιώδης).[86]

"Feeble" puns, however, allow us to ask an important question about Aristophanes and the art of the old comedians. If so many of these puns are "feeble," do these groans suggest that Aristophanes is somehow *failing* time and time again? That is, if jokes are conceived as techniques or a bag of tricks, it seems that Aristophanes, with, for example, his "prising" pun, has detonated a comic device which somehow malfunctions. It leaves the audience "cold" like any poorly executed rhetorical feature. In such a scenario, it seems that Aristophanes wanted the joke to go in one direction (laughter, the comic), but instead it went in another (groans). One might then simply say that Aristophanes fails with his feeble puns, something which as Dover suggests occur often.

There is nothing wrong with such a view, and no reason why one should not leave open the possibility of Aristophanic failure, but it raises the question of why he would make the attempt in the first place, delving into that treacherous territory of the pun, considering how feeble puns tend to be by nature. There seems to be more going on here than a simple divide between "good" and "bad" jokes or puns, and the pun – especially the

---

[84] Van der Stockt (1992) 157: "I cannot see why the pun … would be offensive; even if it is cheap, it does not deserve to serve as an illustration in this sharp condemnation of Aristophanes."

[85] E.g., the specific context of characterization.

[86] Plut. *Comp. Ar. et Men.* 853c19. Although he does not explicitly refer to this aspect of Aristophanic diction as wordplay, it seems to be the logical inference.

"groaner" – allows for an opportunity to explore further this continuum between positive and negative reactions which is the object of study in this chapter. After all, the continuum between laughter and nausea is the pun's most interesting feature. Modern joke theorists who limit themselves to humor's formal features often are unable to explain this laughter–nausea continuum, but instead suggest, for example, that what makes a "bad" pun feel so "bad" is simply its quality[87] – as if the reaction to a poor pun were no different from the reaction to a poorly worded sentence. The "nausea" some puns induce (to use Dryden's and Plutarch's word), however, seems to be altogether of a different class. I would suggest that this irritation arises from the feeling that nonsense, rather than sense, is being produced.

This sets the Aristophanic punning project in a different light: it is not that Aristophanes has aimed his puns in a certain direction (laughter) and they strayed elsewhere (groans), but that these two targets are very much the same direction. That is, this potentially negative phenomenon, the perception of nonsense, appears to be something of a comic goal. Indeed, it may be in "overshooting" (and so, the groan) that Aristophanes makes some of his best attacks into this terrain. If the perception of nonsense is seen as a goal of comedy and not a mistake of comedy, it appears that comic language often desires to approach this boundary of communication. If such perceived nonsense were not a goal of comedy, one would have to explain that Aristophanes simply fails repeatedly with his "feeble" puns. However, when it is seen that it is not sense but nonsense that is being pursued, this aspect of Aristophanic poetics begins to reveal itself.

Extended wordplay in Aristophanes

"Bad" puns suggest themselves as evidence for this negative–positive continuum in the perception of nonsense, and they especially lend support to the idea that although the perception of nonsense can be negative, it nevertheless often appears to be a comic goal. But if this is the case, one would also expect the appearance of those two elements which, as Freud argued, help to prevent those negative reactions from arising: contemporary relevance and aggressive purpose. Since comedy's *onomasti kōmōidein* exhibits both of these elements, the interaction between puns and this category will be particularly valuable (e.g., when is *onomasti kōmōidein* part of verbal

---

[87] See, e.g., Attardo (1994) 143 n. 1.

play, when does it occur *near* verbal play, etc.).[88] I will argue that one function of *onomasti kōmōidein* (and contemporary relevance more generally) is to provide precisely that "sense" that wordplay requires in order to escape that negative aspect of "nonsense."

I will select this extended passage from Aristophanes' *Birds* since the play is often said to be the least overtly political of Aristophanes' works.[89] Unlike *Acharnians, Lysistrata, Frogs,* and others, the plot does not demand contemporary reference, no matter how political the subtext of the play may be.[90] For that reason, it is particularly useful for considering the play's moments of contemporary aggression (and their interaction with wordplay), since such references are more dramatically gratuitous, and can be analyzed more clearly for their technical function. These "contemporary" moments are surprisingly frequent for such a supposed "fantasy" play – with *onomasti kōmōidein* occurring more than fifty times, and contemporary characters like Meton and Cinesias brought on stage for abuse. In the following, I hope to show a formal function for this contemporary relevance that goes beyond the generic necessity of *onomasti kōmōidein* for Old Comedy.

In Aristophanes' *Birds*, like Archippus' *Fish*,[91] there is seemingly endless material for puns in the names of animals. Before the bird-chorus enters, four mute, brightly costumed birds arrive on stage (perhaps on the roof of the *skene*),[92] and a series of puns ensues, as the characters (and audience) try to guess what each bird is. When Peisthetairus remarks on the first bird's crimson costume (272: βαβαί, καλός γε καὶ φοινικιοῦς), the Hoopoe replies, "of course! For in fact its name is flamingo (φοινικόπτερος)." When the Hoopoe explains that the second bird is called a Μῆδος, Euelpides responds Μῆδος; ὦναξ Ἡράκλεις. / εἶτα πῶς ἄνευ καμήλου Μῆδος ὢν εἰσέπτατο; "A *Mede?* Jeez! How then, being a *Mede* did he fly in here without a camel?" (278–9). The third bird gives rise to a rather complicated joke based on *onomasti kōmōidein*: explaining that the bird's lineage is similar to the family of the spendthrift Callias (where each generation alternates between the name Callias or Hipponicus), Peisthetairus decides, "Then this bird is Callias – since he's lost all his feathers (πτερορρυεῖ)" (284). This joke is

---

[88] For *onomasti kōmōidein*, see Chapter 3 n. 27. This feature was not a constant in Old Comedy: Crates and Pherecrates allegedly avoided it (see testimonia in KA).

[89] See, e.g., Asper (2005) 8; Dobrov (1990) 212–18; Sommerstein (1987) 1; Whitman (1964) 169, who stress the difference between *Birds* and Aristophanes' other plays in comparable terms.

[90] For the debate over the alleged political allegory of *Birds*, see Chapter 2 at 81 n. 83.

[91] For the comparable punning in Archippus' *Fish*, see Rothwell (2007) 126–8.

[92] See Dunbar (1995) 227; Dover (1972) 145. Sommerstein (1987) 214 rejects this idea in favor of "little hillocks along the stage-platform in front of the *skene*."

then capped by Hoopoe, who, as if seeing more material in the Callias–bird relationship, unfurls a series of double entendres: "Although he's well-bred (γενναῖος), he's *plucked* (τίλλεται) by sycophants, / and the females also *pluck out* his feathers (ἐκτίλλουσιν)" (285–6).

It would be highly subjective (and probably misguided) to measure somehow the "funniness" of this series of jokes from Flamingo to Mede to Hoopoe–Callias, but there is a certain differentiation between them that cannot be denied: the Hoopoe–Callias joke(s) opens its doors to a richness of "sense" that the previous two do not. By this I mean that if one were asked to explain the Hoopoe–Callias joke, there is much more to articulate than in the first two: there is the moral judgment of the spendthrift Callias, the backstory of political trials, the work ethic of the previous generation and the dissipation of the present one, all combining to produce a considerable amount of material for explaining the joke. But with the Mede–camel joke, articulation becomes more difficult, and sense becomes depleted: "Euelpides has misunderstood" or "Medes usually ride on camels" is the best that one can do; one might even, in the attempt to explain the joke, call it "silly." With the Flamingo joke, on further analysis, it barely seems a joke at all, and if it is one, it is a "feeble" one. That is, if a listener were pressed for the "sense" or "point" of the joke, it would have to be an apologetic "*crimson* (φοινικιοῦς) sounds like *flamingo* (φοινικόπτερος)." The resources for joke-explanation (i.e., "sense") have almost completely dried up. Compared with jokes containing the contemporary relevance and aggression of *onomasti kōmōidein* – like the Callias–Hoopoe jokes – one wonders what to "do" with jokes lacking these, what to "say" about such jokes, what to "take away" from such jokes. This apparent uselessness seems to create the perception that the first two jokes are "sillier" than the third. While a perceived "sense" generates further explanatory language (for example, "Callias is a spendthrift"), these more verbal jests quickly reveal themselves to be sterile for such further discussion.

More remarkable, however, is the continuation of this bird-naming scene. The fourth bird continues the amplification that the previous three began (whereas the Flamingo required fewer than four lines, the Mede required six, and the Callias–Hoopoe and this fourth bird each require eight). It is worth considering the entire interchange here, to gain a sense of the "capping" occurring (287–94):

Eu.   ὦ Πόσειδον, ἕτερος αὖ τις βαπτὸς ὄρνις οὑτοσί.
       τίς ὀνομάζεταί ποθ᾽ οὗτος;
Επ.   οὑτοσὶ κατωφαγᾶς.

Πε. ἔστι γὰρ κατωφαγᾶς τις ἄλλος ἢ Κλεώνυμος;
Επ. πῶς ἂν οὖν Κλεώνυμός γ' ὢν οὐκ ἀπέβαλε τὸν λόφον;
Πε. ἀλλὰ μέντοι τίς ποθ' ἡ λόφωσις ἡ τῶν ὀρνέων;
      ἢ 'πὶ τὸν δίαυλον ἦλθον;
Επ.   ὥσπερ οἱ Κᾶρες μὲν οὖν
      ἐπὶ λόφων οἰκοῦσιν, ὦγάθ', ἀσφαλείας οὕνεκα.
Ευ. ὦ Πόσειδον, οὐχ ὁρᾷς ὅσον συνείλεκται κακὸν
      ὀρνέων;

Eu. Oh Poseidon, here's another colorful bird.
     What ever is this one called?
Ho.   This one's a "gobbler."
Pe. Is there any "gobbler" other than Cleonymus?
Ho. How could it be Cleonymus if he hasn't thrown away his *crest*?
Pe. Well, what ever is this *cresting* of the birds?
     Have they come for the hoplite race?
Ho.   No: they occupy the *crests* like Carians, for
     safety's sake.
Eu. Oh, Poseidon look at all the birds ...

What makes this series remarkable is the unapologetic riffing on "*loph-*,"
first as helmet-crests, then as feather-crests, then as hill-crests (a pun which
had already appeared at v. 279). One is tempted to analyze this segment in
terms of "capping," with each character competing to top the previous joke:
the first joke regarding Cleonymus' corpulence, the second regarding
Cleonymus' cowardice, the third inventing a word "cresting" to play with
the military and ornithological senses of *lophos*, and the fourth adding a
third, topographical sense to the wordplay.[93] If the character assignation is
correct, it can be said that Hoopoe caps Peisthetairus, Peisthetairus caps
Hoopoe, and Hoopoe caps Peisthetairus.[94]

     But is this a correct analysis? Can one really see the quality of these jokes
increasing as each character attempts to "top" the previous joke? It seems, on
the contrary, the opposite: that these jokes are descending in quality, from the
strong attack on chubby Cleonymus to purely verbal jesting. Indeed it is the
last joke, or the last two jokes, that most resemble the "feeble" puns discussed

[93] For a definition of "capping" and bibliography, see Collins (2004) ix–xii; for application of this to
   comedy, 30–53.
[94] See Dunbar (1995) ad loc. for discussion of assignation and the instinct to give Euelpides the "bomolokhic"
   response. For "bomolokhic" asides generally, see Bain (1987[1977]) 87–94; also see Dover (1987) 246–8
   who makes the important point that in Old Comedy jokes are made by whomever is available.

earlier: there seems to be no "point" to the wordplay other than the pre-existing homophony of the *loph-* words – just as with the *kop-* pun from *Clouds*, which strained to unite the verb κόπτω with the κοππατίας horse.[95] While the first and second jokes have ample "sense" to be articulated – Cleonymus is rotund, incontinent with his appetites, despicable; Cleonymus is cowardly, the type to drop his shield, despicable – the latter jokes become considerably more treacherous regarding the articulation or explanation of their "sense" or "point." One is forced to explain somewhat shame-facedly that if it is funny, it is funny because the words sound similar (i.e., "*cresting* is a word that sounds like feather-*crest* but also military *crest*," "military *crest* sounds like hill *crest*," etc.). The requirement of explanation becomes irritating in a way that it does not with *onomasti kōmōidein*: "words sound alike but mean different things" is not a very sensible answer at all.

If it can be accepted that the quality of jokes is not ascending (as one might expect of capping) but devolving into pure verbal soundplay, nevertheless, one might expect that it is still possible to analyze the scene in terms of set-up and punchline. The Hoopoe's information that the present bird is called "gobbler" sets up the punchline about Cleonymus; this in turn is a set-up for the following punchline about losing his crest, which then leads to the next two punchlines about armor-races and Carian hilltops. But even here, things are more complicated than such analysis might yield. The punchlines are clear for the first two Cleonymus jokes, but then what happens in the line ἀλλὰ μέντοι τίς ποθ' ἡ λόφωσις ἡ τῶν ὀρνέων;? It would seem to be a set-up for the δίαυλος punchline, yet at the same time λόφωσις draws attention to itself not only as a play on the previous line's *lophos* (a usual joke feature) but also as a coinage (also a common joke feature).[96] That it is a question might cause it to be felt more as a set-up than as a punchline, but, then again, the δίαυλος punchline is also stated as a question. There seems to be a rather anxious limbo of sorts occurring here: the line is not quite a joke (for how, like the flamingo pun, is it "funny"?), but also not *not* a joke either (for it is too verbally playful).

Rather than trying to differentiate between these two – set-up and punchline – and establishing with certainty where the audience does or does not laugh, a broader unit of analysis may help to explain this broader tract of wordplay. The devolution of sense in this pun series can be seen, not

---

[95] Or not enough point: the birds *do* have crests, they are on elevated positions, and Cleonymus has some associations with military failure, so the language at least fits the Aristotelian requirements for contextual appropriateness.

[96] For comic coinages, see below.

so much as an inadvertent decrease in joke quality, but as an attempt to push language, in play, to a certain volatile boundary. That is, the crescendo or climax that is being created over these eight lines is not one of sense – indeed, the jokes become less and less "pointed" through these lines – but rather a crescendo of meaninglessness, of lines becoming increasingly sense-less. It is as if, in this larger stretch of wordplay, the perception of nonsense is actually being aimed at.

A useful litmus test to grasp this feel of nonsense is a thought experiment: what would happen to these eight lines if Cleonymus were removed at the beginning? What if this series of *loph*-puns had begun not with *onomasti kōmōidein* but rather with a reference to a bird (perhaps a fighting cock) who drops his crest/shield? No longer would there be an initial explosion of contemporary aggression to fuel the following wordplay: instead, as I read it at least, a rather "weak" pun (a bird dropping his "crest") would lead to another "weak" pun (the "cresting" of birds), and so on, and as one pun follows the next, a queasy reaction against this "pointlessness" starts to build. This, I would suggest, is a reaction against perceived nonsense: that is, it is not enough to follow homophones, one must "say something" (*legein ti*), that is, *not* "speak nonsense" (*ouden legein*).

Coinages

The question I have been asking in this chapter is: if the perception of nonsense is some central comic pleasure, why is comedy not an endless procession of Pseudartaban gibberish or random Socratean words like *aerobateo*? The answer I have proposed is that the perception of nonsense can often be a negative experience, due perhaps to nonsense's connotations of delirium, or to a feeling of unjustified play, or to some vague middle-ground between these two. However, despite the potential negative reactions against it, I have been arguing that the perception of nonsense is still a comic goal. I first suggested that evidence of this can be seen in "bad" puns, where it appeared that producing sense may not be the comedian's central goal after all, and then in longer sections of wordplay where it seemed that the appearance of "sense" – particularly the aggression and topicality of *onomasti komoidein* – often was required in order to avoid the potential displeasures of language play.

Now the moment is right to consider further the idea of comic climaxes, those moments of comedy which, as I mentioned in Chapter 2, do not seem confined to the usual descriptions of humor analysis. Instead of laughter being triggered by some formal "punchline" – that moment when a listener registers the "sense" of a joke – with comic climaxes, laughter seems to arise at no particular point and seems to be almost indefinitely extendible. Freud's tidy maxim that "high spirits replace jokes, just as jokes must try to replace high spirits" would help to explain this feature of comedy, if it exists. Comic climaxes may be explained as moments when the mood of the audience has been so heightened that the audience does not require some "sense" to laugh at. For this reason, since audiences appear to be laughing without having something to laugh at and since the comedy itself appears to be insensible, such moments often resemble a sort of delirium. In terms of the question of this chapter, comic climaxes would suggest that a comedy of Pseudartaban gibberish is not impossible, after all: however, raising the mood to such a height where such an extended climax could become possible would require extraordinary comic genius. To approach this idea, I will first take an example from comic coinages and then an example from comic repetitions.

Comic coinages like Socrates' famous ἀεροβατῶ generally create no major obstacles to decipherability. Dover writes on this word in *Clouds* (ad 225): "Given ναυβάτης and the poetic ἱπποβάτης and ὀρεσσιβάτης, it is meant to suggest 'the air is the medium in which I move.'" This is a noted attribute of comic coinages more generally: as Colin Austin claims, unlike Shakespeare's "honorificabilitudinitatibus" and Rabelais's "antipericatametanaparbeugedamphicrationes" which "sound like gibberish," comic coinages like Lysistrata's σπερμαγοραιολεκιθολαχανοπώλιδες and σκοροδοπανδοκευτριαραοπώλιδες are "perfectly intelligible."[97] While Spyropoulos distinguishes between those coinages which appear to create some new sense and those which are an "accumulation" of meanings, Silk notices the "exuberance" and "relish" behind such accumulative words.[98] Because such coinages are usually at a small scale, for example, *aerobatein* or *autotatos*, it is difficult to disentangle them from terms like "punchlines" or from the natural idea that they are risible owing to the new "sense" they produce. Instead, something is required which pushes further into the boundaries of intelligibility, for example, the famous 64-syllable-word that caps the ending of *Ecclesiazusae* (1169–75):

> λοπαδοτεμαχοσελαχογαλεοκρανιο-
> λειψανοδριμυποτριμματοσιλφιο-
> λιπαρομελιτοκατακεχυμενο-
> κιχλεπικοσσυφοφαττοπεριστερ-

---

[97] In Henderson (1987) ad *Lys.* 457–8.   [98] Spyropoulos (1974) 2–5; Silk (2000) 126–36.

αλεκτρυονοπτοπιφαλλι<δ>οκιγκλο-
πελειολαγῳοσιραιοβαφητρανοπτερυγών

fishilydishily … pouredtothebrimmily, etc.

It is difficult here to identify some formal trigger, punchline, or location in this long and rambling word where laughter may be said to arise. Is it at the end when the "sense" becomes finally intelligible (at least for those with such astounding cognitive capabilities)? At some particular syllable, like the overflowing κατακεχυμενο- which doubles the triplet rhythm? At the point where one recognizes a possible parody? It appears that there is no particular point, nor even necessarily one, where laughter can be said to arise. Rather, laughter seems to be skipping around the text and not being triggered by any singular textual spring.

C. C. Jernigan, in an old American dissertation, describes the coinage in this way (41): "Aristophanes often coined words to make fun. The basis of this fun, aside from inherent surprise, is sometimes sheer exaggeration and therefore comic nonsense, as in the case of the long word of 167 letters in *Eccl.* 1169." Like Spyropoulos, Jernigan's desire is more to enumerate different types of incongruity than to analyze them, so one should not press too much the meaning of his throwaway word, "nonsense." Yet, his impulse to characterize the coinage as "sheer exaggeration" is telling. "Sheer" is the key word here: it suggests that the word is nothing more than its exaggeration, as if a word could "just" exaggerate rather than, for example, signify. One might compare van Leeuwen's note here which claims that the word is not worth the "price" of interpretation, as the Latin idiom goes.[99] Whatever the word's value, it seems for these two scholars, it is not in the word's meaning – if the word can even be said to have one.

Silk's observation about comic coinages more generally is also useful here (135): "When Aeschylus is called a 'fancy-phrase-trusser' (κομποφακελορρήμονα, *Frogs* 839) or Lysistrata summons up her 'swede-and-cabbage-women' (σκοροδοπανδοκευτριαρτοπώλιδες, *Lys.* 458), the gusto is palpable, irrespective of the satirical or non-satirical function of the new composite." This observation of "gusto" is sympathetically received yet difficult to pinpoint precisely: as something "irrespective of the satirical or non-satirical function," the "gusto" or "exuberance" Silk detects appears to be something other than the word's meaning or intelligibility. Like Jernigan and van Leeuwen before him, Silk is identifying something else.

---

[99] Ad loc.: "De singulis quae h.l. enumerantur cibis disputare operae pretium non videtur."

If the multisyllable word's enjoyment somehow lies not in its meaning (Jernigan's "comic nonsense"), where does it lie? As has already been noticed, the word appears to have no singular formal trigger, but rather as Silk suggests regarding this particular word, the gargantuan "compound . . . (it would seem) is almost infinitely extendible" (136). However, this observation is both true and (as his parenthetical distancing suggests) not true. One might imagine the joyful conditions in which such a gargantuan word might be "infinitely extendible," yet, at the same time understand why it is not: like Pseudartaban gibberish such a string of syllables and partial meanings, at some point, irritates.

Thus, it is worth considering why it is at this point in the comic play and no other that such a gigantic coinage materializes. Silk points to the "logic" of context: "For such a colossally exuberant moment only a colossally exuberant word-formation will do."[100] The joyful, gustatory end of *Ecclesiazusae* seems to call for such a smorgasborg word-formation. But I would argue that this contextualization ought to be seen in the reverse as well: Aristophanes, in a sense, can only "get away with" such a word within such an exuberant context. After all, a comedian cannot slip in a seventy-some-syllable word just anywhere, and if it were not without such risks, one would expect many more such words in comedy. Freud's observations about the relationship between jokes and mood are salient here: the more heightened the mood, the greater the risks a comedian can take with his audience. At such a moment, the comedian can practically abandon the "satirical . . . function of the new composite" (to use Silk's words) for the exuberance of the language itself (and so Jernigan's observation of "comic nonsense" or "*sheer* exaggeration").

I would like to suggest that with this final word of *Ecclesiazusae* appears an instance of comic climax, a moment where there is laughter without necessarily any articulable "sense" which one can be said to be laughing at. The resources of parody's sense – if the word is parodic at all – seem to be depleted fairly quickly, and its enjoyment quickly enters a different realm. Unlike the cases of language play discussed in the previous section, where aggression's "sense" helped to prevent the negative reactions from arising, here such sense is not required, owing to, it seems, the heightened mood of the finale. Like the other comic climaxes, it would provide evidence for Freud's notion that a heightened mood can substitute the requirement of sense. This large-scale coinage may also help to articulate precisely what

---

[100]   Silk (2000) 135; the quote is in reference to Peace 520–2 but he is referring this logic to Aristophanes' biggest attested compound.

disappears when other small-scale coinages are treated as *merely* intelligible. Jernigan's "comic nonsense," Silk's "exuberance" which lies outside of "satiric function," and even van Leeuwen's withdrawal of the word from the economic values of semantics, point to similar qualities which these coinages share. The thrill of such words may lie not so much in the new sense they create, but in this playful drive of language to a certain subjective boundary, a crossroads of sorts, where one enters either that negative realm of delirium or that related, positive space of comic climax.

To get at the permeability of these two spaces, this idea of a climax being, as Silk writes, "infinitely extendible" yet, at the same time, highly volatile, I will turn, in the next section, to another typically cited comic "technique": repetition. Like the homophony and language play already discussed, such repetition can create highly negative reactions – that difference between "funny-haha" and "funny-strange" to cite Morreall again. Yet, as I have been arguing, this should not be seen as evidence against the idea that the perception of nonsense is a central comic pleasure. Rather it should reveal the stakes and hazards involved in approaching those comic goals.

Repetition

In the *Thesmophoriazusae*, there is a moment which offers a brief glimpse at this boundary between the negative and positive reactions over perceived nonsense. In this scene, the Kinsman, after having successfully infiltrated the women's ranks in his female garb, must watch helplessly as the women hunt for the festival's male intruder. Here he is being interrogated by Cleisthenes, Aristophanes' favorite effeminate, and the bombardment of questions flusters the "female" impostor (618–22):

ΚΛ.   εἰπέ μοι,
      τίς ἐστ᾽ ἀνήρ σοι;
Κη.   τὸν ἐμὸν ἄνδρα πυνθάνει;
      τὸν δεῖνα γιγνώσκεις, τὸν ἐκ Κοθωκιδῶν;
ΚΛ. τὸν δεῖνα; ποῖον;
Κη.   ἔσθ᾽ ὁ δεῖν᾽, ὃς καί ποτε
      τὸν δεῖνα τὸν τοῦ δεῖνα —
ΚΛ.   ληρεῖν μοι δοκεῖς.

Cl.   Tell me,
      who is your husband?

Ki.   You're asking who's *my* husband?
        Do you know what's-his-name, from Kothokidai?
Cl.   What's-his-name? *Which* what's-his-name?
Ki.   *What's*-his-name, the one who once
        what's-his-name's what's his name . . .
Cl.   You're talking nonsense.

An enjoyable interchange: if not quite a "joke," something of a comic "gag" which might be located under the general rubric of "humor." But as Cleisthenes observes, there is another aspect of the Kinsman's speech worth noting: it is, to him, "nonsense" (ληρεῖν μοι δοκεῖς).

Generally, this label "nonsense" should be taken with a grain of salt on the comic stage, since almost everything at one time or another is called "nonsense" by comic characters (something which will be studied in the next chapter), but here Cleisthenes' use of the phrase "you're speaking nonsense" actually describes well the Kinsman's speech. Although the Kinsman has not technically transgressed the rules of grammar (the forms are inflected and all that's needed is a verb),[101] a certain effect is created through his repetition of τὸν δεῖνα. Like someone delirious with a fever – which as I argued in Chapter 1 is a root connotation of ληρεῖν, "to speak nonsense" – here the Kinsman is repeating a certain phrase over and over again, and communication is quickly showing itself to be impossible for Cleisthenes. When Cleisthenes changes tacks and asks who the Kinsman's tent-mate at the festival was last year (συσκηνήτρια), the Kinsman answers (again), ἡ δεῖν' ἔμοιγ' "I had what's-her-name" to which Cleisthenes (again) responds οὐδὲν λέγεις "you're speaking nonsense" (624–5).

Sense, Cleisthenes seems to suggest, can be escaped through repetition. If one repeats a phrase enough times (τὸν δεῖνα . . . τὸν δεῖνα . . . τὸν δεῖνα . . .), one will reach a point where most listeners will, like Cleisthenes, stop trying to interpret. Presumably, after such abandonment of interpretation, other reactions start to occur, for example, irritation, or the desire to stop the speaker from continuing such repetitive, meaningless speech (τὸν δεῖνα . . . τὸν δεῖνα . . . τὸν δεῖνα . . .). This relationship between repetition and non-sense which Cleisthenes indicates is at least partially confirmed by Aristotle, who briefly discusses such verbal repetition in the *Sophistici Elenchi* (he calls

---

[101] The three "what's-his-names" being the husband, the person who is the object of that husband's action, and that person's father, apparently. Frege (1980[1892]) 58 argues that any phrase has a "sense" if it is grammatical. Wittgenstein's definition of "sense" – "It is what is regarded as the justification of an assertion that constitutes the sense of the assertion" – works well in the light of Freud's description of the role of "sense" in jokes (*Philosophical Grammar*, 1: 40, quoted in Dummett (1976) 128–9).

such repetitive speech ἀδολεσχία, "babbling")[102] and groups it along with paradox, solecism, and mistakes/lies, as a type of speech absolutely to be avoided in argument (i.e., if one is caught producing such speech, one will almost certainly lose the argument):

περὶ δὲ τοῦ ποιῆσαι ἀδολεσχεῖν, ὃ μὲν λέγομεν τὸ ἀδολεσχεῖν, εἰρήκαμεν ἤδη. πάντες δὲ οἱ τοιοίδε λόγοι τοῦτο βούλονται ποιεῖν· εἰ μηδὲν διαφέρει τὸ ὄνομα ἢ τὸν λόγον εἰπεῖν, διπλάσιον δὲ καὶ διπλάσιον ἡμίσεος ταὐτό, εἰ ἄρα ἐστὶν διπλάσιον ἡμίσεος διπλάσιον, ἔσται ἡμίσεος ἡμίσεος διπλάσιον. καὶ πάλιν ἂν ἀντὶ τοῦ διπλάσιον διπλάσιον ἡμίσεος τεθῇ, τρὶς ἔσται εἰρημένον, ἡμίσεος ἡμίσεος ἡμισεος διπλάσιον. καὶ ἆρά ἐστιν ἡ ἐπιθυμία ἡδέος; τοῦτο δ'ἐστὶν ὄρεξις ἡδέος· ἔστιν ἄρα ἡ ἐπιθυμία ὄρεξις ἡδέος ἡδέος.

Next, as to making people babble, we have already said what we mean by this term. Arguments of the following kind all have this end in view; "If it makes no difference whether one uses the term or the definition of it, and 'double' and 'double of half' are the same thing, then if 'double' is 'double of half' it will be 'double of half of half'; and if 'double of half' be substituted again for 'double' there will be a triple repetition, 'double of half of half of half.'" Again, "Is not 'desire' 'desire for pleasure'? Now 'desire is an appetite for pleasure': therefore 'desire is an appetite for pleasure of pleasure.'" (3.173a32–40, trans. Forster)

Being forced to define "double" as "double of half of half of half" (ἡμίσεος ἡμισεος ἡμισεος διπλάσιον) or to define desire as "an appetite of pleasure of pleasure" (ὄρεξις ἡδέος ἡδέος) puts one in a precarious position of language.[103] Through the very repetition of words, the words themselves seem to disintegrate as conveyors of meaning: one begins to "babble," and appear no longer to speak sense.

But what is most interesting about this repetitive mistake of language is that this same verbal phenomenon of ἀδολεσχία (repetitive babbling) is listed in the *Tractatus Coislinianus* also as a verbal source of the comic. One need not agree with Janko's thesis regarding the Aristotelian origins of the *Tractatus* to appreciate Janko's position: "Although A[ristotle] nowhere associates [ἀδολεσχία] directly with comedy, as a sophistical fault he can

---

[102] *Soph. el.* 3.165b13: "We must first of all comprehend the various objects at which those aim who compete and contend in argument. They number five: refutation, fallacy, paradox, solecism, and, fifthly, the reduction of one's opponent to a state of babbling, that is, making him to say the same thing over and over again." (ἔλεγχος, ψεῦδος, παράδοχαν, σολοικισμός, τὸ ποιῆσαι ἀδολεσχῆσαι τὸν προδιαλεγόμενον). Trans. Forster 1955.

[103] *Soph. el.* 3.165b16, 3.173a31–40. For further discussion and Aristotelian citations, see Janko (2002 [1984]) 173–4, who wishes to associate this passage with the ἀδολεσχία of the *Tractatus Coislinianus*, where it is listed as a verbal source of the comic.

hardly have failed to note its humorous potential."[104] The "humorous potential" of repetitive babbling is immediately recognizable: one only need to imagine the scene of refutation which Aristotle envisions (and its helplessly stuttering victim) to grasp its potentially comic effect. The question of importance here, however, is what precisely this relationship is between repetitive babbling as a "fault" or a "mistake," and repetition as a "source of the comic."

To consider this question it is worth returning to Cleisthenes and the Kinsman and imagining how the scene would feel if the Kinsman were to *continue* repeating his phrase (τὸν δεῖνα ... τὸν δεῖνα ... τὸν δεῖνα ...). In such a scenario, such repetitive babbling would certainly be humorous at first; but very quickly, I would suggest, a broader array of emotions or effects would begin to announce themselves amidst this repetitiveness: anxiety, irritation, distress, etc.[105] But at what point would this occur? Here humor analysis tends to falter. Although James Robson singles out this passage as one which fails all four of Grice's maxims in order to produce humor,[106] he overlooks the fact that this very failure could quickly become a source of negative reactions as well (i.e., not humor at all).[107] Gerrit Kloss, who devotes an entire chapter to repetitions and "stutters" in Aristophanes, argues that repetitions often become humorous by containing a new humorous "sense" in each iteration: which is clearly not the case for this passage.[108] So too, formal analysis in general would be of little use for the

---

[104] Janko (2002[1984]) 174. But cf. Cooper (1924) 231–3 and Starkie (1909) who, in analyzing the *TC*, interpret the term *adoleskhia* in its broader sense of garrulity or rambing speech. Cf. Theophrastus' *adoleskhos* in *Characters*. For more bibliography on the *SE*, see Fait (2007).

[105] Cf. the actor/director Steven Berkoff who, when playing Herod in Oscar Wilde's *Salome*, would choose a different word or phrase each night to repeat over and over again. The audience would experience the gamut of responses to the spectacle: laughter, anxiety, frustration, rage, panic. I thank Peter Meineck for this anecdote.

[106] Robson (2006) 68–9 with his modification of Grice's (1975) maxims of conversation being quantity (e.g., "make your contribution as informative as is required"), quality (e.g., "do not say what you believe to be implausible"), relation (e.g., "be relevant"), and manner (e.g., "avoid ambiguity").

[107] One might assume that the reason it is "humorous" is because the actor is perceived as speaking "unitary discourse" since, earlier (23–4), Robson distinguishes "nonsense" from "humor" inasmuch as humor is incongruous discourse spoken by one perceived to be capable of unified discourse, while "nonsense" is spoken by one perceived to be incapable of such discourse. Two problems with this are that: (1) it overlooks the fact that the mentally abnormal were found to be comical in the ancient world (see Chapter 1 for discussion); (2) in extended repetition, one does not necessarily perceive the actor to have suddenly become incapable of unitary discourse (cf. the negative reactions to twentieth-century performances of the Theatre of the Absurd; Esslin (1991[1961]), 19–20, 27, 179), but perhaps that the play has become no longer "safe" or "in control," and that one's superior position of control and mastery over the play has disappeared.

[108] Kloss (2001) 204–37. He does not discuss this passage, although his theoretical source, Stierle, isolates repetition as comical inasmuch as it recalls a "stutter" (Kloss (2001) 15 on Stierle (1976) 257);

passage (e.g. "is it the second or the third 'what's-his-name' that is funny?" "where, exactly, is the incongruence? the punchline?"), not least since it would overlook the fact that a talented comic actor could extend this senseless stutter for even longer periods, expanding or contracting the repetition according to the audience's response. Although Harold Miller in his exhaustive studies of Aristophanic repetition misses this example, he may have such moments in mind when he writes of the "humorous effect" which arises "merely because of the repetition of a line" (i.e., not thanks to some new meaning): "the exact comic force here would be difficult to describe and its intensity varies considerably, but ... they appear unquestionably to be deliberate on the part of Aristophanes."[109]

I would suggest that instead of formally searching for a particular punchline or moment of incongruence in this passage, one ought instead to observe the boundary itself between nonsense *qua* producer of pleasure and nonsense *qua* producer of displeasure. The Kinsman in his repetition playfully approaches a certain boundary, and the audience laughs, but if that boundary were to be transgressed (i.e., if he continued in his repetitions), such nonsense would become a "mistake" pure and simple, with all the discomfort and irritations that such high-order mistakes involve. The fun would largely disappear. Although many sources of humor might be identified in this passage (not just the linguistic repetition, but also the social aspects: e.g., perhaps Cleisthenes, by becoming irritated, becomes a "Butt" of the comic gag), the humor *per se* is not the primary interest: rather it is this boundary between "babbling repetition" as an irritating mistake, and one which is capable of producing pleasure. Although I will examine this passage further in the next chapter (where I argue that one of the elements that protects the utterance from producing distress is Cleisthenes' serious scolding of the "nonsensical" utterance), for now, what is important to see is this same phenomenon in two different guises: the "infinitely extendible" comic climax and the rather negative experience of delirium. Despite the negativity of such delirium, however, one can sense the comedian's eager approach toward it.

---

he suggests that such pure stuttering repetitions do not occur in Aristophanes ("Gerade das Stottern scheint in den Stücken des Aristophanes nicht vorzukommen"; Kloss (2001) 205), but this passage might have changed his views.

[109] Miller (1944) 31.

Conclusions

In the last two chapters, I argued that the discovery of nonsense in comedy ("this is nonsense") is a central pleasure of the genre. But a question about the nature of such nonsense then follows: why, if the discovery of nonsense is some central pleasure, is comedy not exclusively Pseudartaban gibberish or Socrates playing with words like *aerobateo*? It would certainly be possible to "discover nonsense" in such a performance, but it would be difficult to imagine how such a performance could be enjoyable. Instead, such a delirious "comedy" would likely irritate within the first few minutes and be unbearable soon thereafter. The answer that I offered is that although the perception of nonsense can be a negative experience (not least owing to its associations with delirium), this perception is nevertheless a comic goal. In the case of language play, rather than thinking of comedy as deploying certain comic techniques in the production of sense or meaning, I suggested that one might envision comedy exploring perceived nonsense with certain assurances of sense.

To consider this once more, it is worth returning to Silk's chapter on Aristophanic style (which is probably the best discussion to be found), where, at the end, he makes some gestures toward the relationship between comic techniques and comic meaning. Summarizing the formal elements of Aristophanes' language (which are, incidentally, also the usual suspects rounded up by those studying Aristophanic humor), Silk concludes (2000, 156–7, his italics): "Aristophanic poetry is not *all* physical, *all* accumulative, *all* discontinuous, or else it would be tedious, endless and unintelligible. Rather, it uses these qualities, freely, in expression of a fully intelligible – and intelligent – vision." Here is a return to the concept of, *mutatis mutandis*, comic technique: that is, the comedian is applying these linguistic aberrances in the expression of his "fully intelligible vision." Not unlike the concept of a "comic veil" discussed in this book's introduction, here comic exuberance is in service to the intelligible idea, and not vice versa.

Yet there is a catch, and this catch is reminiscent of de Ste. Croix's "pure comedy," also discussed in the introduction. In the last line of his chapter, Silk articulates this free application of formal elements like discontinuity as a sort of comic essence: "If comedy means freedom, this is comedy at its most comic." If I understand Silk correctly here, he is identifying what is "comic," perhaps comedy's essential element, in linguistic exuberance itself (i.e., "freedom," "mobility") and not in the "fully intelligible" ideas which this exuberance is serving. If this is his position, it is not hard to appreciate:

surely it is by the removal of elements like the accumulative κομποφακελορρήμονα or the Kinsman's repetitive τὸν δεῖνα ... τὸν δεῖνα ... τὸν δεῖνα ..., and not the intelligible ideas, that comedy would appear less "comic."

But what of the removal of the "intelligible vision"? As Silk writes (already quoted), comedy would then simply be "tedious, endless and unintelligible." This is something I have been emphasizing in this chapter: if such an excessive neologism appeared outside the context of an exuberant comic ending, it is not simply that some comic faucet would shut off, but a new realm of irritability would be upon the spectator ("tedious, endless, unintelligible"). The question that remains, of course, is: if the "comic" part of comedy lies in that freedom to apply the discontinuous, the accumulative, and so forth, rather than the idea for which this freedom is "used," should not the terms of employment be reversed? That is, should it not be said that the "perfectly intelligible" idea is in service to the "comic" part of comedy, and even renders, as Freud would say, the comic part possible? After all, this intelligible part prevents those very same elements from being experienced in a negative and "unintelligible" way.

To conclude this chapter, I would like to draw together briefly the argument here with that of the previous chapter, where I explored the phenomenon of "discovering nonsense" in mockery, since a number of mirror-like relationships have arisen between the two arguments. In that chapter, regarding aggressive play, it seemed that for aggression to become enjoyable it required the form of nonsense, that is, the inconsequential nature of play where one can insult and not "mean" it. In this chapter, where I have been studying language play, the opposite seems to be occurring: in order for perceived nonsense to become enjoyable it often requires the form of consequence or, one might even say with Freud, aggression. Without such assurance of "sense"[110] the negative reactions against unjustified play or delirium may begin to arise. But what is the relationship between these two forms of play, that is, the language play and aggressive play? To think a few final thoughts about this, I would like to turn to a rambling speech from Antiphanes' *Cleophanes* (120 KA):

> τὸν σπουδαῖον ἀκολουθεῖν ἐρεῖς
> ἐν τῶι Λυκείωι μετὰ σοφιστῶν νὴ Δία
> λεπτῶν, ἀσίτων, συκίνων, λέγονθ' ὅτι

[110] For definitions of "sense," see above note 101. Cf. Freud's (1989[1905]9) extended quote of Lipps (1898) (from whom Freud takes his starting point: cf. 5 n. 1) regarding a joke's "sense," "truth," or "consequence."

τὸ πρᾶγμα τοῦτ' οὐκ ἔστιν, εἴπερ γίγνεται,
οὐδ' ἔστι γάρ πω γιγνόμενον ὃ γίγνεται,
οὔτ' εἰ πρότερον ἦν, ἔστιν ὅ γε νῦν γίγνεται,
ἔστιν γὰρ οὐκ ὂν οὐδέν· ὃ δὲ μὴ γέγονέ πω,
οὐκ ἔσθ' ἕωσπερ γέγονε † ὃ δὲ μὴ γέγονέ πω.†
ἐκ τοῦ γὰρ εἶναι γέγονεν· εἰ δ'οὐκ ἦν ὅθεν,
πῶς ἐγένετ' ἐξ οὐκ ὄντος; οὐχ οἷόν τε γάρ.
† εἰ δ' αὐτόθεν ποι γέγονεν, οὐκ ἔσται
κηποι δεποτις εἴη, πόθεν γενήσεται
τοὐκ ὂν εἰς οὐκ ὄν· εἰς οὐκ ὂν γὰρ οὐ δυνήσεται.†
ταυτὶ δ' ὅ τι ἐστὶν οὐδ' ἂν Ἀπόλλων μάθοι

Will you say it's the serious fellow who follows the sophists in the Lyceum –
god! thin, hungry, worthless – saying that "this thing is not, if it is becoming,
nor is something becoming which becomes, nor if it was earlier, is yet that
thing which is now becoming, for nothing not being *is*; but that which has
not yet become is until it has become, †seeing that it has not yet become†;
for it has become from being; but if there were not a whence, how did it
become from what is not? That is impossible.†But if it became from something somewhere, it cannot be ... from where something which is not will
become something which is not; for into what is not it cannot pass."† What
all this means not Apollo himself could understand.

This ten-line speech of the "serious" fellow is impressive: indecipherable, yet
playfully so. However, like the examples discussed in this chapter, instruments of formal humor analysis like "set-up," "punchline," "connector,"
"disjunctor," and so forth, are of little help to articulate the nature of its
comic effect. That is, despite the contortions of argument, the repetitions of
gignetai, and so forth, there seems to be no single cognitive spring that one
can identify and no single point at which one might be said to laugh.
Rather, like the smorgasbord word of *Ecclesiazusae* and the *ho deina*'s of
Thesmophoriazusae it seems that at some subjective moment in these ten lines,
laughter arises: perhaps right around the time that the listener recognizes the
parody, or perhaps when the listener, after trying to make sense of the lines,
recognizes that interpretation is a fool's errand; or perhaps a mixture of both.
The subjective response of laughter (which may be related to the perception
that the speech seems to be "nonsense") may even occur more than once,
taking analysis even further from any concept of a formal trigger.[111]

As with the repetitive stuttering of the Kinsman in the *Thesmophoriazusae*, here is a moment of language at a certain boundary of meaninglessness.

---

[111] Cf. Georges Bataille's laughter at Hegel and his (Bataille's) development of a theory of the "sover-
eignty" of the comic outside that of rationality: see Trahair (2007) 7–8, 15–33 for discussion.

When one removes the parodic frame, focuses on the lines themselves, and demands to know precisely what they mean, one collides with a linguistic brick wall, just as if one tried to articulate what the Kinsman's τὸν δεῖνα . . . repetition "means."[112] It is not difficult to imagine the irritation that these ten lines might conjure in another context or even in the comic context, if the rambling continued beyond the ten lines that Antiphanes allows. Yet, this permeability between the positive response and the negative one (or as Morreall puts it, "funny-haha" and "funny-strange") is what is most revealing: it is not that Antiphanes is "applying" rambling speech somehow as a comic "technique" here, but rather that he is exploring certain boundaries of meaninglessness itself, edging ever closer to those moments where potentially negative responses of perceived nonsense might arise.

Freud might say (as I discussed above) that the aggression of the Eleatic parody is not *itself* the source of pleasure, but rather an intellectual decoy on which to focus (the purpose, or *Tendenz*), in order to reap the pleasures of "childish" nonsense. The parodic frame creates a safe-zone for the playful exploration of language malfunction and an audience can feel the assurance of such sense. But there is something disappointing about such a view, if I understand it, not least because the aggression of the parody *itself* feels pleasurable and not merely some "frame" or "veil" for some other pleasurable source. The dilemma that arises from Freud's position here is that, on the one hand, one does not wish to locate all the pleasure in the judgment "Eleatics are fools," and thereby overlook the magnificent nonsense speech itself; but, on the other hand, one does not wish to overlook the fact that it also feels rather pleasurable to prick the Eleatic-types in the audience.

Bateson's emphasis, like Freud's, was on the mode of play, but he did not entangle himself in ideas about "objective" nonsense as Freud did, and, as I mentioned earlier, this entanglement seems to have caused problems for the latter. Nevertheless, play's relationship to nonsense is a central problem. Via the mode of play, *any* utterance, *any* action can be rendered inconsequential and so "nonsense," and, as I argued in Chapter 3, this mode of play ought to be seen as pleasurable rather than the objects of play themselves (e.g., aggression). But if this is so, there would seem to be something redundant occurring when one plays with language. In rendering inconsequential the potentially inconsequential, one seems to be playing with play itself in some delirious form of "pure" play. So too, the interplay between language play and aggressive play does not really seem separable after all, since, as in the

---

[112] Note too that the discovery of meaning would render the parody less effective.

Antiphanes passage and the puns of *Birds*, the same passage might be described in either way: one is either rendering aggression inconsequential via the signals of language play, or making inconsequence bearable via assurances of aggression. And the two are more connected still: to explore aggression in play is not *just* to explore how aggressive one can be, but also to explore how much can be said in a context where (aggressive) words mean nothing (i.e., play): which is itself, at least in form, an exploration of play/ nonsense itself.

CHAPTER 5

Playing it straight: comedy's "nonsense!" accusations

Ray, you're never gonna solve it. It's not a riddle because Who is on first base. That's a joke, Ray, it's comedy, but when you do it you're not funny. You're like the comedy of Abbott and Abbott.

Rain Man (1988)

In Chapter 4, I argued that comedy exhibits a tension between sense and nonsense, and focused on the difference between (and balance of) wordplay and political (or contemporary) aggression. Wordplay, unlike usual sentence syntax, bears a real threat of "going nowhere."[1] In the production of sense, it seems one must move forward: one makes a "point," and then moves on to the next "point"; a listener takes this "point" and moves on with his or her own "point." Wordplay, however, has the ability to delay or even defeat this relay race of the forward motion of sensible communication: ideas do not move forward, but swim laterally across pre-existing homophony. If one, through this senseless lateral motion, is able to move forward and end up making sense, one has successfully produced a pun or a joke or perhaps a clever rhetorical effect. If, however, that lateral homophonic motion is all that is occurring and it is clear that no forward motion has happened, such utterances tend to be rejected as nonsense. The same can be said for other devices like repetition: so long as one can prove that one is moving forward with sensible communication, one is safe and using repetition as a proper rhetorical (or joking) effect. If not, it becomes clear that one is standing still and no sense is being produced.

---

[1] For more on the opposed relationship between nonsense and motion, see Stewart (1979) 3–12, e.g., at 5: "Nonsense is an impediment ... It trips us up. It gets in the way." It should be noticed here that the Greek *spoudaios* ("serious" but also "quick") contains both notions, as if one who is intent on moving somewhere is *spoudaios* or "serious" about their daily business, while those uninterested in such motion are not "serious," e.g., jesters, idlers, etc. Cf. Chantraine (1968–80): s.v. σπεύδω "Dans cette famille de mots, on observe le champ sémantique de σπουδή qui du sens de 'hâte' est passé au sens de 'application, sérieux, études'." Beekes (2010) does not discuss the relationship further between these two senses.

As I have been arguing, comedy's vital opposition is between not sense (or meaning) and humor, but sense and nonsense. Humor and jokes are properly (and have been called) the offspring of the marriage between these two poles. Sense makes the negative aspect of nonsense – the one which resembles delirium – bearable, I have argued, and unless there is enough effort to show that sense is indeed being produced, the resulting nonsense is seldom pleasurable at all. In this section, I will continue the exploration of this tension between comedy's two poles by examining a particular problem of the genre: the way that comic jokes or gags are received by other characters on stage.

It is clear that jokes or comic gags are intended to draw laughs from the audience, but do the on-stage characters react to jokes in the same way? Some have suggested that laughter on stage was a fairly common occurrence, and so, it might be expected that characters react symmetrically to the audience, laughing right along after a joke's detonation.[2] But others have suggested an opposite reaction, noticing that often when characters crack jokes, these jokes are then ignored by the other characters. In such situations, it seems that the other characters either pretend the joke-utterance had never occurred, or they "translate" the utterance into some serious, non-joke form. The reason, some scholars have suggested, is that if a character were to explain or apologize for a joke, the comic rhythm would be broken: too much dramatic time would be consumed, and the very act of forcing the joke into sensible communication would kill the joke.

But there is also another way of reacting to jokes on stage. Sometimes when one character tells a joke, the other character will actually scold the jester for his jesting as if trying to maintain the "seriousness" of the on-stage discourse. What is most interesting is the form that this "serious" reprimand often takes: the scolder scolds the jester specifically for speaking "nonsense" or engaging in "nonsense" behavior (τί ληρεῖς;, οὐδὲν λέγεις, οὐ μὴ φλυαρήσεις ἔχων, etc.) These brief reprimands seem natural enough and editors of comedy have acknowledged this rhythm of punchlines and nonsense-accusations before, as I will show below. But despite the familiarity of this rhythm of the jester and the "straight" man, it leads to some difficult questions: why, if jokes, humor, and comic gags are positive desiderata, do we as spectators seem to require someone on stage who reacts precisely in the opposite way that we do? *We* know that jokes and gags are desirable and so we laugh – but why,

---

[2] See Kidd (2011) for various scholarly opinions about on-stage laughter in comedy (e.g., Taplin (1996) 190: "Performers who want to arouse laughter often enact laughter themselves as a stimulant," and Halliwell (2008) 245). But, as Kidd (2011) argues, there is little evidence for much on-stage laughter and this dearth of evidence may point to the fact that there was not much laughter on stage in the first place.

then, is there this need for a "straight" man, one who often not only
ignores but often rebukes the foolish jester?[3] It is as if there is an on-stage
element in comedy that is rebuking the comedy *itself*. I will argue that this
requirement of on-stage "seriousness" (and its occasional manifestation as
a "nonsense" accusation) can be explained precisely in the same terms as
the previous chapter's argument regarding nonsense and jokes: comic
buffoonery is only pleasurable if the illusion of sense or forward motion
can be maintained. Without this illusion, comedy quickly deteriorates
into senselessness.

Consider, for example, the following scene from *Thesmophoriazusae* that
was examined in Chapter 4. Here the Kinsman begins to stutter his way
through an enjoyable comic gag as he is interrogated by Cleisthenes (618–22):

ΚΛ.   εἰπέ μοι,
    τίς ἐστ' ἀνήρ σοι;
Κη.   τὸν ἐμὸν ἄνδρα πυνθάνει;
    τὸν δεῖνα γιγνώσκεις, τὸν ἐκ Κοθωκιδῶν;
ΚΛ. τὸν δεῖνα; ποῖον;
Κη.   ἔσθ' ὁ δεῖν', ὃς καί ποτε
    τὸν δεῖνα τὸν τοῦ δεῖνα –
ΚΛ.   ληρεῖν μοι δοκεῖς.

CL.   Tell me,
    who is your husband?
KI.   You're asking who's *my* husband?
    Do you know what's-his-name, from Kothokidai?
CL. What's-his-name? *Which* what's-his-name?
KI.   *What's*-his-name, the one who once
    what's-his-name's what's his name . . .
CL.   You're talking nonsense.

The repetitive stutter of "what's-his-name" from the Kinsman is met with
the charge "you're speaking nonsense" not once but twice, as if emphasizing
Cleisthenes' irritation.[4] It raises the question: what is the relationship

---

[3] By the "straight" character, I do not mean a character who is permanently "straight" (as Dover (1987)
246 notices, anyone in Old Comedy can play the jester), but simply the character who functions as a
temporary comic foil for whoever is cracking the joke at the moment. The role of the "straight"
character is rarely studied (despite numerous studies of the "clown" or "buffoon" character). See
McLeish (1980) 129. A non-scholarly, technical treatise on comedy nicely articulates the importance of
the "straight" character in passing (Mendrinos (2004) 267, my italics): "The straight man is the
comedic person in charge of getting out all the information and keeping the rhythm of the piece going.
Without a straight man, the so-called funny ones usually wind up being a buffoon, *wandering aimlessly
from bit to bit.*"
[4] To the Kinsman answer, ἡ δεῖν' ἔμοιγ' "I've got what's-her-name," Cleisthenes (again) responds οὐδὲν
λέγεις "you're speaking nonsense."

between Cleisthenes' negative reaction to the utterance and the positive one of the audience (who are presumably laughing)?[5] Cleisthenes' on-stage resistance to the comic gag seems to create a sort of elastic tension for the scene: he is resisting the very jokes that the scene is deploying. But what if this resistance were removed? What if, for example, when the Kinsman kept repeating this phrase "what's-his-name's what-his-name . . ." Cleisthenes did not resist, but *also* found the repetitive speech funny just as the audience does? This would be quite a different situation: now, one character is repeating an insensible phrase over and over again, and the other character is laughing. In my view, this could potentially be not a comic spectacle at all, but something rather eerie and discomforting. Such an imagined scene recalls something out of David Lynch, or perhaps the eerie scene from the *Odyssey* where the suitors laugh with "jaws not their own."[6]

Of course, in this scene, on-stage laughter is *not* occurring: instead, Cleisthenes becomes more and more irate over the Kinsman's insensibility, and so, that palpable elastic tension between the Kinsman's nonsense and Cleisthenes' "seriousness" is maintained. As I will argue, when this tension of "seriousness" is established (i.e., Cleisthenes rebukes the repetitive nonsense of the Kinsman), the audience is able to enjoy the nonsense *as* comedy, rather than the potential eeriness or discomfort that such language malfunction might otherwise produce. The "straight" character must insist on forward motion: if he were to indulge in the foolishness of the "foolish" character (e.g., by laughing), those on-stage anxieties which had previously been expressed via Cleisthenes' scolding could potentially become the anxieties of the audience.

I will begin this argument with an overview of the evidence for this comic rhythm where an accusation follows a joke's punchline, and show where this phenomenon occurs not only in Aristophanes but in the comic fragments as well. I will then contextualize this phenomenon with the genre's more consistent habit of having its actors ignore jokes or play the comedy "straight." After comparing and contrasting these two ways of responding to jokes (ignoring jokes vs. scolding them), I will consider why this accusation

---

[5] This relationship can be viewed in terms of the third-party nature of many jokes, i.e., the differential effect on the audience who can distance themselves from Cleisthenes' irritation, and thereby laugh at it. This third-party nature is certainly in play but not the focus here. For more discussion on the third-party nature of jokes and the pleasures of aggression against a joke's "Butt" (a version of which can be found as early as Plut. *Mor.* 631c–632a), see Freud (1989[1905]) 118–19; Halliwell (2008) 310–11.

[6] *Od.* 20.347 οἱ δ' ἤδη γναθμοῖσι γελώων ἀλλοτρίοισιν with Halliwell (2008) 92–7 for discussion and bibliography.

of nonsense occurs, and how it helps to explain why comedy so often needs to be played "straight" in the first place. This nonsense-accusation suggests what the comedian is protecting the comedy from becoming: namely, that nonsense which, as I have been arguing, is both the goal and the danger at once.

On-stage accusations of "nonsense!"

In Chapter 1, I studied Greek words for "nonsense" such as *phluaria* and *lēros* in a number of different genres of Greek literature, with a special attention to oratory and medical writing. I generally avoided discussion of the usage of these words in Greek comedy, mostly so that I could gain a lexical footing outside the comic genre, and build a conceptual map before delving into comedy itself. But, arguably, Greek comedy as a genre is the single largest user of Greek words for nonsense – language is constantly being called nonsense, and characters' behaviors are constantly being called nonsensical – as if there were some particular kinship between comedy and nonsense in ancient Greek thought.

Simone Beta devotes a large lexical study to these nonsense-words, analyzing when and where, and especially about whom these words are used, in a chapter devoted to comedy's empty speech – "La parola vuota."[7] He relates, for example, that sophists like Socrates are accused of "chiacchiera" (the chattering of *adoleskhia*, but also *lalia* and *stomulia*),[8] as well as Euripides (*lalein*). Aeschylus, on the other hand, is not accused of *lalia* but is accused of *lēros*.[9] Cleon too is accused of chattering,[10] and so are women,[11] slaves,[12] cooks,[13] and old people.[14] Beta is less interested in "delirious speech" (e.g. *lēros*), since, as he writes, anyone can be accused of "speaking deliriously" – so listing the types of characters who are accused of such nonsense is more haphazard and pointless.[15] Nevertheless, he devotes a number of pages to the occurrences of this (and similar) "nonsense"-words in comedy, reminding the

---

[7] Beta (2004) 148–74.   [8] Beta (2004) 149–53.
[9] Beta (2004) 153–5. Aeschylus is actually called *aperilaleton* at *Ran.* 839 ("ossia incapace di parlare a vuoto," 155).
[10] Beta (2004) 156–7.
[11] Beta (2004) 157–62 at 62: "In definitiva, il λαλεῖν si mostra in assoluto come il tipico verbo delle donne, indipendentemente dal loro lavoro e dalla loro posizione all' interno della società."
[12] Beta (2004) 163–4.   [13] Beta (2004) 164–5.   [14] Beta (2004) 165–7.
[15] Beta (2004) 168: "Non sempre, a dire il vero, le sue ricorrenze nei poeti comici sono particolarmente significative per la mia analisi: nella maggior parte dei casi, la domanda τί ληρεῖς; equivale al nostro 'che razza di stupidaggini stai dicendo' e può essere rivolta a chiunque."

reader when and where they arise.[16] A similar, but less exhaustive analysis of such words can be found in Neil O'Sullivan's study of rhetorical judgments in Aristophanes' *Frogs* and, more contingently, in Nancy Worman's *Abusive Mouths in Classical Athens*.[17] As these studies show, comedy's use of words for "empty" or "nonsensical" language is pervasive: since ridicule of people or characters is to be expected of comedy, it is no surprise to see a well-developed lexicon of negative judgments on their speech.

But what is interesting about this corpus of nonsense-words is that, often enough, these accusations of "nonsense" refer to the ongoing comedy itself – particularly in response to jokes or comic gags. Take the following example from *Clouds*. Here, Socrates is attempting to teach Strepsiades poetic meter, but with less success than he might prefer (641–4):

Σω. οὐ τοῦτ' ἐρωτῶ σ', ἀλλ' ὅτι κάλλιστον μέτρον
          ἡγεῖ, πότερον τὸ τρίμετρον ἢ τὸ τετράμετρον;
Στ. ἐγὼ μὲν οὐδὲν πρότερον ἡμιέκτεω.
Σω. οὐδὲν λέγεις, ὤνθρωπε.

so. I'm not asking you this, but what you think the most
          beautiful measure is: the trimeter or tetrameter?
st. For me, nothing's better than the half-pint.
so. You're speaking nonsense, man.

A clear set-up and punchline here via Socrates and Strepsiades – a nice joke for the audience. But Socrates' reaction is telling: he does not ignore the joke, nor does he laugh along with the audience. Rather, he calls Strepsiades' response about the half-pint "nonsense" (οὐδὲν λέγεις), presumably in a sober, scolding fashion. Later, a similar interchange occurs with almost precisely the same rhythm, with οὐδὲν λέγεις inserted at exactly the same point – namely, that post-punchline pause which occurs after a joke. At 776:

Σω. ὅπως ἀποστρέψαις ἂν ἀντιδικῶν δίκην,
          μέλλων ὀφλήσειν, μὴ παρόντων μαρτύρων.
Στ. φαυλότατα καὶ ῥᾷστ'.
Σω.   εἰπὲ δή.
Στ.   καὶ δὴ λέγω.
          εἰ πρόσθεν ἔτι μιᾶς ἐνεστώσης δίκης
          πρὶν τὴν ἐμὴν καλεῖσθ' ἀπαγξαίμην τρέχων.
Σω. οὐδὲν λέγεις.

---

[16] Note the categorical mistakes of not putting οὐδὲν λέγεις (43) among "empty speech" with ληρεῖν, etc. (148–74), as well as discussing the habit of "saying one thing while meaning another'" under empty speech rather than deceptive speech (an overlap which he admits at 173–4).

[17] O'Sullivan (1992) 106–50; Worman (2008) 62–107.

so. Tell me how you, as a defendant, would rebut a lawsuit that you
    were about to lose due to a lack of witnesses.
st. Most simply and easily.
so.   Tell me.
st.   All right.
    If I, while there's still one case left on the docket before mine's
      called, would run off and hang myself.
so. You're speaking nonsense.

Again: a nice set-up and punchline, with, one imagines, audience laughter
in response. But Socrates, again, does not laugh along with the audience,
nor does he ignore Strepsiades' answer. Instead he scolds the line and calls
it "nonsense." As the interchange continues, Strepsiades protests, milking
some more laughs out of his comic logic, and Socrates again accuses him of
nonsense (ὑθλεῖς):

Στ.   νὴ τοὺς θεοὺς ἔγωγ', ἐπεὶ
     οὐδεὶς κατ' ἐμοῦ τεθνεῶτος εἰσάξει δίκην.
Σω. ὑθλεῖς. ἄπερρ'. οὐκ ἂν διδαξαίμην σ' ἔτι.

st.   By the gods, I am too [making sense];!
    Since no one will bring a suit against me when I'm dead.
so. You're blathering. Go away. I won't teach you anymore.

Punchline followed by οὐδὲν λέγεις or in this case ὑθλεῖς. Is it a coincidence? It
may seem rather obvious that Socrates should be calling Strepsiades' absurd
answers "nonsense" here, whether these answers are perceived by him to be
jokes or not. But this comic rhythm occurs frequently enough that it raises
questions about why jokes or punchlines are being called "nonsense." Take,
for example, the following passage from *Birds*. Here the servant of Hoopoe
answers the door and Peisthetairos and Euelpides try to persuade him that
they are not two men, but two birds (64–6):

Πε. ἀλλ' οὐκ ἐσμὲν ἀνθρώπω.
Θε. τί δαί;
Πε. ὑποδεδιὼς ἔγωγε, Λιβυκὸν ὄρνεον.
Θε. οὐδὲν λέγεις.

pe. No: we're not two men.
se.   What, then?
pe. I'm a fearfowl [Somm.], a Libyan bird.
se. You're speaking nonsense.

There is little that this passage has in common with the *Clouds* schooling
passages, except for this set-up and punchline rhythm; and this same

punchline rhythm followed by οὐδὲν λέγεις occurs again at *Birds* 986,[18] as well as at *Thesmophoriazusae* 625[19] and 634.[20] The very similar line τί ληρεῖς "why are you blathering/talking nonsense?" often fulfills an identical function to οὐδὲν λέγεις (or the lone ὑθλεῖς) within that post-punchline pause. At *Clouds* 499, when Socrates asks Strepsiades to remove his cloak and Strepsiades counters that he is not looking for stolen goods (thereby riffing on an Attic law and triggering the joke), Socrates replies τί ληρεῖς;.[21] When Strepsiades explains his new-found knowledge to his son (829), parroting and bungling Socrates' earlier lesson about Dinos and Zeus (379) – something of a "boomerang" joke[22] – Pheidippides responds with τί ληρεῖς;.[23] Similarly, when Euelpides in *Birds* comically turns one of Peisthetaerus' phrases, Peisthetaerus demands of him why is he speaking nonsense (341).[24] When Bdelycleon proposes the outlandish idea that Philocleon set up trials at home, trying the slaves (767), he receives a τί ληρεῖς; in response.[25] When the third wife in *Lysistrata* rushes in attempting to malinger with an absurdly fake pregnancy, it is τί ληρεῖς; that meets her (743).[26] When the Kinsman, depilated and singed, exclaims to the effeminate

[18] Peisthetaerus, in response to the oracle-monger's oracles, creates one of his own regarding a certain charlatan who annoys sacrificers and needs a beating. To the oracle's punchline δὴ τότε χρὴ τύπτειν αὐτὸν πλευρῶν τὸ μεταξὺ, the oracle-monger responds οὐδὲν λέγειν οἶμαι σε (986), which Henderson suggestively translates as "you must be kidding," overriding the divide between nonsense and joking.

[19] This passage where the Kinsman repeats the phrase τὸν δεῖνα (vel sim.) under Cleisthenes' interrogation was discussed in Chapter 4 (and in this chapter's introduction). At the fourth τὸν δεῖνα Cleisthenes responds ληρεῖν μοι δοκεῖς (622); at the fifth, οὐδὲν λέγεις (625).

[20] Here the Kinsman, now being interrogated by Critylla, delves into aischrologic territory for his third answer of what occurred at last year's Thesmophoria σκάφιον Ξένυλλ' ᾔτησεν· οὐ γὰρ ἦν ἁμίς "Xenylla asked for a basin, since there was no piss-pot." For the argument (originally in Pollux) that the σκάφιον is a female urine-receptacle and ἁμίς a male urine-receptacle, see Austin and Olson ad loc. Henderson's translation reflects the latter (which adds to the humor: "Xenylla asked for a potty because there wasn't a urinal.").

[21] Streps: ἀλλ' οὐχὶ φωράσων ἔγωγ' εἰσέρχομαι. Soc: κατάθου. τί ληρεῖς;. The joke is based on an Attic law whereby one is required to remove one's cloak before inspecting a house for stolen goods, in order not to plant a stolen object in the house. See Dover (1989[1968]) ad loc.

[22] For "boomerang" jokes, see Kloss (2001) 205; MacDowell (1971) ad *Vesp.* 989.

[23] Cf. 829 Δῖνος βασιλεύει τὸν Δί' ἐξεληλακώς with 379 where Socrates explains that Dinos compels the clouds to move.

[24] In response to the question, "why did you lead me here?," Peisthetaerus' ἵν' ἀκολουθοίης ἐμοί becomes Euelpides' turned ἵνα μὲν οὖν κλάοιμι μεγάλα; this, in turn, sets up Peisthetaerus' next joke πῶς κλαύσει γάρ, ἢν ἅπαξ γε τώφθαλμὼ 'κκοπῇς. The question τί ληρεῖς; often both follows a joke and is a launch-pad for the next one. See discussion below, e.g., of Eupolis' *Flatterers* and Aristophanes' *Wealth*.

[25] Note in this line the final position of the word "slaves" (an important linguistic marker of verbal humor) to highlight the absurdity.

[26] The woman, being the *third* attempted sex-starved malingerer, makes it clear that her pregnancy is a fake one even before Lysistrata's line ἀλλ' οὐκ ἐκύεις σύ γ' ἐχθές at 744). Note too her para-tragic lament of oncoming childbirth ὦ πότνι' Ἰλείθυ...

Cleisthenes "what man would be stupid enough to endure depilation?" Cleisthenes responds with ληρεῖς (595).[27] At *Frogs* 1197, Euripides responds with ληρεῖς in response to Dionysus' gratuitous *onomasti komoidein* against Erasinides (one of the generals put to death after Arginusae).[28] In *Ecclesiazusae*, when a man aischrologically airs the possibility of newly ruling women pissing down on him, the response is, again, "nonsense" (833).[29] In short, when one character offers a joke or punchline, often enough they receive in response some form of the accusation "you're speaking nonsense!"

Nor is it only verbal jokes which are accused of being nonsense on stage, but also other comic gags of a more physical nature. Consider the following scene from *Frogs*. Charon is ordering Dionysus to adopt his position at the oars, but, instead, Dionysus engages in typical comic foolery (198–203):

Χα. κάθιζ' ἐπὶ κώπην. εἴ τις ἔτι πλεῖ, σπευδέτω.
      οὗτος, τί ποιεῖς;
Δι. ὅτι ποιῶ; τί δ' ἄλλο γ' ἢ
      ἵζω 'πὶ κώπην, οὗπερ ἐκέλευές με σύ;
Χα. οὔκουν καθεδεῖ δῆτ' ἐνθαδί, γάστρων;
Δι. ἰδού.
Χα. οὔκουν προβαλεῖ τὼ χεῖρε κἀκτενεῖς;
Δι. ἰδού.
Χα. οὐ μὴ φλυαρήσεις ἔχων. . .

CH. Sit at the oar. If anyone else wants to come on board, hurry up!
     You! What are you doing?
     (*Di. sits on the oar*)
DI. Doing? What other than sitting *on* the oar, where you
     ordered me.
CH. Sit down *here*, fatso.
DI. OK.
CH. Move forward and stretch out your hands.
DI. OK. (*he stretches his hands out but without the oar*)
CH. Stop your nonsense!

Dionysus is being particularly playful (or foolish) here. When Charon orders him to sit at the oar (ἐπὶ κώπην), he sits *on* the oar. When Charon

---

[27] Not just the comic irony, but also Cleisthenes is implicated in this joke. The Kinsman's para-tragic female oath οὐκ οἴομαι 'γωγ', ὦ πολυτιμήτω θεώ caps the humorous question.

[28] Here it is questionable whether he is ignoring Dionysus' interjected line and responding to Aeschylus' criticism, or responding to Dionysus' line. I would argue that it is a mixture of the two, rather like Cleon's line in *Eq.* 902 βωμολοχεύμασιν ταράττεις "you're confusing me with your buffooneries." There Cleon seems to be referring more to the fact that a climax of punning and irrationality is occurring, rather than to either the Sausage-Seller's particular argument or Demos' pun.

[29] Again the joke arises from the context, as Ussher explains ad loc. since κατουρήσωσι is the third of three kata- compounds at 826 and 829.

tells him to reach out for the oar (προβαλεῖ τὼ χεῖρε κἀκτενεῖς), he simply reaches out in any odd direction. It is a comic gag, of course, and one which is presumably enjoyable for the audience, just like the jokes listed above. But the question is this: if these jokes or comic gags are enjoyable for the audience, indeed, seem to be the "comic" part of comedy ("comedy itself"), why are they scolded by other characters on stage? And why does this scolding take the particular form of "you're speaking nonsense"? Surely, it would make more sense that such jokes would be celebrated upon their on-stage deployment. But, instead, as if on cue, often when one character gives a punchline, the other character actually scolds the jester for his jesting – *even though this jesting is precisely what the comedy is trying to do.*

"Nonsense!" accusations in uncertain comic fragments

Even when jokes are not clear, or texts are uncertain, this accusation of nonsense, I would argue, is a common enough refrain that it can suggest the presence of a joke. Take the following passage from Eubulus' *Sphinx-Karion* (106 KA = Athen. 10.449e–f), for example. Here, Speaker A is telling Speaker B a riddle: "it is a tongueless chatterer, with the same name for male and female, steward of its own winds, hairy, at another time smooth, speaking indecipherable things to those who understand, drawing *nomos* from *nomos*; both one and many, if one wounds it, it's unwounded."[30] The interchange that follows between Speakers A and B is, as Kassel and Austin print it:

> τί ἔστι τοῦτο; τί ἀπορεῖς; (Β.) Καλλίστρατος.
> (Α.) πρωκτὸς μὲν οὖν οὗτος <γε'> σὺ δὲ ληρεῖς ἔχων.
> οὗτος γὰρ αὐτός ἐστιν ἄγλωττος λάλος,. . .

> What's the answer? Are you stumped? (B.) Callistratus.
> A. No: it's the anus. You keep talking nonsense.
> It's really one and the same thing – a tongueless chatterer. . .

Two answers are given to the riddle: "Callistratus" and an "anus." It is clear that the first answer from Speaker B – Callistratus – is a fine *onomasti* joke: Callistratus was a leading politician during the Second Athenian Confederacy, and long speeches (λαλῶν) as well as a possible penchant for "dragging in law after law" in his speeches (νόμον ἐκ νόμου ἕλκων) might be

---

[30] Eubulus 106 KA: ἔστι λαλῶν ἄγλωσσος, ὁμώνυμος ἄρρενι θῆλυς, / οἰκείων ἀνέμων ταμίας, δασύς, ἄλλοτε λεῖος, / ἀξύνετα ξυνετοῖσι λέγων, νόμον ἐκ νόμου ἕλκων· ἓν δ' ἐστὶν καὶ πολλὰ καὶ ἂν τρώσηι τις ἄτρωτος.

imagined here.[31] One can even imagine a slight pause after the answer "Callistratus" for the audience to laugh at the unexpected *onomasti* joke.

But then what of the "anus"? This too would be a nice joke, but one which may become lost in the shuffle depending on how the speakers are assigned. Note the way that Kassel and Austin (as well as Hunter and others) edit the text: assigning σὺ δὲ ληρεῖς ἔχων to Speaker A has the effect of muddling the second punchline, or perhaps suggests that the "anus" is not a punchline at all. Speaker A's "No: it's the anus; you're speaking nonsense," is certainly a satisfactory example of an ordinary conversation, but in comedy, it seems to fumble the expected rhythm (or, again, suggests that the "anus" answer is not a joke at all). When one adds to this idea the number of times that "you're speaking nonsense" actually occurs in response to a joke, it seems that this instinct over comic rhythm is substantiated by a significant number of parallels. Surely, what is needed here is a post-punchline pause after Speaker A's revelation of the anus, and the perfect way to harness this post-punchline pause is to adopt the speaker assignment that Gulick and others adopt:[32] namely that it is Speaker B, not Speaker A who says "you keep speaking nonsense."[33] Otherwise, there is no possibility for the "anus-answer" to stand as a punchline at all – it gets passed over, and any possible audience laughter is stifled.

Not just speaker-assignment but textual conjectures have been helped along by recognizing this recurrent punchline-then-"nonsense!" pattern of comedy. Take, for example, the following passage from Antiphanes' *Sappho* (fr. 194 KA = Athen. 10.450e–451b).[34] As in Eubulus' fragment, here are two speakers, with the first speaker (probably Sappho) providing a riddle and another speaker giving a humorous answer. Sappho's riddle is about a feminine creature with a voice which reaches across the sea, even though she cannot hear anything: the answer, as Sappho later explains, is a letter, ἐπιστολή. But before she can provide this "correct" answer, as in Eubulus, a

---

[31] The emphasis on speaking – λαλῶν, ἀξύνετα ξυνετοῖσι λέγων, as well as "interposing law after law and so delaying the case" νόμον ἐκ νόμου ἕλκων (so Headlams's (1922) interpretation ad Herodas 5.5, with Hunter (1983)) – may be more obvious than the sexual connotations of δασύς and λεῖος. Eubulus' *Antiope* (fr. 10 KA) may discuss Callistratus' once-plump bottom in sexual terms, but the passage is corrupt. Elsewhere he is described as a pleasure-seeker but attentive to political matters (Theopompus FGrH 115 F 97), and in regards to food at Antiphanes fr. 293 KA. For more bibliography on Callistratus, see Hunter (1983) ad Eub. fr.11.1 and Olson (2006–12) ad loc. (n. 216).

[32] Hunter (1983) 203 writes: "this verse is normally divided between the two speakers, but this is far from certain..."

[33] Hunter (1983) for the question of whether to print σὺ δέ or emend to σὺ δή which is related to the question of speaker division.

[34] For discussion of Antiphanes' *Sappho* in general, see especially Kostantakos (2000a) 157–80.

comic answer occurs in between which references the contemporary politics of the day. Here is Speaker B's satirical answer:

B. ἡ μὲν φύσις γὰρ ἦν λέγεις ἐστὶν πόλις,
   βρέφη δ' ἐν αὐτῆι διατρέφει τοὺς ῥήτορας.
   οὗτοι κεκραγότες δὲ τὰ διαπόντια
   τἀκ τῆς Ἀσίας καὶ τἀπὸ Θράικης λήμματα
   ἕλκουσι δεῦρο. νεμομένων δὲ πλησίον
   αὐτῶν κάθηται λοιδορουμένων τ' ἀεὶ
   ὁ δῆμος οὐδὲν οὔτ' ἀκούων οὔθ' ὁρῶν.
Σα. – – – – πῶς γὰρ γένοιτ' ἄν, ὦ πάτερ,
   ῥήτωρ ἄφωνος;

B. The being of which you speak is a city,
   and the young it nourishes in itself are the rhetors.
   They yell and drag in here
   international revenues from Asia and Thrace.
   While they're living off the fat of the land
   and constantly abusing each other, nearby sits
   the demos seeing and hearing nothing.
SA. – – – – how could a rhetor, father,
   be voiceless?

Speaker B's seven-line political satire ends with the sting in its tail: the "demos" bears the final ridicule of the last line.[35] Like Eubulus' riddle where the unexpected, humorous answer draws criticism, here too, Sappho rejects the political answer. The problem is that in Sappho's rejection, an iamb has fallen out. The conjectures that have filled this iambic lacuna are telling: first, Friedrich Jacobs in 1809 suggested οὐδὲν λέγεις "you're speaking nonsense," and, later, Georg Kaibel in 1887 suggested the similar ληρεῖς ἔχων.[36] What is interesting to note here is that both editors seem to be aware of this comic rhythm that I have been outlining: namely, that when one character speaks in a humorous vein, often enough the other character will respond with something like οὐδὲν λέγεις or ληρεῖς ἔχων.

Finally, in Eupolis' *Flatterers* – the comedy about the spendthrift Callias and the drainage of his wealth via banquets, parasites, and courtesans – there is a joke which has been lost in transmission, although it seems almost certain that a joke is present. Here is the fragment (171 KA):

---

[35] Note here that the object of ridicule is not an individual but the demos, which is evidence contrary (along with, of course, Demos in *Knights*) to the notion that the demos could not be ridiculed (found first in the Old Oligarch 2.18). See Halliwell (2008) 250 n. 84 for more discussion.
[36] Kostantakos (2000) 176 lends support to Jacobs.

(A.) Ἀλκιβιάδης ἐκ τῶν γυναικῶν ἐξίτω. (Β.) τί ληρεῖς;
    οὐκ οἴκαδ' ἐλθὼν τὴν σεαυτοῦ γυμνάσεις δάμαρτα;

A. Let Alcibiades out from the women. B. Why are you blathering?
    Won't you go home and exercise your own wife?

There seems to be general agreement that at least one joke lies in these lines. As Kassel and Austin explain the lines, there is some pathic implication regarding Alcibiades here.[37] Speaker A wants to have his way with Alcibiades and Speaker B tells him to relieve himself with his own wife. The preconditions for a joke seem right: there is clearly something involving sex here, perhaps pathic sex, as well as abuse of a political figure. Alcibiades, who was Callias' brother-in-law at the time of *Flatterers*, may have been one of the roles in the play, or the present joke may have been a one-off *onomasti komoidein*.[38] Sommerstein, however, locates another joke, or perhaps a second joke, in Speaker A's line Ἀλκιβιάδης ἐκ τῶν γυναικῶν ἐξίτω playing on the Athenian rite-of-passage formula, ἐκ τῶν παίδων ἐξίτω "let [him] leave the the ranks of the boys."[39]

In favor of Sommerstein's second joke being present is, I would argue, this line that separates Speaker A's possible joke from Speaker B's possible follow-up joke: τί ληρεῖς; "why are you blathering?" Even though the context of the fragment is unclear, there is a rhythm to these two lines which is immediately recognizable: that often directly after a punchline is this quick accusation of "you're speaking nonsense" or "stop speaking nonsense." Phrases like τί ληρεῖς; or οὐδὲν λέγεις or οὐ μὴ φλυαρήσεις ἔχων and such – namely, the on-stage accusations of nonsense – appear often to be markers of jokes or comic gags. So, it is probable that this is another case of the phenomenon, and Sommerstein is correct about this Alcibiades joke.

"Nonsense!" accusations in view of other responses to jokes

In the previous two sections, I collected evidence for a particular phenomenon which occurs with some frequency on the comic stage – the accusation of "nonsense!" in response to jokes or comic gags. Socrates scolds Strepsiades for his "nonsense" during their lessons (οὐδὲν λέγεις, ὑθλεῖς),

---

[37] Kassel and Austin regarding Athenaeus' misinterpretation of Eupolis here: "pathicum potius quam virum *akolaston pros gynaikas* notari crederes, siquidem qui Alcibiadem petit admonetur ut suam ipsius uxorem subigitet." Cf. Rusten (2011) 247; Napolitano (2005) 57–8.

[38] See Storey (2003) 194–6 for the possibility of Alcibiades in this play. He feels that Alcibiades, being roughly thirty years old at this point, is too old for the pathic joke that Kassel and Austin suggest.

[39] Cf., e.g., Dem. 18.257 ἐξελθόντι δ' ἐκ παίδων "when I had come of age" (lit. "left the ranks of the boys"), and 21.154; also Isoc. 15.289, Aeschin. 1.40, 2.167, Arist. *Ath. Pol.* 42.1 with Sommerstein (1997) 54 for discussion of the *dokimasia* wherein boys enter manhood with enrollment into the deme's citizen list.

Charon scolds Dionysus for his "nonsense" during their attempt to cross the Styx (οὐ μὴ φλυαρήσεις ἔχων), Cleisthenes scolds the Kinsman for his "nonsense" during his interrogation (ληρεῖς, οὐδὲν λέγεις) – and the list goes on. Although this phenomenon must certainly be familiar to readers of comedy (see, e.g., Kaibel's and Jacobs' conjectures for Antiphanes' *Sappho* above), it must be admitted that, when one thinks about it, the phenomenon is rather strange. Jokes and comic gags, after all, are the bread and butter of comedy – as it were, the "comic" part of comedy. To scold a comic character on stage for telling a joke with "stop your nonsense!", theoretically, would be like scolding a lamenting tragic actor on stage with "quit your belly-aching!": the desired dramatic effect would be ruined. Yet, unlike such a hypothetical situation in tragedy, the "nonsense!" accusation in comedy does not ruin the joke's effect at all; rather, the accusation seems to be perfectly natural.[40] So, it raises the question: what role is this scolding playing in the ongoing comic program?

A first attempt at answering this question is to notice that in all of the comic scenes discussed above, there is a certain forward motion that can be perceived: a certain palpable drive towards a dramatic telos. Whether it be the physical motion of trying to cross the river Styx, or the forward progress of instructing Strepsiades through catechism, or the hunt for the intruder at the women's festival, in each case the drama sets up a certain forward motion or telos.[41] In such dramatic scenarios, very often the jokes or foolery that the characters engage in work against that forward motion, often effectively stopping it. Charon and Dionysus cannot advance if Dionysus continues to misinterpret Charon's commands; Socrates and Strepsiades can make no forward progress in the *Thinkery*'s project if Strepsiades keeps being foolish; the Kinsman cannot be discovered if he keeps repeating "what's-his-name": it is as if that ultimate tool for forward progress and accomplishing things – language – is disintegrating in the users' hands, and for that reason, forward motion becomes impossible. The scene must move forward, however, these "straight" characters insist, and, in this section, I will consider this requirement for dramatic forward motion more broadly. In particular, I will examine comedy's habit of having characters ignore each other's jokes, or "translate" them into flattened utterances, and argue that this (already-noticed)

---

[40] For the "asymmetry" of comedy (that is, the audience's reactions are not in line with the on-stage reactions) unlike tragedy, where sympathy (and its correspondent symmetry of emotion) is a necessity, see, e.g., Asper (2005); cf. von Möllendorff (1995) who argues for "symmetrical" laughter (190) and Sommerstein (2009) 104–15 who concludes with a similar claim.

[41] This dramatic motion and the discomfort of its breakdown is something played with by, e.g., writers of the so-called "Theatre of the Absurd" (Beckett, Ionesco, etc.) See Esslin (1991[1961]) for discussion.

phenomenon nicely highlights comedy's requirement for forward dramatic motion. Like the accusations of nonsense which seem to recognize that certain jokes violate the forward motion of sense, the ignoring or "translation" of jokes indicates the same fact: that dramatic motion must be maintained, and therefore certain jokes must be overlooked and swiftly passed over.

The observation that comedy has a certain forward motion or dramatic rhythm that must be maintained is not a particularly new one: Kenneth Dover (and later, David Bain) noticed something similar years ago, and argued that often enough in comedy, jokes are ignored.[42] As Dover and Bain describe it, many jokes cannot easily be reabsorbed into regular dialogue (i.e., they would require too much time to explain) and so, often enough the best option is simply to ignore the joke altogether. A punchline is given; then, one imagines, a silence or beat where the audience can respond with laughter, and then, a continuation of the conversation as if the interjected joke had never happened. This last step is critical, since otherwise the forward motion of the dialogue or scene could be imperiled. Dover draws attention to this fact specifically in regards to comic insults: "a character may say something which in reality would defeat the purpose of his speaking, and the character to whom it is said may react as he would to a different utterance," and he uses Groucho Marx as a contemporary example of this technique.[43] Dover's Aristophanic example of this phenomenon is from *Thesmophoriazusae* where the Kinsman asks the Prytanis (936–8):

Κη. ὦ πρύτανι πρὸς τῆς δεξιᾶς, ἥνπερ φιλεῖς
    κοίλην προτείνειν ἀργύριον ἤν τις διδῷ,
    χάρισαι βραχύ τί μοι καίπερ ἀποθανουμένῳ.
Πρ. τί σοι χαρίσωμαι;

---

[42] I will disregard the term "bomolokhic response" – which even Bain (1987[1977]) suggests is not a useful term (it was invented by Schaffner (1911) – in favor of the simpler (albeit vague) "joke." As Dover (1987) 246 writes, anyone on the comic stage who has the opportunity to crack a joke will crack a joke. Schaffner's "bomolokhic response" is based on yet another modern invention – that there was a certain "bomolokhos" character or "jester" to be found on the comic stage (first in Zielinski 1885). This causes more confusion than valuable discussion and those attempting to study this alleged character (recently, e.g., Kloss 2001) expand the term further. If *anyone* can say something "bomolokhic," or play the "bomolokhos," then the term "bomolokhos" *qua* on-stage role is useless. For more on the history of this word, see Kidd (2012).

[43] Dover (1972) at 60 n. 9: "This technique was taken to extremes by the Marx Brothers; people seldom react to Groucho's insults except by a fleeting expression of indignation, and it is often possible to tell how long the script-writer has allowed for the audience laughter before the next line is uttered." Bain (1987[1977]), agreeing with Dover, supplements Dover's observation with an example (88 n.4): "Since classical scholars are proverbially insatiable for parallels, here is an extract from *Duck Soup* to illustrate Dover's point: Margaret Dumont 'As chairman of the reception committee I welcome you with open arms.' Groucho 'Is that so? How late do you stay open?' Groucho's reply is ignored by his interlocutrix."

κ. Prytanis, I beg you, by your right hand – which you are accustomed
to hold out palm upwards, when anyone offers you money – grant me
one little favour, although I will soon die.

p. What favor can I grant you?

Dover argues, reasonably, that here the Prytanis does not register the
Kinsman's joke at all. Although, I would argue, there is probably some
wiggle room for the actor to give a "fleeting expression of indignation"
(with gestures, not facial expressions, of course, if the actor wished to step
slightly out of character), any permanent or actual offense from the
Prytanis would ruin the rhythm of the scene. Probably the Kinsman's
quip, as Dover says, is simply ignored. Bain, agreeing with Dover,
emphasizes that the joke ought to be an audible one, not an "aside"
(88): "The audience does not have time or inclination to speculate on
why the person insulted does not react to the insult: it spoils the joke if we
assume that the insult is not expressed aloud," and Austin and Olson in
their commentary for this scene express similar views.[44] All of these
scholars show a sensitivity to a certain comic rhythm wherein the pragmatic effectiveness of dialogue would be spoiled by certain jokes (in this
case, insults) which function in the opposite direction to the dialogue's
dramatic goal. Although this ignoring of jokes is not quite the same
phenomenon as calling them "nonsense," what the two phenomena
share is an allegiance to this requirement of forward, dramatic motion.
Since scenes and dialogues have certain dramatic goals, the jokes which
work against those goals become problems that need to be dealt with. One
way, as Dover and others have noticed, is for the on-stage characters to
ignore the joke altogether and continue as if nothing had happened.

It is important to see, however, that this ignoring of jokes does not just
occur with insults. In *Birds*, for example, often when Euelpides tosses a joke
into the conversation, it must be simply ignored – for example, the Mede
joke from Chapter 4 where Euelpides, upon being introduced to
the Mede bird, asks "how being a *Mede* did he fly in here without a
camel?"[45] Neither Hoopoe nor Peisetaerus acknowledge this question,
because if the question were acknowledged it would ruin the pace of the
scene (and, conversely, kill the joke with a lengthy explanation). So too,

---

[44] Austin and Olson (2004) ad loc.: "In real life, a gratuitous insult of this sort would ensure that the
favour being requested was denied. But different standards apply on the comic stage, and the Prytanis
reacts (939) as if nothing untoward had been said."

[45] The Hoopoe explains that the second bird is called a Μῆδος, and Euelpides responds: Μῆδος; ὦναξ
Ἡράκλεις. / εἶτα πῶς ἄνευ καμήλου Μῆδος ὢν εἰσέπτατο; (278–9). For discussion of this passage, see
Chapter 4.

when Calonice in *Lysistrata*, for example, mentions *para prosdokian* that her husband has been away guarding not a city, but the general Eucrates (who apparently *himself* needs to be guarded) – ὁ γοῦν ἐμὸς ἀνὴρ πέντε μῆνας, ὦ τάλαν, / ἄπεστιν ἐπὶ Θρᾴκης φυλάττων Εὐκράτη (102–3) – the dialogue continues as if nothing abnormal had been said.[46] In such cases the jokes are ignored not because they are insulting, but because they violate the overarching requirement that dramatic motion move forward. For that reason, the insults which Dover and Bain specify, such as that of the Prytanis scene, should be seen more as a sub-category of this same overarching requirement: that is, the reason that these jokes are ignored is not simply that they are poorly timed insults, but because they, like a much broader range of jokes, require too much dramatic time to be dismantled. Mollifying the insult for the Prytanis or explaining to Euelpides the true nature of the Mede bird would be both time-consuming and terribly boring.

So too, when jokes become "translated" or, as Dover writes, when "the character to whom [the joke] is said may react as he would to a different utterance," it applies to a number of different types of jokes in comic dialogue, not just insults. An interesting example can be seen with the phrase εὖ λέγεις or καλῶς λέγεις ("good point," "good idea") which, on a first reading, might seem to represent a character's acknowledgment of a joke's quality, but actually signals the character's obliviousness to a joke's presence. Characters who say εὖ λέγεις seem to be in some sense "translating" the joke for themselves into an ordinary phrase – they are playing the scene "straight," as it were. Consider the following passage from *Lysistrata* (1095). After an extended time of sex deprivation, the Athenian and Spartan ambassadors come to Lysistrata for terms. Their erections are obvious to both the audience and the chorus, and the chorus advises them to cover up their hard-ons in the following terms:

Χο.   εἰ σωφρονεῖτε, θαἰμάτια λήψεσθ᾽, ὅπως
        τῶν Ἑρμοκοπιδῶν μή τις ὑμᾶς ὄψεται.
Αθ.   νὴ τὸν Δί᾽ εὖ μέντοι λέγεις.

CH.   If you think straight, you'll grab your cloaks,
        so that none of the *hermokopidai* see you.
ATH. Gosh! Good idea.

A nice reference to contemporary events and a successfully triggered joke. But how should the Athenian ambassador's response εὖ μέντοι λέγεις be read here? Should he be imagined as laughing and saying something to the

---

[46] Henderson (1987) ad loc.: "A surprise for a place-name (Eukrates himself must be guarded!)" The identification of this man is uncertain.

effect of "that was a good joke"? Should he be imagined as "playing it straight," and taking this advice of the chorus seriously? Or perhaps a mixture of both? Nan Dunbar's note about the phrase εὖ λέγεις is particularly useful here (ad *Birds* 1124, my italics): "More often the phrase expresses agreement with a statement . . . or approval of advice . . ., but εὖ *always refers to content, not to style or delivery.*" This content-vs.-style distinction is particularly important regarding on-stage jokes: the listener who says εὖ λέγεις in response to a joke seems interested only in the "content" of the joke (e.g. the advice to cover one's erection), not in its status *as* a joke (i.e., the "style or delivery").[47]

Consider the following interchange from *Knights* as well, where a similar recognition of a good idea or piece of advice takes place (εὖ λέγεις), which seems to speed past the recognition of there being a joke present. When the Sausage-Seller is about to run off to face the Paphlagonian in debate, the slave Demosthenes offers him some ointment in the following terms (490–2):

Δε. ἔχε νυν, ἄλειψον τὸν τράχηλον τουτῳί,
    ἵν' ἐξολισθάνειν δύνῃ τὰς διαβολάς.
Αλ. ἀλλ' εὖ λέγεις καὶ παιδοτριβικῶς ταυταγί.

DE. Here, slather your neck with this,
    so you can slip out of his slanders.
SA. Good idea, and really well-coached.

Here again, the question arises as to how this interchange ought to be imagined: is the Sausage-Seller laughing at Demosthenes' joke or playing the scene "straight"? It seems that, as Dunbar suggests, the εὖ λέγεις of the Sausage-Seller points exclusively to the content of the advice, not to the fact that the advice is a joke. It is as if he is ignoring that the advice is a joke altogether, as if greasing up a neck in order to slip out of slanders were actually a good idea and not a joke at all. This same joke-translation or disinterest in the presence of a joke occurs at *Clouds* 1092,[48] *Peace* 934,[49]

---

[47] Although the late fifth-century connotations of the phrase also should be taken into account: see Fournier (1946) 69–71; Ford (2001) 89–90.

[48] Regarding where different groups of Athenian citizens come from (e.g., prosecutors, tragedians, politicians, etc.), the first ἐξ εὐρυπρώκτων receives πείθομαι in response; the second εὖ λέγεις "correct." What register as jokes to the audience are received as actual arguments by the actors.

[49] When the slave suggests saying the Ionic ὀί in the Assembly, Trygaeus replies "Good idea!" εὖ τοι λέγεις (Henderson).

Plato Com. 175 KA,[50] and *Birds* 1614.[51] What all of these lines have in common is that they do not appreciate jokes as jokes, but as some more serious form of utterance. Just as with Dover's and Bain's examples, these jokes are ignored *as* jokes because to acknowledge them as jokes would counteract the forward motion of the dramatic action. Because the scene must move forward, certain interchanges must be played "straight" either by ignoring jokes completely, or by somehow translating them into ordinary utterances.

One final example is of particular interest because it involves actors breaking the "fourth wall" (or "dramatic illusion").[52] Here one might expect a recognition of a joke's status as a joke since the actors are no longer playing their putative dramatic roles. But even here the actors who seem to be no longer "acting" are still playing the scene "straight." At *Wealth* 788–801, Chremylus' wife is offering Wealth a customary sprinkling (καταχύσματα) to greet him as their houseguest. This leads to a breaking of the fourth wall, wherein the actors discuss the comic pastime of sprinkling spectators with treats at comedies.[53] It would be base, Wealth says, to receive the sprinkling outside the house, since (797–800):

> οὐ γὰρ πρεπῶδές ἐστι τῷ διδασκάλῳ
> ἰσχάδια καὶ τρωγάλια τοῖς θεωμένοις
> προβαλόντ' ἐπὶ τούτοις εἶτ' ἀναγκάζειν γελᾶν.
> Γυ. εὖ πάνυ λέγεις...

> it is not fitting for the producer
> to throw figs and goodies at the spectators
> and then to compel them to laugh on that account.
> wɪ. Really good point.

Even here, I would suggest, Dunbar's explanation of εὖ λέγεις holds very well. In response to Wealth's incongruous remark, the Wife/Actor is surely not saying "good joke" or "that's funny" but, now in the guise of an actor, not a wife (or perhaps somewhere in between), is treating the "joke" as a sensible utterance, not a joke (i.e., playing the scene "straight").[54] Even here,

---

[50] A. ὁδὶ μὲν Ἀναγυράσιος ὀρφώς ἐστί σοι. / B. οἶδ', ὧι φίλος Μυννίσκος ἔσθ' ὁ Χαλκιδεύς. / A. καλῶς λέγεις. "Here you have Mr. Perch, from Anagyrus." B. "I know, the man whose friend is Mynniscus of Chalcis." A. "Right!" (Gulick, trans.)

[51] Peisthetaerus explains that whenever someone swears "By the Raven and by Zeus," a raven will swoop down and peck out his eyes, to which Poseiden replies (1614) νὴ τὸν Ποσειδῶ ταῦτά γέ τοι καλῶς λέγεις "By Poseidon, that's a very good point" (Henderson, trans.)

[52] Sifakis' (1971) argument that Old Comedy had no dramatic illusion is corrected by Bain (1987[1977]).

[53] For this "sprinkling" in comedy, see *Vesp.* 58–9, *Nub.* 524, *Pax* 748, *Lys.* 1218, and Sommerstein ad *Plut.* 796.

[54] Like many of the εὖ λέγεις (and "nonsense!") examples, this line also launches into a second joke.

even when a breaking of the fourth wall is occurring, a certain seriousness overrides – namely, that seriousness which does not acknowledge a joke as a joke, but as though it were a flattened proposition or piece of advice.

So, to conclude this section, this accusation of nonsense can be seen within a much broader spectrum of reactions to jokes wherein jokes are treated "seriously" – by being either ignored, translated, or simply not registered. What these phenomena share is a commitment to the imperative that comic action move forward (a commitment to "seriousness"), and a recognition that certain jokes violate that forward motion. However, before proceeding to the next section, it is worth reminding again that this rhythm of ignoring or scolding jokes is not comedy's only rhythm. Some jokes are particularly flexible and capable of being integrated into the comic action, especially aggressive jokes. Unlike the case with the Prytanis discussed above, some characters *are* aware when they are being mocked (and this acknowledgment of pain seems to be part of the audience's pleasure). So too, characters *can* have on-stage battles using highly aggressive, aischrologic language – to the glee, of course, of the audience.[55] Aggression, after all, is a great pragmatic force of language, and, as such, provides much of the "sense" for many of comedy's jokes (e.g., judgments like "Hyperbolus is an idiot," "Cleon's policies are harmful," "Cleonymus is fat," etc.), and so it is understandably a much-studied topic.[56] The interest of this chapter, however, is not those jokes which are perceived by characters to maintain the forward motion of sense, but those which are seen to transgress it. This on-stage accusation of nonsense, I think, points to a less-studied aspect of comedy, but a vital one: specifically, that which this on-stage "seriousness" is protecting the comedy from becoming.

Why "nonsense"?

It has long been noticed by scholars of comedy that comic characters often ignore each other's jokes, and play the comedy "straight." Comedy needs its jokes, of course, but if its characters were to register these jokes, often enough the dramatic flow of the scene would be ruined – for example, too

---

[55] For moments where characters acknowledge they are being mocked on stage (to the delight of the audience) see, e.g., *Ach.* 1081 where Lamachus acknowledges he is being mocked οἴμοι κακοδαίμων· καταγελᾷς ἤδη σύ μου; and similar moments at *Eq.* 161, *Nub.* 1238, *Vesp.* 1406, *Pax* 1245, *Av.* 1407, *Plut.* 880. For on-stage battles, see especially the aischrologic slug-fest between Sausage-Seller and Paphlagon, with Halliwell (2008) 256–63 and Rosen (1988) 68–9.

[56] See, e.g., recent monographs on comic *loidoria* and abuse like Stark (2004), Saetta-Cottone (2005), and Brockmann (2003).

much time would be spent trying to explain a joke, or trying to mitigate the effects of an off-hand insult. This phenomenon of ignoring or "translating" jokes resembles the nonsense accusations discussed in the first section, since both suggest a dramatic need to maintain a scene's forward motion and to avoid entanglement in the senseless traps jokes lay. However, there is a certain respect in which this nonsense accusation is different from the phenomenon of ignoring/translating jokes, since it seems to *draw attention to* that very aspect of the joke which the other phenomena are trying to ignore. Rather than paying attention, for example, to that aspect of the joke that is sensible or translatable (as does, e.g., εὖ λέγεις, "good idea," "good point"), the nonsense accusation seems only to identify that aspect of the joke which is not sensible, not translatable. Now it is time to articulate what this aspect of the joke is, and consider why such "nonsense" might need to be both recognized on stage, and sternly rebuked.

To return to the example used earlier, the school lesson between Socrates and Strepsiades:

Σω. οὐ τοῦτ' ἐρωτῶ σ', ἀλλ' ὅτι κάλλιστον μέτρον
         ἡγεῖ, πότερον τὸ τρίμετρον ἢ τὸ τετράμετρον;
Στ. ἐγὼ μὲν οὐδὲν πρότερον ἡμιέκτεω.
Σω. οὐδὲν λέγεις, ὤνθρωπε.

so.   I'm not asking you this, but what you think the most
         beautiful measure is: the trimeter or tetrameter?
st.   For me, nothing's better than the half-pint.
so.   You're speaking nonsense, man.

Unlike the examples in the previous section, Socrates here does not ignore Strepsiades' joke, nor does he translate it into some sort of useful answer. Instead, he pauses and actually draws attention to Strepsiades' "half-pint" with this reprimand of "nonsense." What exactly does Socrates mean here and what is he identifying? It should be noticed that Socrates is not saying his student's answer is a "bad joke" for which one might expect a response like *psychron*:[57] furthermore, it is not clear whether Socrates registers Strepsiades' answer as a joke at all. So too, it is not clear whether Strepsiades intends his "half-pint" response to be humorous, or whether he is an unintentional victim of his own comic stupidity. But rather than choosing between these two alternatives, what is of interest here is to focus

---

[57] The only response of calling an on-stage joke "*psychron*" is Timocles fr. 19 KA where Speaker A puns laboriously between Tereus and the verb τηρεῖν. For complaints about on-stage jokes, see *Ran.* 1–4, Ter. *Eun.* 426, and, possibly, Plato Com. fr. 16. For complaints about old or lame jokes in general, see *Nub.* 535–6, *Vesp.* 54–66, *Pax* 739–47, *Lys.* 381, 543, 1218, *Ekkl.* 888–9.

on the point of contact between them – that is, Strepsiades' "joke" vs. Strepsiades' "stupidity" (which approaches nicely the two sides of the English word "fool").[58] If Strepsiades had mentioned the "half-pint" out of stupidity, Socrates' reply οὐδὲν λέγεις would nicely fit Strepsiades' answer: his reply has nothing to do with Socrates' question, and so he deserves a verbal slap on the wrist. So too, if Strepsiades had spoken the half-pint as a silly joke, the reply οὐδὲν λέγεις would again fit the bill: a certain aspect of Strepsiades' joke has nothing to do with Socrates' question and so the same scolding is in order.[59]

When one considers the situation in this way, it seems that these two categories – the joke and stupidity – adumbrate that shared territory which this "nonsense" accusation covers. That is, Socrates here is identifying precisely that aspect of a joke which is shared by a much broader range of abnormal discourse: Aristotle calls it the part of the joke that is a "mistake," Freud calls it the part of the joke that is "nonsense," humor theorists in the wake of Austin call it the pragmatic "misfire," and so forth.[60] It is that aspect of jokes which resembles the language of feverish patients or the mentally ill (as was argued about nonsense in Chapter 1): it does not reflect reality, it is not worthy of interpretation, and nothing can be "done" with such language. Strepsiades' "nonsense" answer of the "half-pint," then – whether it be considered an intentional joke or an unintentional display of stupidity – commits the sort of mistake, as Xenophon writes, that the majority of people will never make (namely, confusion over Socrates' meaning of *metron*).[61] Since Xenophon is discussing, in this particular passage, the mentally abnormal, such a mistake is a rather disturbing prospect.

On the other hand, it must not be forgotten that Strepsiades' answer is not the useless language of mental malfunction: rather it is, whether considered at the level of the characters or that of the audience, a joke. Anyone can register that cognitive circuit between *metron* "poetic meter" and *metron* "physical measure," and the process of "getting" the joke seems to rely precisely on the recognition that even if the two lines (or "scripts") are not logically connected, they are linguistically linked. But Socrates'

---

[58] See OED s.v. "fool" which reports that it becomes difficult to distinguish historically between the "fool" (i.e., a person of below-average intellect) and "fool" (comic entertainer) owing to the old English (and perhaps universal in the ancient world) pastime of keeping people with mental disabilities for entertainment. See Chapter 1 for this discussion.

[59] Strepsiades' answer of course is linguistically linked to Socrates via wordplay over *metron*; but Socrates is pointing to the fact that logically there is no link.

[60] For an overview of different theories about the "nonsense" part of jokes, see Chapter 4.

[61] For Xenophon's discussion of the mistakes of mentally abnormal people and its relationship to my definition of nonsense, see Chapter 1.

accusation does not seem to be pointing to that element of the joke which is to be "gotten" (the "sense" or "learning," as I argued in Chapter 4), but drawing attention to something else. It is as if Socrates were overlooking that part of the joke which is relevant (the joke's "truth," as Aristotle calls it)[62] and only notices the "nonsense" part of the joke. It seems that, for Socrates, Strepsiades could have spoken any kind of utterance that did not adequately reflect the context (e.g., "let's roast marshmallows" or νοραρεττεβλο):[63] the response οὐδὲν λέγεις would be just as appropriate.

This returns us to the central problem of this chapter, only now with a more exact wording. The question has been why would an on-stage character scold another character for a joke (i.e., scold the desired or "comic" part of comedy). Now the question can be rephrased more exactly: why would a character, in this act of scolding, be drawing attention specifically to the *negative* aspect of jokes – namely, that part which jokes share with malfunctioning language more generally? It is usually, after all, discomfort not laughter which is the response to such malfunctioning language whether it be gibberish, a repeated phrase, or simply language that has no discernible bearing on the reality of the moment. Why would *that* part of the joke be stressed in the accusation of nonsense?

I would like to suggest that the characters reprimand each other for speaking nonsense and maintain their "seriousness" on stage *so that the audience does not feel the need to do so.* The last thing a comic author would want is for an audience to start feeling that comedy had become too "silly," or that it needed to become more serious. This technique of certain characters playing the comedy "straight" or maintaining that seriousness, then, is precisely to avoid that feeling from arising in the audience. On-stage seriousness and the rebukes about nonsense demarcate clearly the language and action of comedy from the language and action of those more anxious realms of language malfunction. So long as someone on stage is scolding the nonsense, the rest of the audience can enjoy what they otherwise might need to scold themselves.

Consider again the "silliness" of the *Birds* interchange one last time and the role the nonsense accusation seems to play (Peisthetairos and Euelpides

---

[62] Arist. *Rh.* 3.11, with Chapter 4 for discussion. The "truth" of the joke might be that *metron* (poetic meter) is phonetically linked to *metron* (physical measure); or that Socrates' sophistic ideas and discussions of meter are worthy of criticism; or that the language of commoners triumphs over the elite; for the social critiques which might provide a joke's "sense," see Chapter 4 for discussion.

[63] νοραρεττεβλο is a piece of gibberish found on a vase of the Tarpoley painter (400–390 BCE) which represents a comic scene with dialogue. See Csapo (2010) 48; Pickard-Cambridge (1968) 217; Beazley (1952). See Chapter 4 for more discussion of gibberish.

are trying to persuade the Hoopoe's slave that they are not two birds but two men, 64–6):

Πε. ἀλλ' οὐκ ἐσμὲν ἀνθρώπω.
Θε. τί δαί;
Πε. ὑποδεδιὼς ἔγωγε, Λιβυκὸν ὄρνεον.
Θε. οὐδὲν λέγεις.

PE. No: we're not two men.
SE.   What, then?
PE. I'm a fearfowl [Somm.], a Libyan bird.
SE. You're speaking nonsense.

Even more here than in the case of Strepsiades and Socrates, if the servant were to laugh at Peisthetaerus' pretend word, the audience might have to face a rather unjustified on-stage enjoyment. But because the servant reacts negatively to such behavior, it provides the spectators with the perfect tension to rest their enjoyment on.

Conclusions: relationship between sense and the "nonsense!" rebuke

Like every day life, the comic stage needs to make some attempt or some pretense of forward motion – that is, one *really is* trying to get somewhere (across the Styx), one *really is* trying to do something (learn rhetoric, find Tereus, etc.) – and so it (like us) must use the tools at its disposal to effect this motion: especially language. The problem is that there is something in the nature of many jokes or comic gags that works in the opposite direction to this forward progression: Dionysus sits *on* the oars instead of *at* the oars, Strepsiades continually misunderstands Socrates, and so forth. The threat, again, is this: if this tool of forward progression (language) is being rendered useless, forward progression becomes impossible. I have argued that this comic problem is dealt with in a number of ways – sometimes a joke is simply ignored, sometimes it is translated, and, most significantly for this chapter, sometimes it is rebuked as "nonsense."

I concluded with the suggestion that the function of this on-stage rebuke is to anticipate the possible negative reactions of the audience: it creates a pretense that the comic stage is (still) engaging in the forward motion of sensible communication. Those comic gags, which are after all the heart of comedy, must be rebuked on stage so that they can be enjoyed by the audience. What these rebukes highlight is the common area that jokes or comic language share with faulty language, dangerous language, language that causes people to feel uncomfortable, language that ceases to be useful. Rather than somehow discerning a sense of the lines or laughing at them, the characters reject the lines entirely and insist that such abuse of language must be stopped.

This "seriousness" indicates something about the nature of the comic genre that, I think, is particularly important. Comedy, at its best, is always dancing on the edge of a nightmarish world: not just the violence and pain that it enjoys so much but the situations where language – that tool so important for social interaction – fails. If one envisions the scene of Charon and Dionysus on the boat without Charon's reprimands (that is, if Dionysus keeps "getting things wrong" or "making mistakes" and Charon continues to communicate with him in good faith), the situation would become no longer comic but nightmarish.[64] Like the aggression which is shown to be inconsequential in comedy in order to be enjoyed, these moments of language-failure are shown to be under control, either through the creation of sense (a punchline, a frame, a parody), or through the sort of on-stage scolding that I have been examining here.

As a closing note to this chapter, I would like to turn to a more modern exploration of this boundary between comedy and mental illness and the source of this chapter's epigraph – the 1988 Barry Levinson film *Rain Man*. In this film, an unlikely comic duo – a yuppie fortune-hunter played by Tom Cruise and his autistic, older brother, Raymond, played by Dustin Hoffmann – have an opportunity to talk about another, better-known comic duo: Abbott and Costello. One of Raymond's habits throughout the movie is to recite over and over again the famous Abbott and Costello sketch "Who's on first?" where, as will be recalled, Abbott has a baseball team with player-names like "Who," "What," and "I Don't Know," and poor Costello cannot decipher what on earth Abbott is talking about. In *Rain Man*, the autistic Raymond does not recognize the sketch *as* comedy, but rather repeats the routine over and over again, for some reason fixated on this odd gibberish. Raymond's brother, meanwhile, as if mirroring the Costello role, becomes increasingly irritated by this gibberish, mostly because it's irritating to hear anything repeated a hundred times, but also because his brother clearly does not register the joke. At one point, he snaps and yells at Raymond: "Ray, you're never gonna solve it. It's not a riddle

---

[64] The metaphor "nightmarish" actually points to the common ground between play and dreams in an evolutionary sense: both may be providing practice for dangerous situations. See Stickgold *et al.* (2001) for dreams; Burghardt (2005) for review of the educational/practice explanations of play, although he himself does not subscribe to them.

because Who *is* on first base. That's a joke, Ray, it's comedy, but when you do it you're not funny. You're like the comedy of Abbott and Abbott."

What is the difference between "Who's on First?" as a comic gag and "Who's on First?" as the babblings of a mentally ill person? What exactly separates the two? As I have been arguing in this chapter: nothing, really, except for those irritated flailings of that other person, who just wants things to be a little more sensible.

Conclusions

Comedy engages in contemporary debates, it mocks political figures, it denounces religious quacks, and it asserts bold aesthetic judgments on the poetry of rivals: it is, in short, full of meaning. Yet this fullness of meaning, for some reason, does not seem fully to capture "comedy." In other genres, like epic or tragedy, this feeling of incompleteness can be assuaged by new, "deeper" readings: such readings announce that there are richer realms of significance to be explored, "more complex" strains of signification which have been heretofore overlooked, only now to be elucidated. But this seductive invitation from other genres is withheld in comedy: the deeper one delves into the richness of comedy's meaning, the more one unearths complex sets of allusions or allegories, the further one seems to drift from the comedy itself. It is as if in the pursuit of meaning, one becomes distanced from the comedy's center, not closer to it.

The answer that I have offered to this problem of comedy is the concept of nonsense. To discover nonsense in comedy, that is, to reject what might be interpreted, is a central pleasure of the genre. This results from nonsense's relationship with play and the pleasures that arise from such play. However, owing to nonsense's relationship with delirium, certain problems emerge: the tension already present in not interpreting interpretable language is weakened or even absent in cases where meaning is not so readily available – for example, the puns and repetitions studied in Chapter 4. To justify such language play, distinguish it from delirium, and so, create the preconditions for enjoyment, certain markers of "sense" or "seriousness" often need to be present in the comedy, usually consisting of aggressive judgments, parodic frames, or serious scoldings of "nonsense." As I argued in Chapter 5, as long as *someone* on stage is being irritated by potential nonsense, the irritations of such perceived nonsense can still be avoided.

If sense and on-stage punishment assist in providing a safe-zone for nonsense on the comic stage, the question that remains regards the relationship between sense and punishment for comedy. In terms of comedy, is sense punitive? If one considers the reactions against comedy's serious readings, this idea may have some merit. The resistance against serious readings of comedy is rather akin to the on-stage struggle between the clown and the straight man. One feels that the clown is "comedy itself," while the serious character is little more than a comic "foil," one who gives "feeds" for the comedy to work. The "straight" character's seriousness is not the main event, but a mere interlude for the "silliness" and "fun" to occur. But there is more to this: the "straight" admonition of seriousness ("be serious!" "stop speaking nonsense!") creates a resistance or a reaction: the audience doesn't *want* to be serious, the audience wants to "clown around" (and this is why they're watching comedy).[1] It is this which suggests that sense is punitive: from the perspective of clowning or nonsense, sense is the oppressive weight which prevents one from experiencing "comedy itself."

But, like any "itself," "comedy itself" is rarely the delight that desire suggests it will be. Except in the infrequent moments of comic climaxes – where one can laugh without having something to laugh at – to have such "comedy itself" is usually to enter not a world of pure foolish pleasure, but one of potential disease: where language no longer functions, where there is no difference between mental health and mental illness, where the familiar world becomes nightmarish and uncanny. The desire for the "foolery" or "fun" of comedy is both central, then, and centrally misguided: a comic audience desires it, but if they were to obtain it, usually the result would be disappointing and, probably, distressing (so with comic aggression, wherein "real" aggression becomes the polar opposite of what play makes it seem to be). Like on-stage punishment of nonsense, comic meaning functions in a similar vein: it makes comedy possible by regulating that which audiences wish to enjoy. It makes safe that exploration of the "strange," the "outside," that unfamiliar bit which we may play with in order to feel mastery over it. Whether that mastery is gained by sense or by on-stage punishment, what is most important to observe is that sense and punishment for comedy, although not equivalents, nevertheless function in the same direction.

As comedy developed toward the end of the fourth century BCE, becoming "New," its form altered: plots became more organized, language calmed down considerably, and explicit political and personal invective disappeared. Old Comedy's scattered exuberance, its silly relentless wordplay, its fantastic ideas, yielded to new desiderata like realism, characterization, and romantic feelings. Although it is often disputed whether Menandrean comedy loses the comic power of Aristophanes (many claim, rightly, that

---

[1] Cf. Pl. *Resp.* 10.606c6 regarding τὸ . . . βουλόμενον γελωτοποιεῖν.

one must watch Menander in performance to appreciate its humor), it cannot be denied that the wild cognitive storm that is Old Comedy had subsided while more reasonable sources of pleasure arose.

What is interesting to notice is that the decline in comedy's direct aggression, whether political or otherwise, occurred during exactly the same period as the decline of its linguistic deviance. While the traditional story of outside political pressures might explain the former, they cannot explain the latter. But this development might be understood in terms of the symbiotic relationship between nonsense and aggression that I have described above: for aggression to be enjoyable in play it must be deprived of its consequence; for certain experiences of nonsense to be enjoyable they must seem, conversely, to maintain some consequence, which aggression easily provides. When one views this balance or mutual tension in terms of comedy's development, it only seems natural that New Comedy simultaneously became less linguistically aberrant and less politically aggressive: these are not separate developments but mutual ones. One might say, then, that the political aggression of Old Comedy is doubly-determined: inasmuch as it is perceived to be political, it *must be* political; inasmuch as it is perceived to be meaningful, it *must be* meaningful.

This is in no way to undermine the significance of the serious readings of comedy – which are and will continue to be important – but rather to situate them in the light of necessity. Just as it is necessary that the straight character demand seriousness of the comic stage, so too comic scholarship must continue to demand seriousness from the comic text. This is not just because the discovery of meaning is a worthwhile pastime in its own right, but because that seriousness creates something for the rest of us to react against, and so demand again from comedy its foolery and fun – which is precisely what comedy wishes us to do.

References

Adrados, F. R. (1999) *History of the Graeco-Latin Fable*, Vol. 1. Leiden.

Amouroux, I. (1999) "Antiphane et les thèmes de la comédie moyenne : traduction et commentaire des fragments d'Antiphane." Dissertation, Montpellier.

Antonelli, G. and Chiummo, C. (eds.) (2009) *Nominativi fritti e mappamondi: il nonsense nella letteratura italiana: atti del convegno di Cassino, 9–10 ottobre 2007*. Rome.

Ardley, G. (1967) "The Role of Play in the Philosophy of Plato." *Philosophy* 42.161: 226–44.

Arnott, W. G. (1996) *Alexis: The fragments: A Commentary*. Cambridge.

Asper, M. (2005) "Group Laughter and Comic Affirmation. Aristophanes' *Birds* and the Political Function of Old Comedy." *Hyperboreus* 11: 5–29.

Attardo, S. (1994) *Linguistic Theories of Humor*. Berlin.

Austin, J. L. (2000[1962]) *How to do Things with Words*. Cambridge, MA.

Austin, C. and Olson, S. D. (2004) *Aristophanes. Thesmophoriazusae*. Oxford.

Bain, D. (1986) "More Light on the *Peace*: Review of *Commedia e partecipazione: La Pace di Aristofane*." *CR* 36.2: 201–3.

   (1987[1977]) *Actors and Audience: A Study of Asides and Related Conventions in Greek Drama*. Oxford.

Baker, G. and Hacker, P. (1984) *Language, Sense, and Nonsense: A Critical Investigation into Modern Theories of Language*. Blackwell.

Bakola, E. (2010) *Cratinus and the Art of Comedy*. Oxford.

Barnes, J. (1971) "Homonymy in Aristotle and Speusippus." *CQ* 21: 65–80.

Bateson, G. (2000[1972]) *Steps to an Ecology of mind*. Chicago. (Originally: 1955, "A theory of play and fantasy." *Psychiatric Research Reports* 2: 39–51.)

Bayard, L. (1920) "Aristophane, *Oiseaux*, 1615–1616." *Revue de Philologie* 44: 30.

Beazley, J. D. (1952) "The New York 'Phlyax' vase." *AJA* 56.4: 193–5.

Beekes, R. (2010) *Etymological Dictionary of Greek*. Leiden.

Bekoff, Marc. (1972) "The development of social interaction, play, and metacommunication in mammals: an ethological perspective." *Quarterly Review of Biology* 47: 412–34.

   (1975) "The communication of play intention: are play signals functional?" *Semiotica* 15.2: 231–9.

(1995) "Play signals as punctuation: the structure of social play in canids." *Behavior* 132: 419–29.

(1998) "Intentional communication and social play: how and why animals negotiate and agree to play," in *Animal Play: Evolutionary, Comparative, and Ecological Perspectives*, ed. M. Bekoff and J. Byers. Cambridge: 97–114.

Bergson, H. (1980[1956]) "Laughter," in *Comedy*, ed. W. Sypher. Baltimore: 61–190. (First published 1900.)

Beta, S. (2004) *Il linguaggio nelle commedie di aristofane: parola positiva e parola negativa nella commedia antica*. Rome.

Betz, H. D. (2007[1986]) *Greek Magical Papyri in Translation*. Chicago.

Bierl, A. (2002) "'Viel Spott, viel Ehr!' – Die ambivalenze des onomasti komoidein im festlichen und generischen Kontext,' in *Spoudaiogeloion: Form und Funktion der Verspottung in der aristophanischen Komödie*, ed. A. Ercolani. Stuttgart and Weimar: 169–87.

Biles, Z. (2011) *Aristophanes and the Poetics of Competition*. Cambridge.

Black, M. (1983) *The Prevalence of Humbug, and Other Essays*. Ithaca.

Blanchard, A. (2007) *La comédie de Ménandre: Politique, Éthique, Esthétique*. Paris.

Bliquez, L. (2008) "The purrikhē of Kinesias, a pun?: Aristophanes *Frogs* 153." *CQ* 58.1: 320–6.

Bonnano, M. (1979) "La Commedia," in *Storia e civiltà dei Greci*. III. *La Grecia nell' età di Pericle: Storia, letteratura, filosofia*, ed. R. Bandinelli. Milan: 311–50.

Bonner, R. J. (1920) "Notes on Isocrates' *Panegyricus* 188." *CP* 15.4: 385–7.

Borthwick, E. (1968a) "Beetle, bell, goldfinch, and weasel in Aristophanes' *Peace*." *CR* 18.2: 134–9.

(1968b) "Notes on the Plutarch *de Musica* and the *Cheiron* of Pherecrates." *Hermes* 96.1: 60–73.

Bowie, E. (1993) "Lies, fiction and slander in early Greek poetry" in *Lies and fiction in the Ancient World* ed. C. Gill and P. Wiseman. Austin: 1–37.

(1995) "Wine in old comedy." In *In vino veritas*, ed. O. Murray and M. Tecusan. London: 113–25.

Boys-Stones, G. R. (ed.) 2003. *Metaphor, Allegory, and the Classical Tradition*. Oxford.

Brock, R. (2004) "Review of Hesk, J. (2000) *Deception and Democracy in Classical Athens*." *CR* 54.1: 144–6.

Brockmann, C. (2003) *Aristophanes und die Freiheit der Komödie*. Munich.

Buchner, E. (1958) *Der Panegyrikos des Isokrates: eine historisch-philologische Untersuchung*. Wiesbaden.

Burghardt, G. (2005) *The Genesis of Animal Play*. Cambridge, MA.

Cameron, A. (1995) *Callimachus and his Critics*. Princeton.

Cavey, C. (1993) "The purpose of Aristophanes' *Acharnians*." *RhM* 136: 245–63.

Cassio, A. (1985) *Commedia e partecipazione: La pace di Aristofane*. Naples.

Catto, B. (1991) "The fear of mockery: a tragic motivation." *CB* 67: 17–26.

Chadwick, J. (1996) *Lexicographica Graeca: Contributions to the Lexicography of Ancient Greek*. Oxford.

Chantraine, P. (1968–80) *Dictionnaire étymologique de la langue grecque: histoire des mots.* Paris.

Chick, G. (2001) "What is play for? Sexual selection and the evolution of play." *Play and Culture Studies* 3: 3–25.

Chomsky, N. (1957) *Syntactic Structures.* London.

Chronopoulos, S. (2011) "Re-writing the personal joke: some aspects in the interpretation of onomasti komoidein in ancient scholarship," in *Ancient Scholarship and Grammar: Archetypes, Concepts and Contexts,* ed. S. Matthaios, F. Montanari, and A. Rengakos. Berlin: 207–23.

Classen, J. (1963[1869]) *Thukydides.* Berlin.

Collins, D. (2004) *Master of the Game: Competition and Performance in Greek Poetry.* Cambridge, MA.

Colvin, S. (1999) *Dialect in Aristophanes.* Oxford.

Conrad, C. (2002) *New Observations on Voice in the Ancient Greek Verb.* [online: http://artsci.wustl.edu/~cwconrad/docs/NewObsAncGrkVc.pdf]

Cooper, L. (1920) "A pun in the Rhetoric of Aristotle." *AJP* 41.1: 48–56.
    (1924) *An Aristotelian Theory of Comedy.* Oxford.

Cooper, C. L. (2010) "Review of (D.) Walsh, 2009, *Distorted Ideals in Greek Vase-Painting.* Cambridge." *JHS* 130: 268–9.

Cope, E. M., and Sandys, J. E. (1973[1877]) *The Rhetoric of Aristotle.* Cambridge.

Copjec, J. (1994) *Read my Desire: Lacan against the Historicists.* Cambridge, MA.

Csapo, E. (2010) *Actors and Icons of the Ancient Theater.* Malden, MA.

Culler, J. D. (ed.) (1988) *On Puns: The Foundation of Letters.* Oxford.

Deleuze, G. (1990) *The Logic of Sense.* New York. (Trans. M. Lester from 1969, *Loqique du sens.* Paris.)

De Luca, K. M. (2005) *Aristophanes' Male and Female Revolutions: A Reading of Aristophanes Knights and Assemblywomen.* Lanham, MD.

De Ste. Croix, G. (1996) "The political outlook of Aristophanes," in *Oxford Readings in Aristophanes,* ed. E. Segal. Oxford: 42–64. (Originally as appendix in G. de Ste Croix, 1972. *The Origins of the Peloponnesian War.* Ithaca).

Dettwyler, K. A. (1991) "Can paleopathology provide evidence for 'compassion?'" *American Journal of Physical Anthropology* 84: 375–84.

Di Florio, M. (2003/4) "L'estetica del comico e la Aristophanis et Menandri Comparatio." *Ploutarkhos* 1: 21–34.

Diggle, J. (2004) *Theophrastus. Characters.* Cambridge.

Dillon, M. (1991) "Tragic laughter." *CW* 84: 345–55.

Dobrov, G. (1988) "Winged Words/Graphic Birds: The Aristophanic Comedy of Language." Dissertation, Cornell University.
    (1990) "Aristophanes' *Birds* and the metaphor of deferral." *Arethusa* 23.2: 209–33.
    (1995) "Language, fiction, and utopia," in *The City as Comedy: Society and Representation in Athenian Drama,* ed. G. Dobrov. Chapel Hill: 93–132.
    (2010) (ed.) *Brill's Companion to the Study of Greek Comedy.* Leiden.

Dobrov, G. and Urios-Aparisi, E. (1995) "Gender, genre and the *Chiron* of Pherecrates," in *Beyond Aristophanes: Transition and Diversity in Greek Comedy,* ed. G. Dobrov. Atlanta: 139–74.

Dodds, E. (1959) *Plato. Gorgias*. Oxford.

(1960) *Euripides. Bacchae*. Oxford.

(1973[1951]) *The Greeks and the Irrational*. Berkeley.

Douglas, M. (2002[1966]) *Purity and Danger: An Analysis of Concepts of Pollution and Taboo*. London.

Dover, K. J. (1958) "Aristophanic Studies: Review of H.-J. Newiger, 1957, *Metapher und Allegorie*." *CR* 8.3–4: 235–7.

(1972) *Aristophanic Comedy*. Berkeley.

(1979) *Plato. Symposium*. Cambridge.

(1987) "Language and character in Aristophanes," in K. Dover, *Greek and the Greeks: Language, Poetry, Drama*. Oxford. 237–48.

(1989[1968]) *Aristophanes. Clouds*. Oxford.

(1994) *Aristophanes. Frogs*. Oxford.

(2004) "The limits of allegory and allusion in Aristophanes," in *Law, Rhetoric, and Comedy in Classical Athens*, ed. D. A. Cairns and R. A. Knox. Swansea: 239–49.

Dummett, M. (1976) "The appeal to use and the theory of meaning," in *Meaning and Use*, ed. A. Margalit. Boston: 123–35.

Dumortier, J. and Defradas, J. (1975) *Plutarque Traités de morale*. Paris.

Dunbar, N. (1995) *Aristophanes. Birds*. Oxford.

Düring, I. (1945) "Studies in Musical Terminology in 5th Century Literature." *Eranos* 43: 176–97.

Eastman, M. (1921) *The Sense of Humor*. New York.

Eco, U. (1998) *How to Travel with a Salmon and Other Essays* (trans. W. Weaver). London.

Eden, K. (1987) "Hermeneutics and the ancient rhetorical tradition." *Rhetorica* 5: 59–86.

Emerson, J. (1969) "Negotiating the serious import of humor." *Sociometry* 32.2: 169–81.

England, E. B. (1921) *The Laws of Plato*. London.

Erard, M. (2010) "The life and times of 'colorless green ideas sleep furiously.'" *Southwest Review* 95.3: 418–25.

Esslin, M. (1991[1961]) *Theater of the Absurd*. New York.

Fait, P. (1996) "Il linguaggio e l'abaco (Aristotele, Soph. El. 1, 165a6–17)," in *Hodoi Dizesios: Studi in onore di Francesco Adorno*, ed. M. S. Funghi. Florence: 181–90.

(2007) *Organon 6, Le confutazioni sofistiche: con testo greco a fronte*. Rome.

Ferrari, F. (1988) "P. Berol. Inv. 13270: i Canti di Elefantina," *SCO* 38: 181–227.

Fisher, N. (1992) *Hybris: A Study in the Values of Honour and Shame in Ancient Greece*. Warminster.

Ford, A. (2001) "Sophists without rhetoric: the arts of speech in fifth-century Athens," in *Education in Greek and Roman Antiquity*, ed. Y. L. Too. Leiden: 85–109.

(2002) *The Origins of Criticism: Literary Culture and Poetic Theory in Classical Greece*. Princeton.

Forster, E. (1965[1955]) *Aristotle. On Sophistical Refutations*. Cambridge, MA.

Fournier, H. (1946) *Les verbes "dire" en grec ancient*. Paris.

Fowler, H. N. (1936) *Plutarch's Moralia X*. Cambridge, MA.

Frankfurt, H. (2005) *On Bullshit*. Princeton.

Frege, G. (1980[1892]) "On sense and meaning," in *Translations from the Philosophical Writings of Gottlob Frege*, ed. P. Geach and M. Black (trans. M. Black). Oxford: 42–55.

Frese, R. (1926) "Die 'aristophanische Anklage' in Platons Apologie." *Philologus* 81: 377–90.

Freud, S. (1927) "Humour," in *The Standard Edition of the Complete Psychological Works of Sigmund Freud, Volume XXI (1927–1931): The Future of an Illusion, Civilization, and its Discontents, and Other Works* (trans. J. Strachey). New York: 159–166.

(1989[1905]) *Jokes and their Relation to the Unconscious* (trans. J. Strachey). New York.

Frisk, H. (1973) *Griechisches etymologisches Wörterbuch*. Heidelberg.

Fry, W. F. (1963) *Sweet Madness*. Palo Alto.

Fyfe, W. H. (1927) *The Poetics of Aristotle*. Cambridge, MA.

Garland, R. (1995) *The Eye of the Beholder: Deformity and Disability in the Graeco-Roman World*. Ithaca.

Gentili, B. and Prato, C. (1985) *Poetarum elegiacorum testimonia et fragmenta*. Leipzig.

Gerber, D. E. (1999) *Greek Elegiac Poetry*. Cambridge, MA.

Gigon, O. (1960–87) *Aristotelis Opera*. Berlin.

Gill, C. (1993) "Plato on falsehood – not fiction," in *Lies and Fiction in the Ancient World*, ed. C. Gill and P. Wiseman. Austin: 38–87.

Giora, R. (1991) "On the cognitive aspects of the joke." *Journal of Pragmatics* 16: 465–85.

Glotz, G. (1929) *The Greek City and its Institutions*. London.

Goffman, E. (1974) *Frame Analysis*. New York.

Gomme, A. W. (1996) "Aristophanes and Politics," in *Oxford Readings in Aristophanes*, ed. E. Segal. Oxford: 29–41. (First published 1938.)

Gomme, A. and Sandbach, F. (1973) *Menander: A Commentary*. Oxford.

Goodman, F. D. (1972) *Speaking in Tongues: A Cross-Cultural Study of Glossolalia*. Chicago.

Gow, A. S. F. (1950) *Theocritus*. Cambridge.

Graves, C. (1958) *The Fourth Book of Thucydides*. London.

Grice, H. (1975) "Logic and conversation," in *Syntax and Semantics, Vol. III: Speech Act*, ed. P. Cole and J. Morgan. New York.

Groos, K. (1898) *Die Spiele der Tiere*. Jena. (Translated but modified by E. L. Baldwin, 1898. *The Play of Animals*. New York.)

Gulick, C. B. (1927–41) *Athenaeus. The Deipnosophists*, 7 vols. London.

Gundert, H. (1965) "Zum Spiel bei Platon," in *Beispiele. Festschrift für Eugen Fink zum 60 Geburtstag*, ed. L. Landgrebe. The Hague: 188–221.

Gutzwiller, K. (1969) "Psychros und Onkos: Untersuchungen zur rhetorischen Termonologie." Dissertation, Zurich.

(2007) *A Guide to Hellenistic Literature*. Oxford.

Haesler, B. (1978) *Plutarch. Moralia* (Vol. v.2.2). Leipzig.

Halliwell, S. (1984) "Ancient interpretations of onomasti komoidein in Aristophanes." *CQ* 34: 83–8.

(1991) "Comic satire and freedom of speech in classical Athens." *JHS* 116: 48–70.

(2002) *The Aesthetics of Mimesis: Ancient Texts and Modern Problems*. Princeton.

(2008) *Greek Laughter: A Study of Cultural Psychology from Homer to Early Christianity*. Cambridge.

Hamilton, E. (1993[1930]) *The Greek Way*. New York.

Hamilton, J. T. (2003) *Soliciting Darkness: Pindar, Obscurity, and the Classical Tradition*. Cambridge, MA.

Harrison, A. R. W. (1968) *The Law of Athens*, Vol. 1. Oxford.

Hausrath, A. (1970) *Corpus fabularum aesopicarum*, Vol. 1. Leipzig.

Headlam, W. (1922) *Herodas. The Mimes and Fragments*. Cambridge.

Heath, M. (1987) *Political Comedy in Aristophanes*. Göttingen. (Revised 2007.)

(2003) "Pseudo-Dionysius Art of Rhetoric 8–11: figured speech, declamation and criticism" *AJP* 124: 81–105.

(2007) *Political Comedy in Aristophanes* (Revision of 1987 edition at http://eprints.whiterose.ac.uk/3588/1/Political_Comedy_in_Aristophanes.pdf).

(2010) "ΤΟ ΓΕΛΟΙΟΝ." *CR* 60.1: 1–3.

Hegel, G. W. F. (1975[1835]) *Aesthetics: Lectures on Fine Art*, Vol. 1. (trans. T. M. Knox). Oxford. (German edition used: 1966[1835], *Ästhetik*. Frankfurt.)

Helmbold, W. C., and O'Neil, E. N. (1959) *Plutarch's Quotations*. London.

Henderson, J. (1987) *Aristophanes. Lysistrata*. Oxford.

(1990) "The demos and comic competition," in *Nothing to Do with Dionysus?*, ed. J. Winkler and F. Zeitlin. Princeton: 271–313.

(1991) "Women and the Athenian dramatic festivals." *TAPA* 121: 133–47.

(1991[1975]) *The Maculate Muse*. Oxford.

(1998a) *Aristophanes. Acharnians. Knights*. Cambridge, MA.

(1998b) *Aristophanes. Clouds. Wasps. Peace*. Cambridge, MA.

Hershkowitz, D. (1998) *The Madness of Epic: Reading Insanity from Homer to Statius*. Oxford.

Herwerden, H. van. (1897) *Eirene: cum scholiorum antiquorum excerptis passim emendatis*. Leiden.

Hesk, J. (2000) *Deception and Democracy in Classical Athens*. Cambridge.

Hochberg, H. (2003) *Introducing Analytic Philosophy: Its Sense and its Nonsense, 1879–2002*. Frankfurt.

Hubbard, T. K. (1991) *The Mask of Comedy: Aristophanes and the Intertextual Parabasis*. Ithaca.

Huizinga, J. (1949) *Homo Ludens: A Study of the Play-Element in Culture* (trans. R. Hull). London.

Hunter, R. (1983) *Eubulus: The Fragments*. Cambridge.

Hurley, M., Dennett, D., and Adams, R. Jr., (2011) *Inside Jokes: Using Humor to Reverse-Engineer the Mind*. Cambridge, MA.

Hutchinson, G. O. (1985) *Aeschylus. Septem Contra Thebas*. Oxford.

Immerwahr, H. R. (2006) "Nonsense inscriptions and literacy." *Kadmos* 45: 136–72.

Innes, D. (2003) "Metaphor, Simile, and Allegory as Ornaments of Style," in *Metaphor, Allegory, and the Classical Tradition*, ed. G. R. Boys-Stones. Oxford: 7–27.

Jacobs, F. (1809) *Additamenta animadversionum in Athenaei Deipnosophistas*. Jena.

Janko, R. (2002[1984]) *Aristotle on Comedy*. London.

Jernigan, C. C. (1939) *Incongruity in Aristophanes*. Menasha.

Jouet-Pastre, E. 2006. *Le jeu et le sérieux dans les "Lois" de Platon*. Sankt Augustin.

Kaibel, G. 1887. *Athenaei Naucratitae Deipnosophistarum libri XV*.

Kaimio, M. and Nykopp, N. (1997) "Bad poets society: censure of the style of minor tragedians in old comedy," in *Utriusque linguae peritus. Studia in honorem Toivo Viljamaa. Annales Universitatis Turkuensis. Ser. B. Tom. 219. Humaniora*, ed. J. Vaahtera and R. Vainio. Turku: 23–37.

Kaplan, R. (2000) *The Nothing That Is*. Oxford.

Kassel, R. (1976) *Aristotelis ars rhetorica*. Berlin.

Katz, B. (1976) "The *Birds* of Aristophanes and politics." *Athenaeum* 53: 353–81.

Kennedy, G. A. (2007) *Aristotle. On Rhetoric: A Theory of Civic Discourse*. Oxford.

Kidd, S. (2011) "Laughter interjections in Greek comedy." *CQ* 61.2: 445–59.

   (2012) "The meaning of bomolokhos in classical Attic Greek." *TAPA* 142.2: 239–55.

Kloss, G. (2001) *Erscheinungsformen komischen Sprechens bei Aristophanes*. Berlin.

Kock, T. (1880) *Comicorum atticorum fragmenta*. Leipzig.

Konstan, D. (1995) *Greek Comedy and Ideology*. Oxford.

   (1997) "The Greek polis and its negations: versions of utopia in Aristophanes' Birds", in *The City as Comedy. Society and Representation in Athenian Drama*, ed. G. Dobrov. Chapel Hill: 3–22.

   (2006) *The Emotions of the Ancient Greeks: Studies in Aristotle and Classical Literature*. Toronto.

Körte, A. (1904) "Die Hypothesis zu Kratinos' Dionysalexandros." *Hermes* 39.4: 481–98.

Kostantakos, I. (2000a) "A Commentary on the Fragments of Eight Plays of Antiphanes". Dissertation, Cambridge.

   (2000b) "Notes on the chronology and career of Antiphanes". *Eikasmos* 11: 173–96.

Koster, W. J. W. (1975) *Scholia in Aristophanem*. Groningen.

Kronauer, U. (1954) *Der formale Witz in den Komödien des Aristophanes*. Zurich.

Kugelmeier, C. (1996) *Reflexe früher und zeitgenössischer Lyrik in der Alten attischen Komödie*. Stuttgart.

Laistner, M. L. W. (1927) *Isocrates: De Pace and Philippus*. New York.

Laland, K. and Brown, G. (2002) *Sense and Nonsense: Evolutionary Perspectives on Human Behaviour*. Oxford.

Laporte, D. (2000) *History of Shit* (trans. N. Benabid and R. el-Khoury of 1978, *Histoire de la merde (Prologue)*). Cambridge, MA.

Lauriola, R. (2010) *Aristofane serio-comico: paideia e geloion*. Pisa.

Lecercle, J. (1990) *The Violence of Language*. London.

(1994) *Philosophy of Nonsense: The Intuitions of Victorian Nonsense Literature*. London.

Lefkowitz, J. B. (2009) "Aesop's Pen: Adaptation, Authorship, and Satire in the Aesopic Tradition". Dissertation, University of Pennsylvania.

Lesky, A. (1966) *A History of Greek Literature* (trans. J. A. Willis and C. de Heer). London.

Lever, K. (1953) "Poetic metaphor and dramatic allegory in Aristophanes". *ClW* 46.15: 220–3.

Lewontin, R. (2010) "Not so natural selection". *New York Review of Books* 57.9.

Lipps, T. (1898) *Komik und Humor*. Hamburg and Leipzig.

Lipsius, J. H. (1984[1905–15]) *Das attische Recht und Rechtsverfahren*. Leipzig.

Lowe, N. (2008) *Comedy (New Surveys in the Classics)*. Cambridge.

Lucas, D. W. (1968) *Aristotle. Poetics*. Oxford.

MacDowell, D. M. (1971) *Aristophanes. Wasps*. Oxford.

(1990) *Demosthenes. Against Meidias*. Oxford.

(1995) *Aristophanes and Athens: An Introduction to the Plays*. Oxford.

McGhee, P. (1979) *Humor: Its Origin and Development*. San Francisco.

McGlew, J. (2002) *Citizens on Stage: Comedy and Political Culture in the Athenian Democracy*. Ann Arbor.

McLeish, K. (1980) *The Theatre of Aristophanes*. Thames and Hudson.

Malcolm, N. (1997) *The Origins of English Nonsense*. London.

Martin, R. A. (1998) "Approaches to the sense of humor: a historical review", in *The Sense of Humor*, ed. W. Ruch. Berlin: 15–60.

Mastromarco, G. (1974) *Storia di una commedia di Atene*. Florence.

(2002) "Onomasti komodein e spoudaiogeloion", in *Spoudaiogeloion: Form und Funktion der Verspottung in der aristophanischen Komödie*, ed. A. Ercolani. Stuttgart and Weimar: 205–23.

Mathieu, G. and Brémond, E. (1987[1938]) *Isocrates: Discours Tome II*. Paris.

Meineke, A. (1970[1839]) *Fragmenta comicorum Graecorum*, Vol. 1. Berlin.

Mendrinos, J. (2004) *The Complete Idiot's Guide to Comedy Writing*. Indianapolis.

Menke, B. (2000) "Allegorie", in *Historisiches Wörterbuch Ästhetischer Grundbegriffe*, Vol. 1, ed. K. Barck, M. Fontius, F. Wolfzettel, and B. Steinwachst et al. Stuttgart: 49–104.

Menninghaus, W. 1995. *Lob des Unsinns: Über Kant, Tieck, und Blaubart*. Frankfurt.

Michael, C. (1981) *Ho kōmikos logos tou Aristophanous*. Athens.

Miller, H. W. (1944) "Repetition of lines in Aristophanes." *AJP* 65: 26–36.

(1945) "Comic iteration in Aristophanes." *AJP* 66: 398–408.

Millis, B. (2001) "A Commentary on the Fragments of Anaxandrides". Dissertation, University of Illinois, Urbana-Champaign.

Mitchell, R. (1991) "Bateson's concept of 'metacommunication' in play." *New Ideas in Psychology* 9.1: 73–87.

Morreall, J. (1987) "Funny ha-ha, funny strange, and other reactions to incongruity", in *The Philosophy of Laughter and Humor*, ed. J. Morreall. Albany: 188–207.

(2009) *Comic Relief: A Comprehensive Philosophy of Humor.* Malden, MA.

Marrow, G. (1993) *Plato's Cretan City*, 2nd edition. Princeton.

Most, G. (2010) "Hellenistic allegory and early imperial rhetoric", in *Cambridge Companion to Allegory*, ed. R. Copeland and P. Struck. Cambridge: 26–38.

Murray, G. (1964) *Aristophanes: A Study.* New York.

Murray, O. (1990) "Sympotic history", in *Sympotica: A Symposium on the Symposion*, ed. O. Murray. Oxford: 3–13.

Napolitano, M. (2005) "Callia, Alcibiade, Nicia: I 'Kolakes' di Eupoli come commedia politica." *Seminari romani di cultura greca* 8: 45–66.

Nash, W. (1985) *The Language of Humour: Style and Technique in Comic Discourse.* London.

Nesselrath, H.-G. (1990) *Die attische mittlere Komödie.* Berlin.

Newiger, H.-J. (1957) *Metapher und Allegorie: Studien zu Aristophanes.* Stuttgart.

Nisbet, G. (2003) *Greek Epigram in the Roman Empire.* Oxford.

Norlin, G. (1928) *Isocrates.* Cambridge, MA.

Norwood, G. (1931) *Greek Comedy.* London.

Obbink, D. (2003) "Allegory and exegesis in the Derveni papyrus", in *Metaphor, Allegory, and the Classical Tradition*, ed. G. R. Boys-Stones. Oxford: 177–88.

(2010) "Early Greek allegory", in *Cambridge Companion to Allegory*, ed. R. Copeland and P. Struck. Cambridge: 15–25.

O'Brien-Moore, A. (1924) *Madness in Ancient Literature.* Weimar.

Olson, S. D. (1998) *Aristophanes. Peace.* Oxford.

(2002a) *Aristophanes. Acharnians.* Oxford.

(2002b) "Review of M. S. Silk (2000) *Aristophanes and the Definition of Comedy.*" *CW* 96: 108–9.

(2006–12) *Athenaeus. The Learned Banqueters*, 8 vols. Cambridge, MA.

(2007) *Broken Laughter: Select Fragments of Greek Comedy.* Oxford.

(2010a) "Comedy, politics, and society", in *Brill's Companion to the Study of Greek Comedy*, ed. G. Dobrov. Leiden: 35–69.

(2010b) "The comic poet Pherecrates, a war-casualty of the late 410s BC." *JHS* 130: 49–50.

O'Regan, D. (1992) *Rhetoric, Comedy, and the Violence of Language in Aristophanes' Clouds.* Oxford.

Orth, C. (2009) *Strattis. Die Fragmente. Ein Kommentar.* Berlin.

O'Sullivan, N. (1992) *Alcidamas, Aristophanes, and the Beginnings of Greek Stylistic Theory.* Stuttgart.

Padel, Ruth. (1995) *Whom Gods Destroy: Elements of Greek and Tragic Madness.* Princeton.

Page, D. L. (1941) *Select Papyri III: Literary Papyri.* Cambridge, MA.

(1981) *Further Greek Epigrams.* Cambridge.

Palagi, E. (2008) "Sharing the motivation to play: the use of signals in adult bonobos." *Animal Behaviour* 75: 887–96.

(2011) "Playing at every age: modalities and potential functions in non-human primates," in *The Oxford Handbook of the Development of Play*, ed. A. D. Pellegrini. Oxford: 70–82.

Parker, L. P. E. (1997) *The Songs of Aristophanes*. Oxford.

Pellis, S. M. (1996) "On knowing it's only play: the role of play signals in play fighting." *Aggression and Violent Behavior* 1.3: 249–68.

Pervukhina, N. (1993) *Anton Chekhov: The Sense and the Nonsense*. New York.

Phillips, E. D. (1973) *Greek Medicine*. Thames and Hudson.

Pianko, G. (1963) "Un comico contributo alla storia della musica greca: *Chirone* di Ferecrate." *Eos* 53: 56–62.

Pickard-Cambridge, A. W. (1962) *Dithyramb, Tragedy and Comedy*. 2nd edition revised by T. B. L. Webster. Oxford.

(1968) *The Dramatic Festivals of Athens*. Oxford.

Pirandello, L. (1998(1988)) *Collected Plays*, Vol. II, ed. R. Rietty. New York.

Plass, P. (1967) "'Play' and philosophic detachment in Plato." *TAPA* 98: 343–64.

Platnauer, M. (1964) *Aristophanes. Peace*. Oxford.

Platter, C. (2007) *Aristophanes and the Carnival of Genres*. Baltimore.

Plebe, A. (1952) *La teoria del comico da Aristotele a Plutarco*. Turin.

Pomeroy, S. (1994) *Xenophon. Oeconomicus: A Social and Historical Commentary*. Oxford.

Porter, J. I. (2007) "Review of Struck (2004) *Birth of the Symbol*," *CR* 57.1: 50–2.

Post, L. A. (1932) "Catana the cheese-grater in Aristophanes' Wasps," *AJP* 53: 265–6.

Preisendanz, K. (2001(1974)) *Papyri Graecae Magicae*. Leipzig.

Pütz, B. (2007) *The Symposium and Komos in Aristophanes*. Warminster.

Quadlbauer, F. (1960) "Die Dichter der griechischen Komödie im literarischen Urteil der Antike." *Wiener Studien* 73: 64–7.

Raskin, V. (1985) *Semantic Mechanisms of Humor*. Dordrecht, Boston, and Lancaster.

(1990) "Sophisticated jokes," in *Whimsy VII*, eds. V. Raskin and S. Hughes. West Lafayette: 125–7.

Raspe, G. C. H. (1832) *De Eupolidis Δήμοις ac Πόλεσιν*. Leipzig.

Reckford, K. J. (1987) *Aristophanes' Old-and-New Comedy*. Chapel Hill.

Redfern, W. D. (1984) *Puns*. New York.

Restani, D. (1983) "Il *Chirone* di Ferecrate e la 'nuova' musica greca." *Riv. Ital. di Musicologia* 18: 139–92.

Ricœur, P. (1977) *The Rule of Metaphor*. Toronto.

Robert, L. (1968) "De Delphes a l'Oxus: inscriptions grecques nouvelles de la Bactriane." *Comptes Rendues de l'Académie des Inscriptions et Belles Lettres*. 112.3: 416–57.

Robson, J. (2006) *Humour, Obscenity and Aristophanes*. Tübingen.

Rochefort-Guillouet, S. (ed.) 2002. *Analyses & réflexions sur Aristophane La Paix*. Paris.

Rogers, B. (1906) *Aristophanous Ornithes. The Birds of Aristophanes: Acted at Athens at the Great Dionysia 414 BC*. London.

Rose, V. (1886) *Aristotelis qui ferebantur librorum fragmenta*. Leipzig.

Roselli, D. (2011) *Theater of the People: Spectators and Society in Ancient Athens*. Austin.

Rosen, G. (1968) *Madness in Society: Chapters in the Historical Sociology of Mental Illness*. Chicago.

Rosen, R. (1984) "The Ionian at Aristophanes *Peace* 46." *GRBS* 25: 389–96.

(1988) *Old Comedy and the Iambographic Tradition*. Atlanta.

(1989) "Euboulos' *Ankylion* and the game of kottabos." *CQ* 39.2: 355–9.

(1997) "The gendered polis in Eupolis' *Cities*," in *The City as Comedy: Society and Representation in Athenian Drama*, ed. G. Dobrov. Chapel Hill: 149–76.

(2007) *Making Mockery: The Poetics of Ancient Satire*. New York.

(2010) "Aristophanes," in *Brill's Companion to the Study of Ancient Greek Comedy*, ed. G. Dobrov. Leiden: 227–78.

Rösler, W. (1995) "Wine and truth in the Greek symposion," in *In Vino Veritas*, ed. O. Murray and M. Tecusan. London: 106–12.

Ross, W. (1959) *Aristotelis ars rhetorica*. Oxford.

Roth, P. (2003) "Die Dialogszene im 'Panathenaikos.'" In *Isokrates–Neue Ansätze zur Bewertung eines politischen Schriftstellers*. Trier: 140–9.

Rothwell, K. (2007) *Nature, Culture, and the Origins of Greek Comedy: A Study of Animal Choruses*. Cambridge.

Rotman, B. (1987) *Signifying Nothing*. New York.

Rowe, C. (1986) *Plato. Phaedrus*. Warminster.

Ruch, W. (ed.) (1998) *The Sense of Humor: Explorations of a Personality Characteristic*. New York.

Ruffell, I. (2011) *Politics and Anti-realism in Athenian Old Comedy: The Art of the Impossible*. Oxford.

Russell, D. A. (1978) "Classicizing rhetoric and criticism: the pseudo-Dionysian Exetasis and Mistakes." *Entretiens sur l'antiquité classique* 25: 113–34.

Russell, D. A., and Wilson, N. G. (1981) *Menander Rhetor*. Oxford.

Russo, C. F. (1994) *Aristophanes: An Author for the Stage*. London (trans. K. Wren, from Italian edition, 1962. *Aristofane autore di teatro*. Florence).

Rusten, J. (ed., and trans.) Henderson, J., Kansian, D., Rosen, R., and Slater, N. W. (trans.) (2011) *The Birth of Comedy: Texts, Documents, and Art from Athenian Comic Competitions*, 486–280. Baltimore.

Saetta Cottone, R. (2005) *Aristofane e la poetica dell'ingiuria: per una introduzione alla loidoria comica*. Rome.

Sandbach, F. H. (1970) "Menander's manipulation of language for dramatic purposes," in *Ménandre*, ed. E. Turner and E. Handley. Geneva: 113–36.

Schaffner, O. (1911) "De adversum loquendi ratione in comoedia." Dissertation, Giessen.

Schenkeveld, D. M. (1994) "*Ta asteia* in Aristotle's Rhetoric," in *Peripatetic Rhetoric after Aristotle*, ed. W. W. Fortenbaugh and D. C. Mirhady. New Brunswick, NJ: 1–14.

Schlegel, A. W. (1809) *Vorlesungen über dramatische Kunst und Litteratur*, Vol 1. Heidelberg. (Trans. by A. J. W. Morrison 1973, as Course of Lectures on Dramatic Art and Literature. London.)

Schofield, M. (1983) "The syllogisms of Zeno of Citium." *Phronesis* 28: 31–58.

Schönewolf, H. (1938) *Der jungattische Dithyrambos. Wesen, Wirking, Gegenwirkung.* Dissertation, Giessen.

Schubart, W. (1907) *Griechische Dichterfragmente.* Berlin.

Schultz, T. R. (1996[1976]) "A cognitive-developmental analysis of humour," in *Humour and Laughter: Theory, Research, and Application,* ed. A. J. Chapman and H. C. Foot. New York: 11–36.

Seaford, R. (1987) "Pentheus' vision: Bacchae 918–22." *CQ* 37.1: 76–8.

Searle, J. R. (1975) "The logical status of fictional discourse." *New Literary History* 6.2: 319–32.

Sewell, E. (1952) *The Field of Nonsense.* London.

Sider, D. (1992) "*Lēkythion apōlesen*: Aristophanes' limp phallic joke?" *Mnemosyne* 45.3: 359–64.

Sidwell, K. C. (2009) *Aristophanes the Democrat: The Politics of Satirical Comedy during the Peloponnesian War.* Cambridge.

Sifakis, G. (1971) *Parabasis and Animal Choruses.* London.

Silk, M. (2000) *Aristophanes and the Definition of Comedy.* Oxford.

(2003) "Metaphor and metonymy: Aristotle, Jakobson, Ricouer and others," in *Metaphor, Allegory, and the Classical Tradition,* ed. G. R. Boys-Stones. Oxford: 115–47.

Slater, N. W. (2002) *Spectator Politics: Metatheatre and Performance in Aristophanes.* Philadelphia.

Sommerstein, A. H. (1981) *Aristophanes. Knights.* Warminster.

(1983) *Aristophanes. Wasps.* Warminster.

(1985) *Aristophanes. Peace.* Warminster.

(1986) "The decree of Syracosios." *CQ* 36: 101–8.

(1987) *Aristophanes. Birds.* Warminster.

(1996) *Aristophanes. Frogs.* Warminster.

(1997) "Response to N. W. Slater," in *Education in Greek Fiction,* ed. A. Sommerstein and C. Atherton. Bari.

(2001) *Aristophanes. Wealth.* Warminster.

(2004a) "The alleged attempts to prosecute Aristophanes," in *Free Speech in Classical Antiquity,* ed. R. Rosen and I. Sluiter. Leiden: 145–74.

(2004b) "Comedy and the unspeakable," in *Law, Rhetoric, and Comedy in Classical Athens,* ed. D. A. Cairns and R. A. Knox. Swansea: 205–22.

(2009) *Talking about Laughter and Other Studies in Greek Comedy.* Oxford.

Spencer, H. (1872) *Principles of Psychology.* 2nd edition, Vol. II. New York.

Spyropoulos, E. (1974) *L'accumulation verbale chez Aristophane.* Thessaloniki.

Staiger, E. (1946) *Grundbegriffe der Poetik.* Zurich.

Staples, D. (1978) "Pea Pteroenta: Plot and Metaphor in Aristophanes." Dissertation, Boston University.

Stark, I. (1995) "Who laughs at whom in Greek comedy," in *Laughter Down the Centuries,* Vol. II. Turku: 99–116.

(2004) *Die hämische Muse: Spott als soziale und mentale Kontrolle in der griechischen Komödie.* Munich.

Starkie, W. (1909) *Aristophanes. Acharnians.* London.

Stewart, J. A. (1892) *Notes on Nicomachean Ethics of Aristotle*. Oxford.

Stewart, S. (1979) *Nonsense: Aspects of Intertextuality in Folklore and Literature*. Baltimore.

Stickgold, R., Hobson, J., Fosse, M., and Fosse, R. (2001) "Sleep, learning, and dreams: off-line memory reprocessing." *Science* 294: 1052–7.

Stierle, K. (1976) "Komik der Handlung, Komik der Sprachhandlung, Komik der Komödie," in *Das Komische*, ed. W. Preisendanz and R. Warning. Munich: 237–68.

Stockton, W. (2011) *Playing Dirty: Sexuality and Waste in Early Modern Comedy*. Minneapolis.

Stone, L. M. (1981) *Costume in Aristophanic Comedy*. New York.

Storey, I. (2003) *Eupolis*. Oxford.

    (2011) *Fragments of Old Comedy*, 3 vols. Cambridge, MA.

Storey, I. and Allan, A. (2005) *A Guide to Ancient Greek Drama*. Malden, MA.

Stroup, S. C. (2004) "Designing women: Aristophanes' 'Lysistrata' and the 'hetairization' of the Greek wife.' *Arethusa* 37.1: 37–73.

Struck, P. (2004) *Birth of the Symbol: Ancient Readers at the Limits of their Texts*. Princeton.

Süss, W. (1954) "Scheinbare und wirkliche Inkongruenzen bei Aristophanes." *RhM* 97: 115–59.

    (1967) "Über den *Chiron* des Pherekrates." *RhM* 110: 26–31.

Süvern, J. W. (1827) "Über Aristophanes Vögel." *Abhandlungen der Akademie der Wissenschaften, Berlin, historisch-philologische Kl. 1–109.* (Trans. W. R. Hamilton, 1835, as *Essay on "The Birds" of Aristophanes*. London.)

Taaffe, L. K. (1993) *Aristophanes and Women*. Routledge.

Taillardat, J. (1965) *Les images d'Aristophane*. Paris.

Tambiah, S. (1985) *Culture, Thought, and Social Action: An Anthropological Perspective*. Cambridge, MA.

Taplin, O. (1993) *Comic Angels: And Other Approaches to Greek Drama through Vase-Paintings*. Oxford.

    (1996) "Comedy and the tragic," in *Tragedy and the Tragic*, ed. M. Silk. Oxford: 188–202.

Tarantino, E. and Caruso, C. (eds.) (2009) *Nonsense and Other Senses: Regulated Absurdity in Literature*. Newcastle upon Tyne.

Teodorsson, S. (1989) *A Commentary on Plutarch's Table Talks*, Vol. III. Goteborg.

Thompson, K. V. (1998) "Self assessment in juvenile play," in *Animal Play: Evolutionary, Comparative, and Ecological Perspectives*, ed. M. Bekoff and J. Byers. Cambridge: 183–204.

Thompson, W. (1973[1868]) *The Phaedrus of Plato*. New York.

Tigges, W. (1988) *An Anatomy of Literary Nonsense*. Amsterdam.

Tissol, G. (1997) *The Face of Nature: Wit, Narrative, and Cosmic Origins in Ovid's Metamorphoses*. Princeton.

Trahair, L. (2007) *The Comedy of Philosophy: Sense and Nonsense in Early Cinematic Slapstick*. Albany.

Ussher, R. (1973) *Aristophanes. Ecclesiazusae*. Oxford.

Van der Stock, L. (1992) *Twinkling and Twilight: Plutarch's Reflections on Literature*. Brussels.

Van Hook, L. (1917) "Ψυχρότης ἤ τὸ ψυχρόν." *CP* 12.1: 68–76.

Van Leeuwen, J. (1968[1900]) *Aristophanis Equites*. Leiden.

(1968[1905]) *Aristophanis Ecclesiazusae*. Leiden.

(1968[1906]) *Aristophanis Pax*. Leiden.

Veatch, T. 1998. "A theory of humor." *Humor* 11: 161–215.

Vickers, M. J. (1997) *Pericles on Stage: Political Comedy in Aristophanes' Early Plays*. Austin.

Von Arnim, H. F. A. (1968) *Stoicorum veterum fragmenta*. Leipzig.

Von Möllendorff, P. (1995) *Grundlage einer Ästhetik der Alten Komödie*. Tübingen.

Von Reden, S. and Goldhill, S. (1999) "Plato and the performance of dialogue," in *Performance Culture and Athenian Democracy*, ed. S. Goldhill and R. Osborne. Cambridge: 257–92.

Wallace, R. (2005) "Law, Attic comedy, and the regulation of comic speech," in *Cambridge Companion to Ancient Greek Law*, ed. M. Gagarin and D. Cohen. Cambridge: 357–73.

Walton, F. R., and Geer, R. M. (1967) *Diodorus Siculus: in Twelve Volumes*. Cambridge, MA.

Warning, R. (1976) "Elemente einer Pragmasemiotik der Komödie," in *Das Komische*, ed. W. Preisendanz and R. Warning. Munich: 279–333.

Wehrli, F. (1969) *Die Schule des Aristoteles. Klearchos*. 2nd edition. Basel.

Weinreich, O. (1933) *Menekrates Zeus und Salmoneus: Religiongeschichtliche Studien zur Psychopathologie des Gottmenschentums in Antike und Neuzeit*. Stuttgart.

Wellershoff, D. (1976) "Infantilismus als Revolte oder Das ausgeschlagene Erbe – zur Theorie des Blödelns," in *Das Komische*, ed. W. Preisendanz and R. Warning. Munich: 335–57.

West, M. L. (1968) "Two passages of Aristophanes." *CR* 18.1: 5–8.

(1974) *Studies in Greek Elegy and Iambus*. Berlin.

(1982) *Greek Metre*. Oxford.

White, A. (1981) *The Uses of Obscurity: The Fiction of Early Modernism*. London and Boston.

White, E. B. (1977) *Essays of E. B. White*. New York.

Whitman, C. H. (1964) *Aristophanes and the Comic Hero*. Cambridge, MA.

Whittaker, M. (1935) "The comic fragments in their relation to the structure of old Attic comedy," *CQ* 29: 181–91.

Willi, A. (2002) (ed.) *The Language of Greek Comedy*. Oxford.

(2003) *The Languages of Aristophanes: Aspects of Linguistic Variation in Classical Attic Greek*. Oxford.

Wilson, A. M. (1977) "The individualized chorus in Old Comedy," *CQ* 27: 278–83.

Wilson, N. G. (2007) *Aristophanis Fabulae*. Oxford.

Wittgenstein, L. (1974) *Philosophical Grammar*, 2 vols. Bereeley.

Woodhouse, S. (1971[1910]) *English–Greek Dictionary*. London.

Worman, N. (2008) *Abusive Mouths in Classical Athens*. Cambridge.

Wright, M. (2012) *The Comedian as Critic: Greek Old Comedy and Poetics*. London.

Yunis, H. (2011) *Plato. Phaedrus.* Cambridge.

Zacher, K. (1902) "Review of O. Koehler, *Adnotationes ad comicos Graecos.*" *Berliner Philologische Wochenschrift* 40: 1218–22.

Zielinski, T. (1885) *Die Gliederung der altattischen Komödie.* Leipzig.

Zimmermann, B. (1993) "Comedy's criticism of music," in *Intertextualität in der griechisch-römischen Komödie*, ed. N. Slater and B. Zimmerman. Stuttgart: 39–50.

(2010) "Structure and Meter," in *Brill's Companion to the Study of Greek Comedy*, ed. G. Dobrov. Leiden: 455–69.

Zweig, B. (1992) "The mute nude female characters in Aristophanes' plays," in *Pornography and Representation in Greece and Rome*, ed. A. Richlin. Oxford: 73–89.

General index

adoleskhia, 17, 40, 152–4
aggression, 120
aggressive play, *see* play with aggression
alazoneia, 31
allegory, 11, 53, 56, 69, 77
  without allegorized or "broken" allegories,
    69–83
asteion, 124

Bateson, Gregory, 109–12, 159
bomolokhos, 107, 111

Carroll, Lewis, 5–6, 19
Chomsky, Noam, 4–5
Cinesias, the case of, 89–117
clown, *see* fool
coinages, 147–51
comic, 3
comic climax, 56, 86, 123, 148, 151, 188
convention, 96–7, 114

deception, 21
deformity, 43
delirium, 12, 112–15, 121–3, 148, 152, 155, *see*
    nonsense and mental illness
Dionysiac festival, 94, 109
dithyrambic language, 65

eu legeis, 177–80

fantasy, 1, 115
fiction, 96–7, 114, 115
fool, 42, 163, 164, 182, 188
foolery, 1–4
Freud, Sigmund, 86, 116, 123,
    151, 159
fun/funny, 1–4, 149

games, 49–50
gibberish, 5–7, 123, 136

Harpaste, the case of, 42
homonymy, 129
hubris, 101–3
humor, 3–4, 81, 119, 142, 155
hythlos, 7, 167, *see also* nonsense
    etymology of, 16

iambic poetry, 96
incongruity, 3, 116, 121, 149
interpretation, 10, 12, 17, 54
    as Clearchus of Soli's "searching", 60,
        62, 81
    loss incurred by, 75, 81
    rejection of, 13, 121, 187
    symptomatic, 88, 90, 112–17

joke, 183
    aggressive, 120, 180
    explaining a, 107, 115, 147
    "getting" a, 126, 133
    ignoring an on-stage, 162, 175–7
    responding with "nonsense!" to a, 162, 165–73,
        184, 188
    translating an on-stage, 162, 177–80
    verbal, 120

kalōs legeis, 177–80
komoidoumenos, 89, 93, 103

lalia, 17, 38–40
laughter, 2, 149, 158
    and mental illness, 40–3
    and nonsense, 40–3, 44–6
    on stage, 162, 164
Lear, Edward, 5–6, 19
lēros, 7, 166, 169, 173, *see also* nonsense
    defined, 31
    and drunkenness, 28–9
    etymology of, 16
    and linguistic features, 35–40

lēros (cont.)
  as mental impairment, 25–9
  and play, 43–50
  as rhetorical accusation, 20–6,
    29–31
  vs. madness, 33–35

meaning
  behind the comic, 2, 115
  beneath the comic, 2
Menecrates, the case of, 32, 35, 42
mental illness, *see* nonsense and
    mental illness
metaphor, 11, 53, 56
  without tenor, 83–6
mistake, 122, 132, 155
  of homonymy, 130
  as pragmatic "misfire", 128
  see also nonsense vs. mistakes
mockery, 89, 91–7, 102, 109, 113

nonsense, 152, 165
  as accusation in response to jokes, *see* joke,
    responding with "nonsense!" to a
  discovery of, 157, 187
  Freud's notion of, 122, 132–7
  as gibberish. *See* gibberish
  and laughter, 40–3
  as meaningless language, 4–7, 10
  medical vs. sympotic, 113
  and mental illness, 11, 12, 26–9, 31–5, 50,
    183, 185
  perception of, 87, 123, 147, 151
  as physical object, 20
  and play, 11–12, 19, 50
  as rejection of interpretation, 81, 84
  as symptom, 29, 40
  as unworthy of interpretation, 8, 60
  as useless language, 7
  vs. falsehood, 22–6, 29–31
  vs. Greek terms for "nonsense",
    19–20
  vs. mistakes, 33, 131
  vs. noise, 4, 77
  vs. useful speech, 23–6, 51
  as waste, 8

obscurity, 55, 57, 61, 66, 85
onomasti komoidein, 93, 96, 142–7,
    170, 173
oracles, 64
ouden legein, 17, 167, 172

paidia, 107
paizein, 104, 105
personification in Old Comedy, 78
phenakismos, 31
phlēnaphia, 7, *see also* nonsense
phluaria, 7, 169, *see also* nonsense
  defined, 29–31
  and drunkenness, 29
  etymology of, 16
  and linguistic features, 35–40
  as mental impairment, 25–9
  and play, 43–50
  as rhetorical accusation, 20–6, 29–31
  vs. madness, 33–5
phluax, 19
play, 12, 43–50, 88, 103, 107–17, 119, *see also*
    nonsense as play
  with aggression, 120, 143, 157–60
  with language, 122, 156, 157–60
play boundary, 120
play signal, 12, 109–13, 160
psychron, 128, 139, 181
punchline, 175
puns, 124–32
  "bad" puns, 124, 129, 137–42

rambling speech, 35–40, 123, 136, 158
reference, 52
repetition, 35–40, 123, 136, 151–5
riddle, 11, 53, 56
  without solution, 57–65
ritual, 95

sense, 52, 123, 135, 143, 152, 157, 159, 163, 181
  defined, 152
  of a joke, 122, 134, 143–7
serious, 1–4, 8–10, 44, 88, 109, 163, 164, 180,
    185, 188
  "serious content", 103, 109, 112, 178
  "taking seriously", 89–117
silly, 183
spoudazein, 104, 105
stōmullesthai, 16
straight character, 163, 164, 183, 188
symptom, 90, 112–17, *see also* nonsense as
    symptom

Thrasyllus, the case of, 33, 35
truth-values, 24, 35, 101–3, *see also* nonsense vs.
    falsehood

wordplay, *see* puns

Index locorum

adespota elegiaca, 44–50
Aelius Aristides
  Pros Platona hyper ton
    tettaron, 38
Alexis
  fr. 9 KA, 46
Antiphanes
  120 KA, 157–9
  122 KA, 58–61
  192 KA, 61–5
  194 KA, 172
Aristophanes
  629 KA, 120
  Acharnians 100, 5–7
  Birds 64–6, 167
  Birds 272–94, 143–7
  Birds 1390–402, 105–9
  Clouds 22–4, 138
  Clouds 222–4, 8–10
  Clouds 641–784, 167
  Ecclesiazusae 328–30, 92
  Ecclesiazusae 1169–75, 148–51
  Frogs 1095–8, 103
  Gerytades, 92
  Knights 490–2, 178
  Lysistrata 102–3, 177
  Lysistrata 1095–7, 178
  Peace 43–8, 65–9
  Peace 702–904, 82–6
  Thesmophoriazusae 618–22,
    151–5, 164
  Thesmophoriazusae 936–8, 176
  Wasps 891–1001, 71–7
  Wealth 788–801, 180
Aristotle
  Nicomachean Ethics 4.14, 108
  Poetics 1458a, 58
  Rhetoric 2.2, 101–3
  Rhetoric 3.10–11, 124–32

  Sophistici Elenchi 165b24–5, 130
  Sophistici Elenchi 173a32–40,
    153
Eubulus
  106 KA, 171
Eupolis
  171 KA, 173
  Cities, 79–83
Hippocrates
  De Morbis 2.22, 27
  De Morbis 2.65, 27
Isocrates
  Antidosis 83.7–8, 36–40
  Panathenaicus 205, 22–6
  Panegyricus 188, 23–6
  Philip 13, 22–6
  Philip 73–5, 30
Lysias
  fr. 195 Carey, 90–1
Pherecrates
  fr. 155 KA, 98–103
Plato
  Apology 19c, 10
  Crito 46d4, 48
  Laws 701c5–d2, 37–40
  Protagoras 347c–d, 47
Plato Comicus
  fr. 200 KA, 91
Plutarch
  Comparatio Aristophanis et Menandri,
    138–41
  De Garrulitate 504c, 36–40
Ps.-Dionysius of Halicarnassus
  Ars Rhetorica 11.8, 40

Seneca
    Epistle 50, 42
Strattis
    fr. 14 KA, 92

Theophrastus
    Characters 7.7, 39

Tractatus Coislinianus, 154

Xenophon
    Cyropaedia 1.4.11, 49
    Cyropaedia 2.18–20, 103
    Memorabilia 3.9.6–7,
      32, 35

Made in the USA
Middletown, DE
25 November 2017